W9-DEP-891

BIOGRAPHY OF A PROGRESSIVE

BIOGRAPHY OF A PROGRESSIVE

Franklin K. Lane, 1864-1921

KEITH W. OLSON

Contributions in American History, Number 78

GREENWOOD PRESS
Westport, Connecticut • London, England

50155

0734254

Library of Congress Cataloging in Publication Data

Olson, Keith W
   Biography of a progressive, Franklin K. Lane, 1864-
1921.

   (Contributions in American history ; no. 78 ISSN 0084-
9219)
   Bibliography: p.
   Includes index.
   1. Lane, Franklin Knight, 1864-1921. 2. Politicians—
United States—Biography. 3. Social reformers—
United States—Biography. 4. Progressivism
(United States politics) 5. United States—Politics
and government—1865-1933. I. Title.
E664.L23O57   973.8'092.4 [B]   78-57766
ISBN 0-313-20613-9

Copyright © 1979 by Keith W. Olson

All rights reserved. No portion of this book may be
reproduced, by any process or technique, without the
express written consent of the publisher.

Library of Congress Catalog Card Number: 78-57766
ISBN: 0-313-20613-9
ISSN: 0084-9219

First published in 1979

Greenwood Press, Inc.
51 Riverside Avenue, Westport, Connecticut 06880

Printed in the United States of America

10 9 8 7 6 5 4 3 2 1

To my daughters,
Paula and **Judy**

Contents

0734254

50155

Acknowledgments

In the course of my work on Franklin K. Lane's career, I benefited from the assistance of numerous individuals. I acknowledge this debt with pleasure and thank all of them.

Most of all, I am grateful to three persons. David A. Shannon, of the University of Virginia, provided a critique and invaluable encouragement and friendship. During the final stage of work, my colleague and friend Horace Samuel Merrill improved the organization, style, and conceptualization of the manuscript and reinforced my confidence. To me, and many others, he always has kept open the door to his office and to his home. My wife, Marilyn, applied her editorial skills to every draft of the manuscript, gave unfailing support, and contributed to a desirable atmosphere in which to work.

Several other persons deserve recognition. Horace M. Albright, who served under Lane, answered my interview questions and letters and read the manuscript. Meeting him proved a pleasant bonus to my work. E. David Cronon, of the University of Wisconsin, helped in many ways, especially sharing with me his knowledge of the Wilson era and his evaluation of my work. Morton Rothstein, also of the University of Wisconsin, offered an assessment of the manuscript. At a later stage in the development of my study, my colleagues Herman Belz, Donald C. Gordon, and George H. Callcott gave their reactions to portions of the work. Merritt Sherman, consultant, Board of Governors, Federal Reserve System, made available to me a box of papers relating to the career of Adolph C. Miller. Robert Wood, of the Herbert Hoover Library, and Renee M. Jaussaud, of the National Archives, took a personal interest in my work that exceeded their professional responsibilities.

Without exception, the staffs of the following libraries answered my questions, located and permitted use of materials, and offered suggestions with model professionalism: Columbia University, Cornell University, Duke University, Franklin D. Roosevelt Library, Herbert Hoover Library, Interstate Commerce Commission Library, Library of Congress, National Archives, New Jersey State Historical Library, New York Public Library, School of Law Library-Northwestern University, Stanford University, Syracuse University, University of California at Berkeley, University of Wisconsin, Washington State Library, Wisconsin State Historical Society, and Yale University.

Two of my departmental chariman, Walter Rundell, Jr., and Emory G. Evans, found money in a tight budget to pay typing expenses. A sabbatical leave from the University of Maryland afforded me a period of sustained research. Finally, the editor of *The Historian* permitted me to use material that first appeared as an article (February 1970) in that journal.

April 1978 Keith W. Olson

BIOGRAPHY OF A PROGRESSIVE

Introduction

Franklin K. Lane's career embraced two streams of interest to students of our past. One is the story of the performance of persons as they helped construct our society into what it has become. The other is the attempt of historians to label and define the many and varied changes those persons contributed to our increasingly complex society as the nation moved into the twentieth century. So many facets of change prevailed that adequate definitions have proved difficult, if not impossible. Early twentieth-century observers found it convenient, as have many subsequent observers, to refer to that period of transition as the Progressive Era. But ever since, historians have been debating the validity and implications of that term. For certain, the Progressive Era included many activities, and for certain, Lane participated in and contributed to a number of those efforts. So to study his career helps us understand what happened during those years and, in a broader sense, sheds light on what those years were all about. If we can label the period and its activities the Progressive Era, as it would appear we can, we also certainly can label Lane a progressive of note.

II

Lane's public life paralleled the reform impulse that quickened in the 1880s, broadened during the 1890s, and reached maturity during the years 1901 to 1916. Like the numerous reform efforts that participants placed under the broad rubric of the progressive movement, Lane expanded his activities through the years from the local, to the state, and eventually to the national scene. Both the man and the movement came of age at the turn of the century. In 1902, Lane attracted national attention in an unsuccessful but surprisingly close attempt to win the governorship of California as a "Roosevelt Democrat." The same year, President Theodore Roosevelt's intervention in the anthracite coal strike and the Justice Department's initiation of an antitrust suit against J. P. Morgan's Northern Securities Company signaled that reform had become a dominant concern within the executive branch of government. Lane maintained a close relationship with Roosevelt, who used the White House as a "bully pulpit" to publicize the progressive movement on the national level. Moreover, Lane held appointments under all three Progressive Era presidents; Roosevelt and William Howard Taft named him to the Interstate Commerce Commission and Woodrow Wilson appointed him to the Cabinet as secretary of the interior. By 1920, when progressivism had lost vitality and much of its leadership, a discouraged Lane, worried about his health and finances, resigned from the Cabinet. He died two months after Wilson left office.

Lane grew up with the fledgling reform activities of his community and state. As a teenager in the San Francisco Bay area during the 1880s, he participated in good-government groups. At age twenty, reflecting his family background, he campaigned for a prohibitionist candidate for governor. Participating in the drafting and adoption of a new city charter for San Francisco spurred him to seek election as city-county attorney in 1898; he was then thirty-four. Lane's political career in California, just as his earlier journalism career in California, New York, and Washington State, revealed his strong identification with and support of a wide range of reform efforts. In California, his activities contributed significantly to a progressive mood that Hiram Johnson and the progressive Republicans nurtured with sufficient success to win the elections of 1910. During his years on the Interstate Commerce Commission, 1906 to 1913, Lane used his position to curb railroad abuses and to advance government regulation. While secretary of the interior, 1913 to 1920, he pushed to fruition several component parts of the conservation movement and supported numerous other reforms of the Wilson administration.

III

Lane, along with most of his reform-minded contemporaries, had little difficulty in talking confidently about the progressive movement with which he identified. But that movement was both more complex and full of ambiguities than individuals such as Lane realized. Essentially, the movement was a response to the events of the preceding quarter century, especially the character and dimensions of industrialization, urbanization, and immigration. Adverse reaction to these forces of change developed as their influence became more widespread and more recognizable. Reaction varied from person to person, group to group, depending upon income, occupation, size and location of community, religion, age, and ethnic background. These reactions produced a multitude of reform efforts, first within cities and states, and, later, on the national level. Eventually reform activities dominated the country. One group of reforms pursued good government, another group sought economic change, and a third group addressed social justice. The groups, however, lacked precise identifying limits. A particular effort sometimes fell within two or even three of these broad categories.

The progressive movement, therefore, consisted of a collection of uncoordinated reform efforts operating at various local, state, and national levels. To obtain legislation or a policy change, a single reform movement forged a transitory coalition from diverse segments of society. Labor unions, intellectuals, the urban working class, social workers, and humanitarian-minded businessmen, for example, all had reasons to support a child labor law. At one time or another, almost every group and individual in the country, including businessmen of different persuasions, probably endorsed one or more reform movements.

Each reform effort had its own distinctive origins, characteristics, leadership, supporters, and success. Progressives disagreed over the magnitude of and the best solutions for the nation's social, political, and economic problems. They exhibited little accord on most issues, including prohibition, entry into World War I, immigration restriction, and regulation of business. Some of the national efforts, such as the campaigns for women's suffrage, the direct election of senators, and the creation of a federal income tax, achieved their objectives. Others, such as the drives to establish a federal minimum wage and old-age pensions, failed. Reforms for prohibition and a Federal Trade Commission won enactment but once in operation disappointed many of their initial supporters. The regulation of corporations and natural resources seemed adequate to some progressives and inadequate to others.

The three progressive presidents set high personal standards of public service when the national government markedly increased its powers. Roosevelt and Wilson transformed the presidency from a relatively passive office into a powerful executive institution with new prerogatives. To significant degrees, for example, Roosevelt used his office to formulate public opinion, and Wilson gave leadership to members of his party in Congress, including a legislative agenda.

Outside governmental chambers and offices, a questioning of values and of the status quo permeated much of society. Intellectual and professional changes abounded in the fields of education, law, economics, history, and philosophy. Muckraking journalism reached its peak, and the American socialist movement experienced its golden age.

The element unifying this aggregate of reform was a widespread mood among middle-class Americans of optimism, morality, and activism, plus a belief that the next level of government could solve problems that once had been more local. People believed they could use existing governmental processes to make government more responsive to the voters; to eliminate corruption in government, business, and society; to eradicate special privileges; and to bring greater order to an expanding, changing country. This mood was crucial, because when it changed during and immediately after the war years, reform lost the pervasiveness it once enjoyed throughout the country. Thereafter only specific reform efforts continued through the 1920s. The diversity of efforts, motivations, and interests, however, offset the common, unifying mood and explains why one individual or group of progressives did not necessarily agree or act in concert with another. The term "progressive" served wide though imprecise use.

IV

Scholars have found the Progressive Era of immense interest because of the changes that took place during it and because of the relationship that the period seemingly has to the present. Accordingly, they have investigated progressivism from a wide spectrum of vantage points. Many have sought to identify the motives of leaders and supporters or to explain the movement's relationship to reform efforts that preceded and followed. Others have examined the essential character, objectives, accomplishments, and failures of the movement. Scholars also have studied ideology, individuals, groups, and institutions. With different perspectives of time and value, historians have applied different research techniques. The result is a rich and varied body of scholarship.[1]

The interpretations of progressivism include five major phases, one roughly following another without necessarily superseding the previous. The phases are the "progressive," the "consensual," the "new left," the "organizational," and the "neo-progressive." Often studies fit into one of these groupings only with some adjustment, and a few exceptions do not fit at all. These groupings, however, offer a discernible pattern for the scholarship of many decades.[2]

The progressive historians, starting with Benjamin Parke DeWitt in 1915, viewed the movement as one of reform, a conflict of democracy and the public versus the forces of privilege. Writing in narrative form, these historians highlighted moral stances and assumed the democratic intentions of progressives and the success of reform. They assumed further that the Progressive Era gave the twentieth century its major characteristics. Historians in this group include Charles A. Beard, V. L. Parrington, and Harold Faulkner.

During the post-World War II decade, a second phase emerged. Richard Hofstadter typified and dominated this consensual phase of scholarship with two of his books, *The American Political Tradition* (1948) and his Pulitzer Prize-winning volume *The Age of Reform* (1955). Although educated in the progressive tradition and sympathetic to most of its ideals, Hofstadter remained professionally skeptical of the progressives. He asked questions about the motives, identity, and success of progressives that his predecessors largely ignored. These inquiries cast progressives in a less favorable light. Rather than being in conflict with business interests, Hofstadter saw progressives sharing with business a commitment to capitalism. Drawing upon earlier work of George Mowry and Alfred D. Chandler, Hofstadter identified the leadership of progressivism as middle class, predominantly urban, and economically successful. Hofstadter's analysis of their motivation was his most original contribution. The progressives became reformers, he maintained, "primarily because they were

victims of an upheaval in status that took place in the United States during the closing decades of the nineteenth and the early years of the twentieth century."[3] In addition to exhibiting status anxiety, progressives,
according to Hofstadter, displayed tendencies toward moral absolutism,
nativism, and nostalgia. He also suggested that progressive economic reform had been less effective than earlier historians believed. Finally, he
assumed that reform provided the dominant theme for twentieth-century politics, although he pointed out the discontinuity of the reform impulse from populism, to progressivism, to the New Deal.

During the 1960s, the new-left historians shifted the focus from Hofstadter's motivational approach to an examination of political economy.
The most important new-left book was Gabriel Kolko's *The Triumph of
Conservatism* (1963), which investigated federal regulatory legislation
and concluded that the progressive impulse "was initially a movement
for the political rationalization of business and industrial conditions . . .
that operated on the assumption that the general welfare of the community could be best served by satisfying the concrete needs of business."
He contended further that "It is business control over politics . . . rather
than political regulation of the economy that is the significant phenom-
enon of the Progressive Era."[4] As historians of the period carefully re-
examined the record of the business-political relations, however, they
one by one rather quickly rejected Kolko's sweeping conclusion. So in
the end, most professional historians concluded that although Kolko's
effort stimulated considerable interest, it added little or nothing of sub-
stance to the history of the period. It was more a diversion than a contribution to the history discipline.[5]

The fourth phase of scholarship regarding the Progressive Era appeared
concurrently with new-left writing but continued longer and with greater
influence. Two historians, Samuel P. Hays and Robert H. Wiebe, stand
out among the organizational writers. They have attempted to move
beyond interpretations focused on conflict between the public and the
expanded corporations, urban machines, and other institutions, whether
psychological or economic in origin. Instead, Hays and Wiebe emphasized
the compatibility between the new institutions and reform. But whereas
Kolko pointed out the continuity of power the older capitalist class
maintained, Hays and Wiebe stressed the power of a new middle class of
bureaucrat-minded professionals whose power derived from expertise and
detached vision, rather than from inherited status or wealth. The objective

of this new middle class was not reform of conventional definition, but a desire to bring order, rationality, and efficiency to a society experiencing just the opposite. To understand the Progressive Era, therefore, the organizational historians suggest the study of a process. In 1973, for example, in a historiographical essay, Wiebe concluded that "The fundamental issue at stake in the history of the progressive period is modernization. . . . What modernization meant to the less articulate . . . stands as the major challenge for another wave of historians."[6] The work of Hays, especially *The Response to Industrialism* (1957) and *Conservation and the Gospel of Efficiency* (1959), and Wiebe, notably *The Search for Order* (1967), undercut Hofstadter's portrait of progressive leadership as slightly irrational, nostalgic, and unable to accommodate themselves to new conditions. Meanwhile, research into the movement in several states indicated that progressives and their opponents shared individual characteristics. Hofstadter, Mowry, and Chandler had not used control groups of nonprogressives to test their theories.

Although Hays and Wiebe have stimulated new research, offered refreshing insights, and demonstrated that Hofstadter's conclusions are unsatisfactory, historians have raised questions about Hays and Wiebe's descriptions of progressive leadership and about their subordination of reform to modernization.

Two excellent case studies of progressivism at the state level, one by David P. Thelen and the other by Sheldon Hackney, provide the core of the neo-progressive phase of scholarship. Both historians found that conflict existed and that for progressives ideology was important. In his study *The New Citizenship: Origins of Progressivism in Wisconsin, 1885-1900* (1972), Thelen discovered that the economic depression of 1893-97 nurtured a coalition of reformers with diverse economic, religious, ethnic, and class backgrounds. In Wisconsin, he concluded, a conscious concern for the general public unified reformers and produced substantial results. Hackney examined *Populism to Progressivism in Alabama* (1969) and also discerned "genuine public spirit" that played a major role in forming a progressive coalition of dissimilar groups. By eschewing interpretative syntheses and attempts to find an all-encompassing definition of progressivism, and by concentrating on reconstructing the activities of a community of persons instead, Thelen and Hackney concluded that the pronounced political partisanship so characteristic of the Progressive Era was more than misleading rhetoric.

V

Because Lane's career touched many areas of progressivism and constituted a component part of that diffuse movement, the story of his public life is relevant to the current conceptions and arguments about the nature of progressivism. Descriptions of his personality and his attitudes and actions regarding reform in general, regulation of business, and conservation reinforces the conclusions of some historians and disputes those of others.

Lane's outgoing, confident personality was one of his major assets and mirrored the optimistic, forward-looking qualities most historians assign to progressivism. The diversity of reform efforts provided opportunities that suited his extroverted personality, for he exhibited throughout life a singular ability to impress people of different interests. He was at ease with wage earners and made them feel at ease with him; he was similarly comfortable with journalists, lawyers, and politiciams. His innate capacity to be friendly, even charming, often had a magnetic effect on others that helped Lane sell himself, for he was ambitious.

The bipartisan aspect of progressivism, even the imprecise meaning of the term, facilitated his association with other reformers, regardless of party affiliation. Large numbers within each major party favored reforms of some kind. Although Lane was a Democrat, the politician he most admired was the Republican Roosevelt. Because of Lane's strong support of organized labor, unusual for the period even among self-styled progressives, he once won endorsement from the Union Labor party in San Francisco. Samuel Gompers, president of the American Federation of Labor, considered Lane a solid friend of labor. Early in 1920, Lane judged Herbert Hoover the most capable progressive in the country and would have supported him for president had he chosen to run, even on the Republican ticket.

To the extent that his origins and values were middle class, Lane easily fits the description of progressive leadership offered by historians such as Hofstadter and Wiebe. But Lane's motivation derived not as Hofstadter and Wiebe, respectively, concluded about progressives, from anxiety over new forces and institutions in society, or from a desire to bring order and direction to a disorganized society. Rather, Lane's motivation stemmed from the Christian tradition to serve and to live a moral life, ideals his parents worked to instill in their children. He also sought leadership positions because he loved the attention and praise that usually accompanied them. Confidence, not anxiety, was the hallmark of his personality. He started his reform activities, moreover, from the perspective of a teenager's reaction to local conditions he observed, read about in local newspapers, and heard criticized at home and in church. Youthful idealism made him a reformer. Perhaps the most remarkable characteristic of Lane's personality was his life-long adherence to this reform impulse.

In addition to certain aspects of his personality, Lane's rhetoric and sense of morality likewise harmonized with values scholars generally agree dominated the Progressive Era. At a time when Americans relied on the written word and public speakers for information about public affairs, the ease with which he expressed himself on paper and in person proved an important advantage. His sense of right and wrong, although keen, was not dogmatic. Growing up, he had abandoned the Protestant mysticism of his parents, but retained the Christian ethic.

By his appearance and his morality, as well as his rhetoric, Lane represented the popular image of an ideal public figure. When he entered the Cabinet in 1913, at age forty-nine, he stood slightly above average in height. What remained of his hair covered only the back of his head and had been prematurely white for some years. A square jaw and clear blue-grey eyes accented his large head and round face. Despite being overweight, he appeared solid and well fed rather than flabby: the dividend of physically active early years, rather than any attempt as an adult to maintain muscle tone by regular exercise. His deep voice emphasized his confidence and sincerity, and his dress proclaimed him a man of affairs.

Starting with passage of the Hepburn Act in 1906, Lane's seven years as a member of the Interstate Commerce Commission (ICC) provide a case study of how one progressive viewed railroad regulation and the appropriate role of a federal regulatory agency, both subjects of paramount interest to recent historians. Lane acted on belief that the public and the railroads were in an adversary relationship, that he and the ICC represented the public interest, and that public ownership of the railroads was the alternative to regulation. He urged federal regulation as a positive good to end the inevitable corruption and misuse of power he associated with railroads. The attitudes Lane held and acted

upon while a member of the ICC run counter to the conclusions of
new-left and organizational historians regarding motivations and intentions of progressives sitting on regulatory commissions.

Although Lane consistently criticized misconduct on the part of
some segments of the business community and favored governmental
restraints, he, like other progressives, remained loyal to the tenets of
capitalism. He believed that railroad owners were entitled to a fair
return on their investment, and that in its work the ICC considered the
interests of the railroads along with the welfare of the public. Senator
Robert M. La Follette, symbolic of left-wing progressivism, affirmed a
similar commitment to capitalism while writing his autobiography in
1912, at the peak of progressivism, He titled one of his chapters "Progressive Government Produces Business Prosperity: What Was Accomplished in Wisconsin." Reform measures, progressives realized, would
stabilize and more firmly entrench capitalism, but it would be a more
humane, regulated capitalism. Had they not had this commitment,
they logically would have joined the Socialist party, an organization
contemporaries judged a viable political force.

Lane, La Follette, and other progressives emphasized their disagreement, not their agreement, with nonreformers. To dismiss the
fierce conflict of the Progressive Era as empty rhetoric among persons
with common values is somewhat akin to dismissing the bloody religious
wars between Catholics and Protestants as intramural because they
shared a fundamental commitment to Christianity. Whether or not
progressives were superficial in their analyses and naive in their expectations depends considerably upon the value judgments of the historian
making the assessment. That does not, however, lessen the intensity of
feelings and actions progressives displayed.

As secretary of the interior for seven years, Lane played an important
role in the conservation movement. Examining how he perceived that
movement and what he hoped to accomplish assists historians to understand the conservation movement, a vital constituent part of the broader
progressive movement. Two studies of the conservation movement offered contradictory conclusions about its essential character. Writing an
influential essay in the progressive tradition, J. Leonard Bates summarized his major point in his title "Fulfilling American Democracy:
The Conservation Movement, 1907 to 1921."[7] Hays, with his organizational approach, also summarized his basic conclusion in his title *Conservation and the Gospel of Efficiency.*

Lane considered the conservation movement a democratic struggle between the public and corporate interests. His objective was federal regulation to guarantee individual opportunity, thwart monopoly, and promote development, with a much greater concern for development than Bates noted. Lane, in his legislative proposals to establish a program of leasing federal lands, included clauses to limit the number of acres an individual or corporation could obtain. He likewise limited the size of farms on reclamation projects. His desire to develop resources helped shape his proposals and policies regarding Indians, World War I veterans, illiteracy, and national parks; at times it also caused him difficulties. Throughout his secretaryship, his dual themes of greater development and greater democracy determined the character of Lane's contributions to the conservation movement.

A study of Lane's life reinforces the scholarship of the past decade that describes progressivism as a many-sided collection of reform movements and depicts progressives as a group of diverse individuals with rational concerns about society. The conclusions of the study underscore the complexity of the Progressive Era and the impossibility of fitting a study of Lane into a historiographical pattern.

1
Preparation, 1864-1894

> *Without the labor unions of our land politi-*
> *cians and political parties would not fear labor;*
> *it is organization that compels recognition. Poli-*
> *ticians and princes are of one stripe—they yield*
> *only to coercion and realize no necessity which*
> *they are not made to feel.*

Lane editorial,
Tacoma Daily News, September 2, 1893

I

During his first thirty years, Franklin K. Lane developed the personality, obtained the education, and gained the experience that prepared him for a successful career in public service. He exhibited, during these years, an ambitious restlessness, rather than a fixation for holding public office. He considered the ministry, then tried journalism, studied law, and returned to journalism, all the while dabbling in political reform and becoming acquainted with active, capable persons who proved useful to him in later years. The path he followed was traditional. In background, values, and personality, he resembled numerous members of his generation who also used law or journalism, or both, as a professional base for reform or as a vehicle to gain public office.

II

Life began for Lane in a minister's home near Charlottetown, Prince
Edward's Island, Canada, on July 15, 1884. His parents, Christopher S.
Lane and Carolina Burns Lane, were Presbyterian prohibitionists of Scotch-
Irish heritage. The seven years following Franklin's birth were important
for Caroline and Christopher. They gave birth to two more sons, George
and Frederick, and a daughter, Maude. Meanwhile, repeated attacks of
bronchitis weakened Reverend Lane's voice and forced him to give up
his ministry. He turned to the study of dentistry. To support the household during his course of study, Caroline maintained a boardinghouse in
addition to caring for her four young children. When Christopher completed his dental training, he first looked for a suitable location in Nova
Scotia, but finally, in 1871, attracted by reports of opportunity, the
Lanes moved to Napa, California, a small town some fifteen miles north
of San Francisco Bay.

The children grew up in the certitude of the Presbyterian faith, impressed with the worth of unselfishness, rules of courtesy, and moral
precepts. Each Sunday evening, parents and children gathered to con-
fess the week's transgressions, to pray, and to sing hymns. Franklin
learned from his father to enjoy the out-of-doors, use guns, care for
horses, fish, camp, and sail. He listened to his mother read aloud and
learned from her to apply himself to his school work.

In 1876, the family moved to Oakland, a growing city across the
bay from San Francisco, an area that offered greater professional opportunities for the father and better schools for the children than could
be found in Napa. Franklin entered Oakland High School where he impressed teachers and students as bright, confident, and gregarious, traits
that won him the honor of delivering the class oration at graduation in
1880.[1]

Franklin seriously considered following his father's first calling, the
ministry, but he questioned some of his parent's religious tenets. When
he appeared before an examining board of the Presbyterian Church, he
underwent two hours of questioning that served to accent his theological
doubts. The board decided his superior ability made him too good a prospect to lose, despite his wavering Presbyterian faith, and they asked him to
return in six months, hoping that time would ease his skepticism. After

the examination, one of his inquisitors continued informally to point out the eternal truths of Presbyterianism. Lane's uncertainty persisted. Finally, the minister remarked, almost flippantly, "Well, Lane, why not become a Unitarian preacher?"[2] This remark, coming from a clergyman, was too much for a teenager struggling with religious doubts. It exhibited such indifference to strict orthodoxy, and thus to eternal damnation, that Lane never again thought about entering the ministry.

With high school completed and the ministry eliminated as a possible career, he took a job as a printer's devil in the office of the *Oakland Times* and quickly earned reporter status with a special interest in politics. The summer of 1883, he supported the efforts of John H. Wigmore, an overzealous Harvard graduate with a plan to reform the city by organizing a reform club. The following year, the twenty-year-old Lane accepted the offer of the prohibitionist candidate for governor to become a regular campaign speaker.

Lane's newspaper work, his college friends from Wigmore's reform movement, and his ambition persuaded him to return to school. In January 1885, he enrolled as a special student at the University of California in nearby Berkeley. Part-time reporting jobs with the *San Francisco News, San Francisco Letter, San Francisco Examiner,* and *Alta California* provided him with an income. As a special student, he choose his own curriculum, mostly courses in political science, economics, and history. He joined a fraternity and the campus's political science club, where he gained the nickname of "Demosthenes Lane." In the spring of 1886, after two and one-half semesters, he left Berkeley to enroll at the Hastings Law School, a branch of the University of California in San Francisco. Before completing the usual course of study, he took and passed the California bar examination in January 1888.[3]

At first, Lane's legal career stopped with his passing the bar examination, because he judged the world of law to lack the excitement he found in the world of journalism. The thought of "quarreling like school boys over a few hundred dollars" held no appeal for him. Passing the bar examination, however, and having been successful in newspaper work heightened his sense of security and contributed to his increasing desire to travel, to earn more money, and to find greater intellectual challenges than those evident to him in San Francisco. He wrote to his friend Wigmore, who by then was a Boston attorney, and inquired about the possibilities of a newspaper job in the East. Before his plans could materialize, the *San Francisco Chronicle* offered Lane a regular staff position, which he accepted for the comfortable sum of $25 a week and which left him with some free time. His major responsibility with the *Chronicle*, that of writing sensational stories, did little to ease his restlessness. He already had done some editorial writing for smaller papers and anything else seemed second-best.[4]

He used his free time to satisfy his compulsion to reform city politics by joining with James P. Phelan, three years Lane's senior and a millionaire by inheritance, to organize the Young Men's Democratic League. The league, one of many San Francisco reform groups, hoped to stimulate political awareness among voters and to press for reform. The new league proved more successful than the Municipal Reform League Lane had helped to found five years earlier. During 1888-89, it served as the nucleus of a drive to bring about ballot reform. Lane worked as a member of the league's committee responsible for drafting a bill the league planned to present to the state legislature. In the autumn of 1888, the league's bill won the support of the Federated Trades and Labor Organizations of the Pacific Coast, and this endorsement won recognition from the legislature. In February 1889, the Legislative Assembly Committee on Election Laws invited Lane to present the league's arguments. He spoke for an hour and a half, armed with a sense of righteousness and examples from his friend Wigmore's new book, *The Australian Ballot System as Embodied in the Legislation of Various Countries,* the first American study of the Australiam ballot. When Lane finished, the Reform Ballot Bill had only one opponent left on the committee, and even he, Lane boasted, acknowledged its virtues. Despite Lane's and the league's efforts, and the backing of those persons he called "the best men in both Houses," the bill failed to pass. Lane blamed the failure on the widespread graft and bribery imbeded in the legislature. Two years later, the legislature introduced the Australian ballot in California, but Lane, once a leader of the movement for ballot reform, was not part of the final victory, having moved from the state.[5]

In May 1889, the *San Francisco Chronicle* finally granted Lane his wish, appointing him its New York correspondent. His primary responsibility was reading the foreign news cables reaching New York and then rewriting and forwarding the ones suitable for the *Chronicle.* It was an important assignment, not usually entrusted to a twenty-four-year-old.

Lane was delighted, not as much with the recognition of his work that the appointment represented, as with the opportunity to see more of the country.

In New York, he found the intellectual atmosphere he desired. Each week, he joined with friends to discuss a variety of topics: poetry, literature, art, and religion, as well as economics and politics. He also joined the Reform Club of New York and came into contact with reformer Henry George, then at the zenith of his popularity and influence. The two men developed a friendship, although Lane never became a single taxer. Lane revered George for reinforcing the foundations of his intellectual house and judged him one of the greatest forces of his generation.[6]

Despite stimulating friendship, participation in reform activities, and a cosmopolitan atmosphere, Lane again was restless. He easily mastered the job of reporting on foreign affairs and soon found his ambition spurred him to seek greater challenges and increased rewards. When he learned, in the spring of 1891, that a daily paper was for sale in Tacoma, Washington, he explored the possibility of buying it. He collected his savings, borrowed a few additional thousands of dollars from his friend from college Sidney Mezes, and at the age of twenty-six acquired his own newspaper. New York City, once so eagerly sought, gave way after two years for the challenge of running his own paper and writing his own editorials.

III

Tacoma, in 1891, was a booming city of fifty thousand, well situated on Puget Sound and at the western terminus of the Northern Pacific Railroad. The city's economic well-being rested upon the vast forests that dominated the northwestern region of the United States, but to sustain its prosperity, Tacoma depended upon investment capital from other parts of the country.

Lane's running of his paper revealed a strain of idealistic reform and a greater interest in national rather than local conditions. He immediately changed the paper's name to the *Tacoma Daily News,* but announced he would continue its traditional support of the Democratic party. Although his editorials ranged from the theatre to French literature, European affairs, and women's rights, most of his editorial writing dealt with politics.

During the campaign of 1892, Lane championed Cleveland's candidacy. Throughout the summer and fall, he carried on his editorial page the inscription "For President, Grover Cleveland, For Vice President, Adlai E. Stevenson," small pictures of the two men, a copy of the Democratic platform, and a quote from a James Russell Lowell speech made before the Boston Tariff Reform Club.

Lane argued that the Democratic party was the friend of the laboring man and the Republican party the friend of the trusts. He criticized Samuel Gompers, president of the American Federation of Labor, for maintaining that laborers had no interest in the success of either party. When the Homestead steel strike occurred during the summer of 1892, Lane defended the strikers, branded the Pinkertons as "men who kill for money, thugs, and toughs ... hired by a purse-proud capitalist." He demanded that the Washington State Democratic party make it impossible for such a tragedy to happen within its state.[7] Although he regretted the violence, he emphatically stood behind labor, which he believed was waging a revolution to assert its rights.[8]

The *Tacoma Daily News,* in addition to being unusual on the West Coast for its prolabor stance, was one of the few anti-silver newspapers in the Pacific watershed. Lane's reason was simple, although probably wrong; he asserted that the ability to earn or borrow money was unrelated to how much the government coined, and therefore the minting of more money would not alleviate the financial woes of the debtor. The champions of a monetary system based on the parity of silver and gold argued that an increased money supply lowered interest rates and encouraged inflation, both of which helped the debtor. Lane dismissed this reasoning and backed Cleveland's gold-standard proposals, although by so doing he took a position similar to that of the corporations and banks he censured for oppressing labor.[9]

While editor, he directed his strongest condemnation to the tariff. He called it a crime against labor, an oppressive tool, and a special privilege for one class. Even after the 1892 election, Lane continued his indignant criticism. According to him, the tariff kept out foreign goods, and promoted an influx of foreign workers; it regulated the price of commodities and left open to free competition the price of labor. He insisted that since the tariff protected only "the millionaire manufacturer," the government either desist in granting this privilege or else extend equivalent privileges to the farmer and laborer. His preference, however, was free trade.[10]

In 1892, the Populist party nominated a national ticket and ran a full slate of candidates in numerous states west of the Mississippi River and in the South. Most people in the states from Wisconsin and Illinois east to the Atlantic coast viewed the Populist platform as dangerously radical, but many in the South and Far West, including Lane, saw no cause for alarm. To him, populism merely represented "a protest against wrong and injustice"; and with the purpose of the party, he believed there was "much to sympathize."[11] Although he labeled the party's presidential candidate, James B. Weaver, a demagogue, he concluded that Walter Q. Gresham, who had declined the nomination, would have added dignity to the movement. Lane saw little basic difference between the Democratic and Populist parties, but to reach that conclusion, he embraced a long list of specific Populist platform demands that few other Democrats accepted. During 1892-94, he endorsed such Populist measures as postal savings banks, immigration restrictions, direct election of senators, direct election of the president and vice-president, the initiative, the referendum, a graduated income tax, an inheritance tax, and a heavy tax on unoccupied land. He found nothing frightening in the possibility of Kansas voters sending to the United States Senate the Populist Mary Elizabeth Lease, who had won fame for her advice to farmers to raise more hell and less corn. If it were right for the eastern manufacturer to have a tariff, Lane believed it only right for the Great Plains farmer to have a government loan and for the western miner to have aid in maintaining the price of silver. Despite his endorsement of many diverse planks from the Populist platform, he believed the party derived its main strength from the silver question. The electoral success of the Populists, therefore, surprised Lane, who nevertheless still predicted an early death for the party. He reasoned that the Populists, once their party's fortunes ebbed, would vote Democratic.[12] By early 1894, however, his newspaper faced a crisis equally severe but more immediate than the demise he prophesized for the Populist party.

The prosperity Tacoma and the country enjoyed in 1891 when Lane bought his paper proved to be temporary. Throughout 1893, banks, railroads, and other commercial enterprises declared bankruptcy with increasing regularity as the country slid into a depression that lasted four years. Lane's rival paper, the Republican-oriented *Ledger,* reduced the wages of the members of the typographical union. His *Tacoma Daily News,* on the other hand, maintained its union wage, the only daily paper in Tacoma to do so, and even allowed the union to use the paper's presses to run off propaganda. For his efforts, Lane won the gratitude of the union, but his prolabor sentiment helped push him into bankruptcy. On June 11, 1894, exactly fourteen months after his marriage to Anne Wintermute of Tacoma, he watched his paper sold at auction. For the next six months, he worked for the new owner. Lane pondered his future, even asking his friend Wigmore, who had been a professor at Fukuzawa University in Tokyo from 1889 to 1892, about employment opportunities in Japan.[13] Still restless and ambitious, the thirty-year-old Lane decided to return to San Francisco. He had been gone five and one-half years. Above all, he needed a job, and in the Bay area's newspaper world he had experience and a favorable reputation. Also, his immediate family lived there and his brother George had opened a law office in San Francisco. He arrived in time to celebrate Christmas, 1894.

2
Politics in California, 1895-1906

*The great struggle of our time is against
special privileges.*

Lane, undated campaign speech
for governor, 1902

*The law must not be severe or lenient with
any man simply because he is rich nor because
he is poor. It must not become the tool of class
antagonism for either the persecution of the
well-to-do or for the repression of the masses
of the people.*

Lane to Orva G. Williams, April 7, 1904

I

In the course of eleven years, 1895 to 1906, Lane shifted his profession
from journalism to law and changed from a political reform advocate to
an elected officeholder. As he made these transitions, he extended his
range of acquaintances, his reputation, and his political ambitions from
the local, to the state, and, finally, to the national arena. He demonstrated in his first four campaigns, starting in 1898, that his extroverted

personality and commitment to progressivism appealed to voters. By 1902, he had fashioned a coalition of labor union and middle-class reform support and stood as California's most prominent Democrat. His narrow failure to win the governorship that year convinced him that his political future lay in Washington and not in a state in which Republican voters vastly outnumbered Democrats. Fortunately for Lane, his ability to win votes had attracted the notice of politicians across the country. His reform bent, moreover, harmonized with the growing reform mood in the White House, in Congress, and in an increasing number of states. His activities in California made a contribution to this mood.

Upon returning to San Francisco, he joined *Arthur McEwen's Letter* as business manager and columnist. McEwen and Lane had known one another for over a decade, and from 1889 to 1891, when they both lived in New York City, they shared a bachelor's apartment. In February 1894, McEwen quarreled with his boss, William Randolph Hearst, quit his job, and started his weekly *Letter* because he wanted "free expression" to denounce the "greed and dishonesty which master this town."[1] Then in Tacoma, Lane followed the launching of the *Letter,* commenting that its owner "cannot be 'reached' in any way, and we may expect his paper to be as honest and fearless as it must be brilliant."[2]

Lane's association with the *Letter* lasted less than seven months, because in June 1895, its owner discontinued publication; he had not found enough readers who appreciated the paper's ardently crusading style. Hearst, who recognized McEwen's ability, rehired him despite their previous quarrels and McEwen's harsh words.[3]

Lane, however, decided to end his journalistic career. Twice within one year, he had found himself unemployed, and in the summer of 1895, securing another newspaper job meant working for a large paper. After running his own paper and experiencing the unrestricted, although financially impoverished, atmosphere of the *Letter,* he lacked sufficient motivation for that prospect. He was ambitious, moreover, and after more than a decade in journalism, he had accumulated little money. In other ways, of course, he had profited from his years of newspaper work.[4] He had developed a direct, easy style of writing that remained a strong asset for the rest of his life, and the experience of writing about subjects as diverse as sensation stories, world politics, and literature had increased his breadth of knowledge.

II

With his newspaper career behind him, Lane turned his energies toward building a private law practice in partnership with his brother, but he found that public affairs continued to dominate his interest. In 1896, he supported William Jennings Bryan for president, because he agreed with Bryan's position that the basic election issue was the emerging class-structured society and the subsequent upper-class exploitation of the working class. Lane, in keeping with his earlier position, disagreed with the young Nebraskan's advocacy of free coinage of silver; nevertheless, he publicly endorsed him. During the campaign, Lane devoted special attention to San Francisco's mayoralty race, which his friend James D. Phelan won. Phelan's victory, less than eighteen months after Lane embarked on a full-time practice of law, led Lane into a political career.

By the time of Phelan's election, he and other reformers realized that San Francisco required more than an honest mayor to clean up the scandalous conditions that plagued the city, especially the administration of public utilities. The reformers reasoned that much of the difficulty resulted from inadequacies of the 1854 city charter and its two hundred-plus amendments.[5] After a year in office, Phelan appointed a nonpartisan committee of ninety persons to draft a new charter. He included his friend because Lane was an attorney, knew the city, and had concern for good government. In addition to his civic interest, Lane no doubt recognized that the association with the committee would be a boost to his law practice. As one of its members, he favored the adoption in the charter of civil service reform, increased power for the mayor, greater home rule, the referendum, the initiative, and the recall. On May 26, 1898, the citizens of San Francisco accepted the new charter by a margin of twenty-three hundred votes. During the campaign for adoption, Lane made speeches, wrote newspaper publicity, and helped organize support.[6]

With his appetite further whetted by his experience with the charter movement, he decided to seek the Democratic nomination for city-county attorney. He gained the nomination by appealing in person to the majority of delegates, many of whom he knew from various reform activities. To run against Lane, the Republicans selected William F. Fitzgerald, the attorney general of the state and, in Lane's words, "the best man on the Republican ticket."[7] Lane aimed his campaign at factory

0734254

workers and middle-class reformers. One noontime, upon the advice of a friend, Lane appeared outside the Union Iron Works plant, climbed upon a wagon, and gave a short campaign speech. The tactic of campaigning outside factories at lunch was new to San Francisco, but made to order for the outgoing, articulate Lane. His teenage printer's devil experience and his consequent honorary typographical (Tacoma No. 175) union memberships strengthened his appeal for union support. His prior legal work also paid political dividends. During 1895-96, Lane and his brother cleared the land titles of some five thousand persons of moderate incomes when the Jose Noe family claimed ownership on the grounds of a technical error in the transfer of titles from an old Spanish land grant. The grateful recipients of the Lane brothers' efforts organized the Franklin K. Lane Campaign Club and worked for his election. On the other hand, not one newspaper supported Lane, who nevertheless won the election by 832 votes. Only two other Democrats, including Phelan as mayor, won office that year, while the Republican candidate for governor carried San Francisco by 12,000 votes.[8]

Lane worked hard and capably as city attorney. The position paid $5,000 annually (compared with the governor's $6,000) and permitted Lane five assistants, a messenger, a clerk, and a typist. Under the new charter, the city attorney served as the legal adviser to all county and city officials; he likewise had "to define and construe" the new charter, and thus give it an "initial construction."[9] Lane appointed his younger brother George as his first assistant. George usually analyzed cases and developed their major legal ramifications, and Lane, more forceful as a speaker and writer, presented the cases in court. The next two elections indicated that the public endorsed the manner in which Lane shifted from a private career to administering a public office.

Although the charter called for municipal elections in odd years, the implementation of such a schedule initially required elections in consecutive years. On October 3, 1899, the Democratic party renominated Lane by acclamation, an action that San Francisco newspapers, in a reversal from the previous year, supported during the campaign. Lane won reelection by a landslide of 12,409, the greatest margin in history for that office. Two years later the Democrats, after Lane had declined their mayoralty nomination, again renominated him for city-county attorney by acclamation, and the newly formed Union Labor party, whose candidate won the mayoralty contest, refused to nominate anyone to oppose Lane.

50155

The city's newspapers again reversed their positions. In fact, Lane wrote to his friend Wigmore, "They hardly mentioned . . . that I was a candidate."[10] Nevertheless, Lane received 62.6 percent of the votes cast, 10,488 more than his opponent and more than twice as many votes as the Democratic candidate for mayor.

As city attorney, Lane handled as many cases in five years as his predecessors had done in sixteen years. The opinions he rendered, moreover, were clear and straightforward in style and legalistically sound in content. In every instance that the Supreme Court of California reviewed one of Lane's opinions, it sustained his work.[11]

The taste of public office stimulated Lane's political ambition. When he began working on the charter committee, he indicated no plans or desire to run for office. Shortly after his first election, he confided to Wigmore that he did not "want to stay in politics." Two years, he thought, "will be long enough for me." Three years and two resounding victories later, however, he talked not about leaving politics but about becoming governor.[12]

III

Lane set out to capture his party's gubernatorial nomination with two strong assets: himself and Gavin McNab. Lane's ability to campaign, his popularity in San Francisco, and his performance in office made him a logical candidate for state office. In 1902, politicians who, in general, shared Lane's reform bent and who also supported the leadership of McNab, dominated the Democratic party. McNab, a San Francisco lawyer, wanted a winner and a progressive for a candidate, backed Lane from the start, and thereby practically assured him of the nomination.

Lane, although grateful for and receptive to McNab's backing, also wanted to generate support for his candidacy on his own. This move, Lane knew, would strengthen his hand at the Democratic convention and weaken the impact of any possible charge of being a boss-promoted candidate. He also thereby would become better known in the state and boost his chances in the election. Aware of his solid public support among San Francisco voters, he visited the Central Valley counties, talked with party officials, gave a few speeches, and enlisted the support of small newspapers. By the middle of July, some nineteen papers endorsed Lane's candidacy, starting with the *Sacramento Bee* and the *Redlands Daily Review,* and the Republican press mentioned Lane as the likely Democratic nominee.

The California Democrats held their convention the first week in September. Behind the scenes, the McNab-Lane wing of the party agreed to support George Patton of Los Angeles for convention chairman in return for Patton's support of Lane's nomination. This arrangement, plus his initial strength, especially among the labor-union delegates, gave Lane the nomination on the first ballot. The convention then adopted a progressive platform restating familiar national demands for low tariffs, trust regulation, direct election of United States senators, and direct legislation through the use of referendum, recall, and initiative. For California, the platform called for removing the Southern Pacific Railroad from politics, levying a franchise tax on corporations, adopting a merit system in the civil service, and establishing a bureau of mines. The platform reflected the strength labor exercised with the party; it also recommended the exclusion of Chinese immigration, the adoption of an eight-hour day on public works, and the creation of a new state labor bureau.[13]

Lane and the Democrats had few grounds to be optimistic about the election. Republican William McKinley had carried the state in the presidential elections of 1896 and 1900, and the last Democratic governor, elected in 1894, had faced a legislature with a Republican majority. In 1902, moreover, the California delegation in Congress was solidly Republican, and the state legislature counted ninety-four Republicans to only twenty-six Democrats. Then, too, the Republicans had nominated for governor Oakland's Mayor George C. Pardee and thereby avoided a party split. The Republican party at that time consisted essentially of two equal factions: supporters and opponents of the Southern Pacific Railroad. Neither group had enough convention votes to nominate a leader from its ranks, so Pardee gained the prize because he was the most prominent of a handful of Republicans who hoped to reconcile the factions by compromise.

Although as a candidate, Pardee wanted to avoid definite commitment to either segment of his party, his record in Oakland indicated that he sympathized more with the aims of the opponents rather than the supporters of the Southern Pacific. In 1888, for example, he had bolted the party when he suspected corruption and had joined a fusion ticket of progressive Republicans and Democrats. Nevertheless, Pardee represented neither of his party's factions and therefore generated little enthusiasm; in that sense, he was a weak candidate. On the other hand, with his party irreconcilably divided, he also was the strongest candidate the Republicans could send against the Democrats.[14]

Lane conducted a campaign noteworthy for its appeal to labor and for its lack of party unity. He often spoke to six or eight audiences a day, in addition to impromptu stops at factories, stores, street corners, and wherever else groups of people gathered. Laborers soon learned that Lane previously had been a union man and held two honorary memberships, that he had been a prime mover in the incorporation of eight-hour-day and minimum-wage clauses in the San Francisco city charter, and that he had led the fight for the policy that required the union label on all goods purchased by the city of San Francisco. Lane defended unions with the phrase "Organized labor is responsible labor" and with opposition to the use of injunctions in labor disputes. He publicized his belief that the laborer did not receive "his full proportion of wealth which he produces."[15]

Although Lane directed his major efforts toward the labor vote, he also campaigned for increased irrigation, reclamation, and conservation programs. He likewise demanded reform of state hospitals, asylums, and prisons. He advocated government regulations of railroads and condemned the influence of the Southern Pacific in California politics. Although pledged to enact the entire Democratic paltform, Lane emphasized the parts of it that called for the improvement of the civil service, highways, public education, and the fair taxation of corporations. In the middle of the campaign, a United States circuit court upheld Lane's suit to have national corporations pay San Francisco city taxes, and thereby added some unexpected substantiation to his previous charges of tax favoritism to corporations.

Lane conducted an issue-oriented campaign; some important Democrats disagreed with its positions and withheld their support. Ex-governor James Budd left California to aid William Randolph Hearst's bid for a New York State congressional seat. Bernard D. Murphy, the party's state chairman, frequently stayed away from party headquarters and provided inadequate leadership; and the chairman of the campaign committee reported that numerous party leaders likewise failed to give full cooperation. The state's largest Democratic newspaper, Hearst's *San Francisco Examiner,*

opposed Lane's candidacy by ignoring most of his campaign effort, praising Pardee, and misrepresenting Lane's positions. The most blatant instance
of the latter occurred when Hearst published excerpts from a small prohibitionist newspaper for which Lane had served as business manager
while in college and incorrectly credited the excerpts to Lane. On election
morning, Hearst dispatched a special train throughout northern California's
wine-growing districts distributing issues of his paper.[16] Lane realized his
image as a friend of labor, an opponent of the South Pacific's influence
in politics, and a champion of increased government programs and regulation alienated some Democrats and appealed to some Republicans. During the campaign, therefore, he called himself a "Roosevelt Democrat,"
frequently expressed hearty sympathy with the President, and asked for
nonpartisan support.[17]

Pardee, like Lane, ran a campaign notable for its lack of personal accusations or bitter recriminations. After Lane won his nomination, Pardee
sent "as hearty congratulations as your Republican opponent can," and
hoped that after the election "there will be between us nothing but the
kindest personal feeling." The Republican nominee then told Lane that
during the campaign he would "take great pleasure in speaking of you
only in the kindest terms." Lane replied, "All that you have said is most
cordially and sincerely echoed by me. . . . I trust we will always be friends."
The two candidates honored their intentions, and publicly took pride in
the first-name friendship they maintained.

As a campaigner, Pardee lacked Lane's personality. He suffered from
his party's internal feud and from Lane's repeated criticism of the Republican party's negative attitude toward labor and close relationship to
the Southern Pacific Railroad. On the other hand, Pardee enjoyed the
benefits of a well-financed, efficient campaign organization and the support of the majority of California's newspapers.[18]

On election day, Lane ran well ahead of his party but lost the governorship by 143,783 to 146,332 votes. Republicans won every state executive
office, the three vacant seats of the state supreme court, five of the state's
eight seats in Congress, and a sufficient number of state legislative seats
to maintain a three-fourths majority in the assembly and a seven-eighths
majority in the senate. But while Pardee defeated Lane by 2,549 votes, an
0.88 percent victory margin, the Republican candidate for lieutenant
governor defeated his Democratic counterpart by 20,290 votes. Lane
finished first in ten counties that the previous Republican gubernatorial

candidate had carried four years earlier and lost only one of the counties that his predecessors had won. In San Francisco, Lane attracted approximately 10,000 more votes than Pardee, whereas four years earlier the Republican candidate for governor had carried the city by 3,400 votes.[19]

The closeness of Lane's defeat led to accusations that the Republicans intentionally miscounted the votes and thereby stole the election for Pardee. The *San Francisco Star,* an ardent Lane supporter, claimed the returns from Mayor Pardee's home town of Oakland "were held back and locked up without any opportunity being given for their examination. Democrats were refused permission to inspect the tally-sheets in the different precincts."[20] Although Lane did not publicly challenge the legality of Pardee's victory, he and his family believed that Hearst had manipulated the election returns.

IV

Despite Hearst's antagonism and the 1902 defeat, Lane's stock among San Francisco Democrats remained high. He was by far the most popular Democrat in the city and enjoyed political support that crossed party lines. In 1903, when the time came to nominate someone for mayor, the majority of Democrats immediately looked to Lane, who in turn wanted them to look elsewhere. For several reasons, he had little desire to run for mayor. If nominated, it would mean his fifth campaign in six years. In the municipal elections of 1901, moreover, the Union Labor party ran candidates for the first time, elected a mayor, and pushed the Democratic party into a minority status. Furthermore, several months before the Democrats met to nominate their mayoral candidate, President Roosevelt had promised Lane the next vacancy on the Interstate Commerce Commission. The reasons not to run were weighty, but the Democrats pleaded, insisting that no other Democrat had a chance to win. Torn both ways, Lane rationalized to his confidant Wigmore, "I acted out of a sense of loyalty to my party and a desire to do something to rid the city of its present cursed administration."[21] In the end, Lane no doubt ran because he believed he could win. His earlier electoral success, however, clouded his political analysis of chances for victory. Considering these chances, and the pending Roosevelt appointment, Lane blundered.

Before accepting the nomination, Lane sent a letter to the convention stating three conditions that had to exist before he would run: the offer had to come from a united party; the loyalty and integrity of those named to run for supervisors had to be above question; and the party had to understand that he would make no promises of patronage and would make appointments on the basis of merit. The convention nominated Lane on the first ballot. In his acceptance speech, Lane emphasized that he meant the conditions spelled out in his prenomination letter, adding that "perhaps some of you have criticized [the letter] on the ground that it was not the work of a shrewd politician, and that is probably so, but I have yet to hear the man who says that it was not forthright, that it was not honest, and that I did not mean every word that was in it." His campaign, he continued before a cheering audience, would be a fight for good government, and would mean "good men in office, good methods, and a square deal to everyone." It would be a "fight for principle."[22]

The campaign developed into a three-corner contest with party lines somewhat blurred. The Union Labor party renominated Mayor Eugene E. Schmitz, and the Republicans nominated a wealthy businessman, Henry J. Crocker, nephew of one of the founders of the Southern Pacific Railroad. To reduce Lane's labor support, Abraham Ruef, the real power of Schmitz's administration, used two campaign stratagems. First, he capitalized on the strong anti-Chinese feeling in the city and the fact that Lane employed a Chinese cook. Ruef devised and widely distributed small cards with a picture of a Chinese man and the line "Me cookee for Lane while Lane talkie for white labor." Second, Ruef emphasized Lane's association with Gavin McNab, whom workingmen despised because they believed McNab was responsible for Phelan's decision, as mayor, to use police to protect strikebreakers. Consequently, labor rallied around Schmitz and conservatives and most business interests united behind Crocker.

Without the labor vote, Lane's basic support consisted of those nonlabor, nonbusiness citizens who wanted good government. He denounced the Schmitz-Ruef corruption and the privilege-seeking Republicans. "I want a San Francisco," Lane campaigned, "that has a moral tone: that goes back to that old commandment, 'Thou shalt not steal.'"[23] Many prominent Republicans and at least one important Union Labor party leader publicly endorsed his crusade for clean government.[24] Lane also enjoyed the support of the *Bulletin* and Hearst's *Examiner*. By this

time, Hearst had announced his candidacy for the 1904 Democratic
presidential nomination and endorsed, therefore, the entire Democratic
ticket. He strongly backed Lane, but at the same time never once criticized Schmitz. The day after the election, the *Examiner* heartily congratulated Schmitz on his victory. Lane's defeat was not close. He received 12,578 votes to Crocker's 19,621 and Schmitz's 26,016.[25]

Lane's loss was understandable. Democrats supporting him had difficulty soliciting campaign funds when Lane refused to promise patronage.
With few exceptions, businessmen refused to contribute money or support because Lane consistently attacked corporate corruption without
reminding voters that many businessmen were honest. But primarily,
Lane lost because Ruef masterfully usurped Lane's labor backing. "The
fight was along class lines entirely," Lane analyzed, with "the employers
on one side and the wage earners on the other. . . . I stood for good
government and in the battle my voice could hardly be heard. It was a
splendid old fight." Undaunted, he stated that "it will, of course, not
lead to my retirement from politics."[26]

V

In January 1904, two months after he failed in his bid to become
mayor, Lane's term as city attorney expired. For the next two and
one-half years, he concentrated on his law practice, enjoyed the steadily
increasing income it provided, and bided his political time, waiting for
Roosevelt to name him to the Interstate Commerce Commission.

Politicians other than Roosevelt had noticed Lane's political career.
Early in 1904, New York's Senator David B. Hill, impressed by Lane's
1902 gubernatorial campaign, informed him through a mutual friend
that the New York delegation would cast its votes for him as vice-
presidential nominee at the national convention scheduled for the summer. Lane had to reply that he had been born in Canada and thus was
ineligible for the honor.[27] In the 1904 session of the California state
legislature, the Democrats cast their votes for Lane for United States
senator, an honorary tribute since the Republicans controlled the body
and elected a Republican.

Lane realized, of course, that his political future lay in Washington, not in Republican-dominated California. Another defeat might irreparably tarnish the reputation he enjoyed as California's most prominent Democrat. Thus, during the 1904 national campaign, he did little on behalf of his party. He occasionally made a speech but never as the principal speaker, and although he consistently celebrated the tradition of Democratic progressivism, and sometimes praised the Democratic ticket, he never criticized the energetic Republican nominee Theodore Roosevelt. The conservative Democratic candidate Alton B. Parker disappointed Lane, especially in relation to Roosevelt, whom Lane had admired for over a decade. In 1892, he had praised Roosevelt's record as civil service commissioner and recommended that President Cleveland reappoint him.[28] For Lane, the election of Roosevelt meant the election of a man with whom he identified politically and who had promised him a new career.

3
On the Interstate Commerce Commission, 1906-1913

*The greatest force standing today between
the United States and government ownership
of railways is the act to regulate commerce,
backed by the opinion of the decent people.*

Lane, speech before the City Club
of Chicago, December 23, 1908

I

On June 26, 1906, when he signed the Hepburn bill into law, Roosevelt completed a legislative process that marked a turning point in the history of the Interstate Commerce Commission. The Hepburn Act granted new powers to the commission and ended the general helplessness that had characterized it during the preceding decade. Because Senate confirmation of Lane's nomination to the ICC was related to passage of the Hepburn proposal, Roosevelt's signature that June day had a special meaning for his friend from California. The President expected him to vitalize the commission. Because the commission had new powers, Roosevelt expected it to establish federal control over the railroads. Lane's work enhanced his national reputation as a capable progressive with leadership qualities; it also fulfilled Roosevelt's expectations.

Lane owed his appointment to Benjamin Ide Wheeler, president of the

University of California. Wheeler and Roosevelt had been friends since the late 1890s, when Wheeler was a professor at Cornell University in upstate New York. Although Wheeler was a Democrat, Roosevelt relied upon him for political advice throughout his governorship and presidency.[1] In the summer of 1899, Wheeler moved to the Berkeley campus as president and soon thereafter met and developed a friendship with Lane. Their mutual interest in politics, in clean government, and in the career of Roosevelt helped forge a strong bond between them.

In March 1903, when Lane prepared to journey to Washington as city attorney to argue a case for San Francisco,[2] Wheeler gave him a letter of introduction to Roosevelt.[3] On March 21, Lane, with the letter in hand, called at the White House. Roosevelt, like so many others, took an instant liking to the friendly "Roosevelt Democrat"; he invited Lane to stay for lunch. Before Lane returned to California, he accepted Roosevelt's invitation and again visited the executive mansion, talking away an evening with the President. By the time Lane left late that evening, the President, impressed by his visitor's quick mind, friendly countenance, and political opinions, had promised him the seat to be vacated upon James D. Yeoman's retirement from the ICC the next year.[4]

In November 1904, however, Roosevelt offered Yeoman's place on the commission not to his "good friend Lane," but to another friend, Senator Francis M. Cockrell, Democrat, of Missouri. Roosevelt apologetically wrote to Wheeler that "I never felt more caught and rarely more chagrined than when I discovered that I had utterly forgotten the promise about Franklin Lane." Roosevelt promised to make amends to Lane, but asked Wheeler if there were any truth in the charge that "Lane did not appear to advantage" in his mayoralty content. Wheeler's reply must have eased Roosevelt's doubt, for the next October, when Joseph W. Fifer resigned from the commission, the President announced his intention of naming Lane to the vacant post. Between the date he voiced his intentions and when he submitted Lane's name to the Senate for confirmation, Roosevelt's faith in Lane wavered again. Roosevelt confided to Wheeler that he had heard "some pretty strong assertions against Lane," adding that he still wanted to appoint him, "but of course under no consideration can I appoint any man who is not just the right man from the government standpoint." Lane told a friend that he believed the railroads, especially the Southern Pacific, worked determinedly to keep any independent West Coast man from membership on the commission and consequently charged they were responsible for any accusation against him. Once again Wheeler reassured Roosevelt that Lane was an exceptionally able, high-minded person.[5]

On December 6, 1905, Roosevelt formally submitted Lane's nomination to the Senate despite the opposition of some senators. The ICC then consisted of five members: two Republicans, two Democrats, and one vacancy. The Republican-controlled Senate found obnoxious the thought of giving Democrats a three-to-two majority of seats, but Roosevelt had no intention of withdrawing Lane's name. If the Senate refused to vote upon the nomination, he planned to resubmit Lane's name as soon as Congress adjourned. Roosevelt also attempted to enlist support for Lane by sending some clippings and letters about him to his friend Lyman Abbott, the editor of *Outlook*. He in turn championed Lane's appointment. Roosevelt concluded that the persons who opposed Lane were the same ones who fought the plan to increase the powers of the ICC.[6]

Although the Senate balked at approving his appointment, Lane's nomination met with considerable approval elsewhere. The California press, including the Republican segment, greeted the nomination with almost unanimous enthusiasm. The *Review of Reviews* called Lane "exactly the sort of man who should be placed on the Interstate Commerce Commission," and concluded that the Senate should immediately confirm "so brilliant an appointment."[7] Many of Lane's friends, including Senator Francis Newlands, William R. Wheeler, Albert Shaw, and John H. Wigmore, also lobbied for his confirmation, or as Lane expressed it: "I don't want to bring pressure to bear upon him [Roosevelt]; but, of course, I want him to know that I have friends who think well of me."[8] But Lane's greatest asset was Roosevelt. He promised that he would "make and am making as stiff a fight as I know how for you."[9] Roosevelt kept the promise and won the struggle; the day after he signed the Hepburn bill, the Senate confirmed Lane. Senate opposition to Lane subsided when Roosevelt agreed that he would appoint Republicans to the two new commissionerships that the Hepburn Act created.[10]

II

The early history of the Interstate Commerce Commission, which the Interstate Commerce Act of 1887 established, divided into three periods:

1887-97, 1897-1906, and 1906-17.[11] Substantial promise characterized the initial decade. The public viewed the act as the beginning of the end of railroad corruption and abuse of power that accompanied the era of massive construction during the latter third of the nineteenth century. The act forbade such practices as rebates, pooling, rate discrimination, and unreasonable rates. From the standpoint of eliminating railroad abuses, however, two major weaknesses plagued the commission. First, it had no power to enforce its decisions. Upon complaint, the commission could investigate a rate, declare it unjust, issue a cease-and-desist order against it, and hope the courts would endorce the order. The courts were sympathetic; they consistently reversed the commission's orders because of legal technicalities or because of differences of judgment about economic policy. During the 1890s, moreover, the average court case dragged on for four years. Meanwhile, the railroads were openly hostile to the commission's orders and worked to discredit its viability. The second major weakness of the commission was the curtailment of its authority through judicial interpretation. Although the original act granted no explicit rate-making power to it, the commission acted upon the assumption that this power was implied because the basic declaration and intent of the act was that all rates must be reasonable and just. For the first ten years of its existence, the commission did prescribe rates, but in 1897, in the *Maximum Freight Rate* case, the Supreme Court declared specifically that the commission did not have the power to set rates. As a result of this decision, the already weak commission lapsed into a state of helplessness; its promise and limited effectiveness virtually disappeared.[12]

From 1897 to 1906, the commission could do little more than publicize the need to amend the Act of 1887 and thereby give it meaningful power, especially in the field of rate control. The commission's best friends in demonstrating the need of a strong railroad regulatory commission were the railroads themselves. During the nineties and the early years of the twentieth century, what had been a network of a large number of independent railroad systems became a network of six or seven giant combinations. Many of the financial manipulations that accompanied this railroad concentration bordered on the unscrupulous. Then, beginning at the turn of the century, railroad rates took a sharp upward turn, while rate discrimination and other abuses remained widespread. The situation became so serious that some of the railroads themselves turned to the federal government for help, in part because some of the practices had become too costly.

The railroad's desire for reform, especially to strengthen the prohibition of rebates, served as a major impetus behind the Elkins Act of 1903. Under this act, the railroads had to file published rates with the ICC, and if the railroads departed in their charges from these rates, the act prescribed penalties. Furthermore, the shippers involved, as well as the railroad corporations, were liable to prosecution, rather than just the railroad officials. Although a step forward, the Elkins Act did not correct the major defects of the Act of 1887; it represented little more than a legal agreement among railroads to abolish some of their own dishonesty. Despite this, the Elkins Act gave encouragement to those seeking more drastic reform.[13]

The most important person who sought reform sat in the White House, and he seemed determined to bring the railroads under stricter control. In his annual message to Congress in December 1904, Roosevelt called the control of railroad rates "the most important legislative act now needed as regards the regulation of corporations." To generate support for rate regulation, he wrote letters, gave speeches, and met with influential persons. The debate he helped fuel led to fears about railroad property rights, which, in turn, Roosevelt tried to lessen in his December 1905 annual message to Congress, recommending that the courts review ICC decisions on rates. This spurred a new debate whether the court's review would be narrow or broad. The debates ended with the Hepburn Act, which included the essential reforms the President wanted.[14]

The act extended the authority of the commission to cover carriers other than railroads, such as pipelines (excluding water and gas) and express and sleeping-car companies. It reinforced the law against rebates, abolished the granting of passes (except to clergy, employees, and charitable cases), and gave broader definition to the term "railroad." The so-called commodity clause prohibited ownership by railroads of products and goods they transported. Of fundamental importance was the provision that the commission's orders were to be effective immediately, and that the burden of proof in the testing of the validity of these orders rested with the carrier. Regarding judicial review of rates, the act stipulated that the courts would have the power and left to the courts the decision whether the power would be narrow or broad. Most important of the amendments embodied in the act was the one that empowered the commission to establish maximum railroad rates. The commission, although essentially still restricted to eliminating specific abuses, made the most of its new powers through vigorous and effective administrative activity.[15]

The third pre-World War I period of the ICC, therefore, dated from passage of the Hepburn Act in 1906 and was a time of expansion of the commission's authority. Roosevelt had played the key role in making this third period possible. His interest in railroad reform seemed to transcend partisan consideration sufficiently to push the nomination of Democrat Lane, despite the fact that the President could have used the appointment to reward a progressive Republican in California and thus help the progressives in their struggle to control the state's party.

III

Four matters dominated Lane's work as a commissioner: rate discrimination, issuance of railroad securities, express companies, and supremacy of federal control over transportation.

Agreeing with Roosevelt, Lane believed rate discrimination was the central problem the ICC faced in regulating the nation's railroads. Through their rates, he concluded, the railroads could make each section of the country virtually independent of the remainder, or they could weld the nation into an economic unit with each section specializing according to its resources. Lane preferred the latter and worked through control of rates to achieve it. The difficulty, he explained in a speech before The City Club of Chicago, after two and one-half years on the commission, was that "No railroad man has as yet arisen before us to define what a reasonable rate is and yet the law declares that the railroad must charge a just and reasonable rate." Recognizing the impossibility of defining "a just and reasonable rate," Lane and the commission confidently worked toward standardization. "The great part of our work is . . . in the destruction of discriminations. We are trying as our first step," he added in his Chicago assessment, "to see if we cannot secure for all shippers the same rates, the same privileges, the same rights."[16]

Because of the Hepburn Act, the ICC, indeed, had considerable power over railroad rates, but Lane wanted the government to have more. He advocated a uniform policy pertaining to railroad rates such as existed in the postal service. In correspondence with Roosevelt, he suggested that

the commission have absolute power to raise and lower rates. Before the
Mann-Elkins Act of 1910 authorized it, he and the commission requested
the power to suspend rate changes or advances while proceedings were
pending before the commission.[17] In 1912, with Lane's contribution
seemingly being decisive, the ICC, in the *Shreveport rate* case, asserted
its authority over intrastate commerce rates when competing with
interstate rates. The commission ruled, with three strong dissenting
opinions, that no state could grant preferential rates to local commerce
and thereby discriminate against goods entering from other states.[18]

Lane's call for greater government regulation, over rates specifically
and railroads generally, was simply to make the system more equitable,
by his definition. "Our laws do not seek to establish dominion over
private capital for any other purpose than to make sure against injustice
being done the public," he concluded in a case he believed touched
"large and fundamental principles of law and governmental policies"
and that dismissed the first major general rate advance proposals the
railroads made after passage of the Hepburn Act.[19] In 1912, after five
and one-half years on the job, he concluded that "The problem of railroad regulation will always be with us, no matter in whom the ownership of the property used many be vested." Drawing upon his studies
of European railroads, as well as his ICC experiences, Lane explained
that regulation involved decisions about "rival communities and rival
industries and competing sections of the country," and that rate setting, therefore, directly influenced the country over and beyond the
annual percentage of profit railroad owners gained from their investment. In Lane's opinion, the persons best suited to deal with the continuing problem of regulation, especially rate regulation, were individuals
who looked at the problem with a national, rather than a private or
sectional, view.[20]

To eliminate stock watering and other abuses and to achieve a harmony
of rates, profits, and service he considered necessary, Lane insisted that
the federal government control the issuance of railroad stocks and bonds,
in addition to the regulation of rates. Railroad expansion and policies,
he advised Roosevelt as early as March 1907, "made imperative the consideration of a national policy."[21]

In June 1908, Lane published a plan that he hoped would form the
skeleton of a bill to establish a national policy. He suggested: (1) that the
government state "affirmatively and negatively, the purposes for which
an interstate carrier may issue stocks, bonds or notes," including a ban

on railroads owning stocks and bonds of a competitor; (2) that "the directors of the road proposing to use such securities should make a record of such proposed issue on the minutes of the corporation"; (3) that each director sign the record and send it to a designated governmental official or body; (4) that "an annual report . . . be sent to the same body, stating with particularity how such securities were disposed of, the proceeds resulting, and their use"; (5) that the government have "direct access to all books and accounts of the railroad,—and by law they may keep only such books, accounts or memoranda as the Interstate Commerce Commission shall authorize"; and (6) that any deviation "from the original declaration of intention made at the time of issuance of the securities . . . should subject the directors personally to such terms of imprisonment as the law may prescribe."[22]

Lane and other forces kept the idea alive. During the presidential campaign of 1908, the Republican party pledged itself to government control of the issuance and sale of railroad securities. In October 1909, he reported to President William Howard Taft that "I found in England and in France a prevailing belief among financiers that hundreds of millions of dollars of American railroad securities could be sold in those countries if this country undertook the supervision of capitalization." The next year, the ICC, in its annual report, recommended security regulation, and in 1911, the Taft administration brought forth a regulatory bill, but the progressives of both houses of Congress deemed it unacceptable, as did Lane.[23]

The case that Lane concluded was "the biggest one" he worked with while on the ICC dealt not with railroads, but with the express companies that transported goods between railroad stations and points of ultimate destination.[24] After the Hepburn Act brought express companies under the jurisdiction of the ICC, complaints against them started to accumulate. The commission requested Lane to conduct a comprehensive investigation into the companies' operations and rates; Lane did so and discovered ample grounds for criticism. Such practices as overcharging, undercharging, indirect routing, and delaying claim settlement were commonplace. As a result of his investigation, the commission issued a number of orders, including demands for "a new and simple method of stating rates by which one who is not an expert in the reading of tariffs may know what rate he should be charged," for a new system of classifying merchandise shipped, and for improved routing. The commission also made some recommendations, including a simplified rate-statement system that Lane had devised and that his fellow commissioner James D. Harlan called "ingenious and entirely original."[25] Not only did the express companies eventually adopt Lane's system, but the United States Postal Department did likewise when it inaugurated its parcel post program on January 1, 1913.[26] Despite the highly creditable work Lane and the commission performed, there remained considerable need for further experss company reform outside of the jurisdiction of the commission.

Early in his investigations, Lane had warned a group of important express company officials that unless they coordinated to improve their service and lower their rates, the public would demand and receive a competing public agency. Slightly over a year later, Lane's prediction came true when Congress established a parcel delivery service within the post office system.[27]

Permeating Lane's work with rates, securities, and express companies was a concern for the principle of federal regulation of transportation. This concern rested upon his assumption of an "inevitable tendency" toward monopoly, the result of many observations, but especially of the detrimental influence of the Southern Pacific Railroad in California. His experience on the ICC only reinforced his beliefs. A few months after joining the commission, he started to investigate consolidation and combination of the railroads and steamship lines controlled by Edward H. Harriman. Eventually he obtained from the magnate a statement of his ultimate objective.

During the hearings before an ICC panel early in 1907, Lane maneuvered Harriman into admitting that if it were not for the ICC, he would try his best to "spread not only over the Pacific coast, but spread out over the Atlantic coast" as well, until he controlled every railroad in the country.[28] Felix Frankfurter, then a young assistant United States attorney, attended the hearings because the Justice Department expected that the proceedings would lead to a lawsuit. The hearings made a profound impression on the young attorney because of Harriman's treatment "of his lawyers and their almost obsequious deference to him" and because of the unusual abilities Harriman and Lane demonstrated. Harriman's testimony, Frankfurter remembered years later, "soon reduced itself to a contest between him and Lane. He [Harriman] was not long on the witness stand before I realized that I was seeing a powerful personality and a keen mind in action." Despite Harriman's exceptional ability, Frankfurter observed that "Lane's quietly skillful cross-examination led . . . [Harriman] to a bluntness of speech which largely established the fears that lay behind the investigation." Lane's work in this case led to the suit that dissolved the merger of the Southern Pacific and the Union Pacific railroads.[29]

Lane believed that only the government could prevent the monopoly that would result if the business activities of persons such as Harriman remained unchecked. Competition in transportation, Lane reasoned, was an unnatural condition, and thus to maintain "regulated monopoly" he insisted that the government scrutinize and approve all consolidations and mergers. "The greatest force standing today between the United States and government ownership of railways," he pointed out in a speech the year following the Harriman hearings, "is the act to regulate commerce, backed by the opinion of the decent people."[30]

IV

Although Lane considered the ICC still in an experimental state in 1913, he concluded that during his seven years as a member, it had produced some notable achievements over and above the success of specific cases. First, he believed the mere presence of the commission was a moral force that resulted in incalculable benefit. Railroad leaders knew that if they did not listen to grievances and attempt to rectify abuses, the commission would. He also was pleased with the commission's successful enforcement of the prohibition against rebates. Another major achievement, according to Lane, was the commission's influence on the stabilization of rates during the financial panic of 1907. Had there "been no Hepburn Act during the last three months," Lane asserted early in 1908, "railroad rates would have been cut to pieces and railroad revenues would have fallen far below what they have."[31] Finally, Lane concluded, "that the effect of regulation has been to increase railroad earnings and put things upon a stable and more satisfactory basis."[32] In an article published in the spring of 1913, Lane pointed out that in 1890, the net operating income per mile of single-track railroad in the United States was $664. He compared this figure with the 1911 net per-mile income of $2,088. Lane realized the higher earnings figure was partly the result of added capital, but he maintained, nevertheless, that railroads had registered a definite increase.[33]

Certainly the work load of the ICC increased markedly during his service as commissioner, which, of course, started at the time the Hepburn Act became law. In 1905, the ICC received 65 formal complaints; in 1907, the first full year of operation under the Hepburn Act, the ICC received 415. By 1909, the number of complaints had climbed to 1,097. Meanwhile, the number of informal complaints filed skyrocketed from 503 to in 1905 to 4,435 in 1909. To help the commissioners handle the mounting work load, the number of ICC employees jumped from 178 to 1905 to 527 in 1909.[34]

Despite definite achievements, Lane believed problems remained. The ICC, for example, consistently but futilely requested Congress "to make provision for a physical valuation of railway property," a procedure long advocated by Senator Robert M. LaFollette and after May 1907 by Roosevelt. Lane confided to a friend that the railroads, to hamper such an evaluation should it become law, "have taken good care to destroy most of the books and papers that show cost."[35] In 1910, Lane supported the provisions of the Mann-Elkins Act, including President Taft's suggestion to establish a Commerce Court to hear appeals on commission decisions. The Commerce Court lasted less than three years. Initially Lane welcomed its creation for he believed such a court would be better qualified than the federal courts to judge the commission's specialized decisions. In fact, Lane remarked in 1909, the commission itself, "some years ago," had recommended just such a court. The commission dealt with economic questions, and Lane and the other commissioners wanted only experienced men to review their work. Before the new court had operated a year, however, Lane reversed his position and favored its abolition, thus joining the Republican insurgents in Congress who always had opposed the court. From the beginning, he concluded, the court had favored the railroads. In Lane's mind, the problem of an adequate review of appeals on ICC decisions remained.[36]

Important and influential persons praised Lane for his attitude toward regulation and his work on the ICC, Roosevelt always found satisfaction in having appointed him. In May 1908, when an article appeared in the British *Fortnightly Review* praising the caliber of public servants that Roosevelt had brought into his administration, the President sent a copy of the article, along with a personal letter, to each member of his Cabinet and to five other men: Robert Bacon of the State Department; Herbert Smith, commissioner of corporations; Charles Neill, commissioner of labor; Gifford Pinchot, chief forester; and Lane. Several years later, as

Lane neared the end of his service on the ICC, Roosevelt wrote about the ICC in his autobiography, praising its work after 1906 and giving special credit to "men like Prouty, Lane, and Clark," who had helped to make the commission "a most powerful force for good."[37]

President Taft respected Lane, reappointed the Californian when his term expired in December 1909, and developed a lasting friendship.[38] In January 1913, Lane's fellow commissioners elected him to the chairmanship of the commission. Three months later, when he resigned from the commission to become President Wilson's secretary of the interior, Wisconsin's distinguished senator, Robert M. LaFollette, paid Lane a tribute he gave to few others. In an editorial in his weekly magazine, LaFollette declared that although a score of men could handle Lane's Cabinet job, "No man can fill the place on the Commission made vacant by his resignation."[39]

Prominent segments of the journalistic community, especially those who endorsed the principle of federal regulation, likewise praised Lane. Before he had been a member of the commission a year, *The World's Work* concluded "that Mr. Lane stands out as probably the most aggressive and certainly the most significant member of the Commission." In January 1913, after he had been on the commission six and one-half years, *The Independent* designated Lane as the type of public official "who renders government by the people effective," calling him "an exceptional man from any viewpoint." Four magazines published articles Lane wrote about his work and a fifth, *Collier's Weekly,* published an extract from an ICC report he wrote.[40] The day after Lane died, the *New York Times* editorialized that during the years he served on the ICC, his "grasp of principles, his mastery of intricate details, his insight into complicated problems were remarkable." At the same time, Edgar E. Clark, a Republican from Iowa who joined the ICC the same month as Lane, remembered him as "one of God's noblemen."[41]

Lane obviously enjoyed the respect he received; he also derived satisfaction from playing a dominant role in the ICC's increased importance, authority, and activity. In October 1912, he told a friend that the ICC was "the most powerful body in the United States."[42] To the extent that one of seven equal commissioners could influence the group by ability, personality, and hard work, Lane proved the major force on the ICC during the years 1906 to 1913.[43] His experience in politics and law, his gift of expression, and his knack of getting along with people had prepared him well for a position from which he could command national attention. The commission's work, moreover, required him to travel both at home and abroad. In 1909, for example, he traveled to England to study government regulation of railroads. During the summer of 1910, he spent two months in Europe as a delegate to the International Railway Congress in Berne, Switzerland. Frequently, he found time to stop at Northwestern University Law School for a visit with his friend John H. Wigmore. Meanwhile, his salary provided him with a comfortable although not lavish standard of living, and extended summer vacations allowed him time with his growing children, a son born in 1898 and a daughter born in 1903. By the time his colleagues elected him chairman of the ICC, however, other persons already had taken the beginning steps that eventually removed Lane from a position he had mastered, to the ICC's and to his own distinct advantage.

4

Joining Woodrow Wilson's Team, 1912-1913

I am persuaded from my experience here that no President can be a success unless he takes the position of a real party leader—the premier in Parliament as well as a chief executive.

Lane to Woodrow Wilson,
November 6, 1912

. . . the new President faces the crises of the whole conservation issue that seems to me inevitable early in his administration.

Walter L. Fisher to Ray Stannard Baker,
December 30, 1912

I

A few days before his inauguration, Woodrow Wilson asked Lane to become secretary of the interior, a position demanding both administrative skills and a talent for formulating and advancing a program. The post held potential for explosive controversy as well as for real accomplishment. Ironically, Lane played no public role in the 1912 election that resulted in his appointment and owed his assignment to Wilson's adviser, Colonel Edward M. House, not the new President.

Lane viewed the 1912 presidential election with special interest be-

cause he was a friend of Theodore Roosevelt and of Wilson's closest
adviser, House. Several times Lane made the trip from Washington to
Baltimore to observe sessions of the Democratic convention. In letters to
friends, he commented on the course of the campaign and the candidates.
From the start of the campaign, he envisioned the contest as a race between Wilson and Roosevelt, who headed a third-party ticket. Lane predicted that Wilson would win and that Taft, the Republican nominee,
would have fewer than five states supporting his candidacy. Although he
admired Roosevelt and supported most of the Progressive party platform, Lane exhibited a stronger allegiance to his own party, especially
on the tariff issue. On the whole, he concluded, Wilson handled himself
well and at times splendidly. Still, Lane harbored fears about Wilson's
possible performance once in office, for he judged him "a bit too conservative." He worried that Wilson would surround himself with southern
reactionaries who opposed the strong central government Lane believed
the country needed. Wilson, Lane lamented, talked "too much like a
professor and too little like a statesman," and at times seemed ill-informed.[1]

The campaign excited Lane, but as an interstate commerce commissioner he could not take an active part. In 1908, when members of Taft's
presidential campaign organization pressured two Republican commissioners to participate in that campaign, Lane vigorously insisted they
should not. The commissioners discussed the matter and agreed with
Lane that the ICC's independence, prestige, and usefulness demanded
that its members remain politically nonpartisan and inactive.[2]

During the autumn of 1912, therefore, Lane resisted pleas from
political friends in California and from the chairman of the Democratic
National Committee, William F. McCombs, to campaign on Wilson's
behalf. "I have never wanted to get into a campaign as much as I have
this one," he replied to McCombs, but "I cannot go to California . . .
without resigning from the Commission," and this Lane refused to do.[3]
"If I wanted a Cabinet position now I would resign from the Commission
and go out to help him [Wilson]," Lane succinctly told one of his former
assistants in the city attorney's office. He also added that he would "probably" follow that course of action "if I felt that California's vote was
necessary to Wilson's success and that I could help to get it."[4] Lane, of
course, believed Wilson would win the election handily and so, with
the exception of encouraging friends to support the Democratic candidate, he remained a sideline observer to the election that placed him in
the Cabinet.[5]

II

The Wilson Cabinet was as much a House creation as it was Wilson's; Lane was a House appointment.[6] The two had known one another since the spring of 1903 when Lane stopped in Austin, Texas, on his return trip from Washington where, as city attorney, he had represented San Francisco at a government hearing. While in Austin, Lane addressed the state legislature and visited with his long-time friend Sidney Mezes, who happened to be House's brother-in-law. Impressed with Lane, House gave a dinner in his honor and in the honor of Mezes and David F. Houston, who recently had become president of the Agricultural and Mechanical College of Texas.[7] Between this first meeting and November 1912, Lane and House met a number of times. Politics and their mutual friend Mezes provided common interests.

Because of his friendship with House, Lane hoped to be close to Wilson and perhaps even advise the President as a member of a "kitchen cabinet." Lane also believed that Wilson would look to him for advice because of his record on the ICC, his favorable press, and his political following on the West Coast.[8]

Some of Lane's friends and admirers, however, wanted him to be more than unofficial adviser to Wilson, and so, even before the election, they started recommending Lane for a Cabinet seat. Lane gave his friends little encouragement, although he admitted to one that "the glamour of intimate association with the President—the honor that comes from such a position—appeals to me, for I still have all my old-time vanity and love of dignity and appreciation." This appeal, Lane pointed out, did not counterbalance the drawbacks. "In the first place," he confessed, "I can't afford it. There is no Cabinet man here who lives on his salary, and as you know, I have got nothing else." Lane also explained, "I am doing just as big work and as satisfactory work as any member of the Cabinet. The work that a Cabinet officer chiefly does is to sign his name to letters or papers that other people write." Although Lane told friends, "I don't want a position in the Cabinet," he never said he would refuse to accept such an appointment.[9]

Between election day and Wilson's inauguration, Lane served as a major consultant in selection of the Cabinet, frequently corresponding and occasionally meeting with House. The Texan had similar contacts with many other prominent politicians for the same reason, but he especially valued Lane's counsel because he believed Lane rendered what aid he could in an intelligent, disinterested way, knew "all the important lawyers in the country," was familiar with California politics, and had "a remarkably strong, virile mind."[10] House particularly wanted Lane's suggestions of Californians of Cabinet stature, as well as an opinion of specific subjects and individuals. Lane responded with the names of a number of friends for a variety of positions: Major James H. Trezevant, for consul general at Mexico City; Joseph N. Teal of Oregon, for secretary of the interior; John H. Marble, secretary of the ICC, for Wilson's private secretary; Adolph C. Miller, professor of finance at the University of California, Berkeley, for secretary of the treasury; John H. Wigmore, dean of the Northwestern University Law School, for attorney general; and James D. Phelan, of San Francisco, for recognition in a "first class manner."[11]

During the months of contact devoted to Cabinet selections, the House-Lane friendship deepened. At the start, House thought highly enough of Lane to consider him fine material for the Cabinet. Lane, equally as early, made it known that he was content on the ICC. He refused to permit anyone to speak on his behalf and repeated that he did not seek a Cabinet position, but on November 25, he also confided to Charles K. McClatchy, editor of the *Sacramento Bee* and a long-time political supporter, "that I would not say that I would not accept an appointment, because I would do almost anything to make Wilson's administration a success."[12] On January 8, House and Wilson had one of their many discussions about the Cabinet and drew up a tentative list of members; they did not include Lane's name. Two weeks later, in a reply to another of House's requests of Cabinet possibilities from California, Lane repeated he was not a candidate and urged the selection of Phelan. The next day, House wrote to Lane that, "If I were Governor Wilson, I would lean upon you heavily when I became President"; and the same week, House told Wilson that Lane was "one of the big men of our party."[13]

When Wilson and House spent two hours before dinner on Valentine's Day going over Cabinet appointments, the list of possibilities had narrowed considerably. Six positions, as it turned out, already were definite. At this time, House at last urged Wilson to put Lane in the Cabinet, either in the War or Interior Department. Wilson inquired about Lane's views on conservation; House had not discussed the topic with Lane, but said he knew they would be sound. To be positive, Wilson and House decided that House would enlist the aid of Norman Hapgood, a confirmed Eastern

conservationist, to sound Lane out. On February 16, Lane, House, and
Hapgood met in House's new York apartment. House explained to Lane
that he might be drafted into the Cabinet. Lane replied that, although he
was content to remain as chairman of the Interstate Commerce Commission, he would take any position for which Wilson and House believed him
to be suited. He added that he thought the Interior Department was the
most difficult department in the Cabinet. House purposefully guided the
conversation that evening over a wide range of subjects. After Lane left,
Hapgood expressed enthusiastic approval and promised to convey his
views to Wilson. House recorded in his diary that his own opinion of Lane
had "increased materially, much as I had thought of him before. There
will certainly not be a stronger or more dominant force in the Cabinet."
A few days later, Lane questioned House about the degree of control
Wilson would exercise over his Cabinet members in the running of the
various departments. House's reply, that Wilson planned to give his department heads a free hand, providing they were capable, pleased Lane,
who by then momentarily expected a letter from Wilson.[14]

Wilson, after accepting House's suggestion to make Lane secretary of
the interior, delayed making the appointment until he settled the other
Cabinet seats. On February 22, therefore, Wilson offered the Department
of War portfolio to A. Mitchell Palmer, who expressed disappointment
because he intensely wanted to become attorney general. Later that day,
when Wilson and House were alone, House suggested that since Palmer
would undoubtedly refuse the offer, the President-elect should move
Lane to the War Department and name Walter H. Page, a North Carolina
journalist, to the Interior Department. Wilson agreed and told House to
contact Page. House could not locate Page immediately, and before he
did, word of the prospective offer leaked out and opposition arose. Politicians explained that no southerner should head a department with jurisdiction of the Pension Bureau and its rolls of Union veterans. Realizing
their error, Wilson and House quickly reversed themselves, decided not
to make Page the offer, planned to keep Lane in the Interior Department,
and looked elsewhere for a secretary of war.[15]

Lane, meanwhile, with the inauguration only a few days away, and the
last word from House over a week past, had heard nothing definite and
had written off the appointment as a near miss. When Wilson's letter finally arrived on February 28 expressing need for Lane's services, Lane said
it hit him "like a blast out of a blue sky." He and his wife worried about

the expense of entertaining that a Cabinet position involved, and he again compared the advantages and disadvantages of remaining on the ICC. In the end, he convinced himself that his duty to the President-elect compelled him to accept. The day before the March 4 inaugural, the newspapers reported the appointment.[16]

Most Washington newspaper correspondents looked upon Lane as the strongest man in the Cabinet, the only member certain to make good. He continued to have mixed feelings about entering the Cabinet, while House still wished that Lane was secretary of war.[17]

On the afternoon of March 5, with his wife, a few officials, and a score of Californians present in the Interior Department, Associate Justice Joseph McKenna of the Supreme Court administered the oath of office. Commissioner Lane officially became Secretary Lane.

III

Upon turning his attention to the new position he was to occupy, Lane soon discovered he had much to learn. In 1913, the Department of the Interior was a collection of unrelated bureaus, miscellaneous federal institutions, and various offices scattered about Washington, the country, and as far afield as Hawaii. Its diversifications and responsibilities ranged from the guardianship of the territory of Alaska to the direction of a foundling hospital. In many cases, the only relationship these conglomerated bureaus, institutions, and offices shared was that the secretary of the interior held direct authority over them; among the majority there was no communication.

The principal constituent units of the department were the Geological Survey, the Bureau of Mines, the Reclamation Service, the General Land Office, the Bureau of Indian Affairs, the Patent Office, the Pension Bureau, and the Bureau of Education. In addition, the department administered the national parks, the Maryland School for the Blind, the Washington Hospital for Foundlings, the Columbia Institution for the Deaf, the Office of the Superintendent of Capitol Building and Grounds, Howard University, Freedmen's Hospital, St. Elizabeth Hospital for the Insane, and the territories and insular possessions of the United States. Finally, the department held guardianship over buildings and land that Congress designated as American antiquities. For the fiscal year 1914, which began July 1, 1913, Congress gave the Interior Department $239,633,001 to carry out its programs and to maintain its responsibilities.[18]

In 1913, the Secretary of the Interior maintained his office, which numbered about twenty persons and constituted the heart of the department, in the old patent building on the corner of Seventh and F Streets. Scattered about the area, but within walking distance, were the bureaus. The Geological Survey, for example, was also on F Street but a few blocks to the west; the General Land Office was across the street from Interior in the old post office building; the Bureau of Mines was directly behind the Land Office; the Pension Bureau, the largest of the department's units, was two blocks to the east in Judiciary Square; the Bureau of Education shared part of the Land Office building; and out in the suburbs were the institutions, such as Howard University and the Freedmen's Hospital.[19] Meanwhile, because of the nature of the department's work, land offices, reclamation projects, national parks, and other departmental offices and officials dotted the western states.

The major challenge Lane faced in his new position transcended the stewardship of this wide array of disconnected administrative units that made up the Interior Department. In the spring of 1913, the country, as represented by politicians, voters, newspapers, journals, and special-interest groups, was in the midst of a debate about the degree and type of control the federal government should exercise over the nation's natural resources, often known as the public domain. The Interior Department, because it administered the federal laws that dealt with the public domain, found itself in transition from an agency dedicated to transferring the nation's resources into the hands of private individuals, to an agency committed to managing and preserving the country's national resources. This debate about federal control of natural resources, and the philosophy behind it, had its origins at least half a century before Lane entered the Interior Department.

Between the Civil War and the turn of the century, the conservation movement consisted of several groups of enthusiastic citizens and a growing number of government administrators and scientists; their effort produced a few national parks and forest reserves, the latter through the Forest Reserve Act of 1891. During the first decade of the new century, however, a group of officials within the Roosevelt administration, supported by the President and led by Gifford Pinchot, chief of the United States Forest Service and Roosevelt's primary conservation adviser, formulated a comprehensive, national-oriented conservation program.

The Roosevelt-Pinchot plan had two major components. First, it called for the federal government to maintain ownership of all lands that contained minerals or had potential for hydroelectric power installations. The government, in turn, would lease the right to extract the minerals and develop the power sites under terms commensurate with their value and consistent with efficient use. With the income from the leasing system, the plan's supporters pointed out, the government could finance additional resource development. The second part of the Roosevelt-Pinchot conservation program called for a federal commission to coordinate national resource development, using the country's major river basins as the foci of planning. This concept paid particular attention to the fact that a resource might have more than one use and that resources within a given area are interrelated. Roosevelt, Pinchot, and their followers believed this twofold plan, with its emphasis on scientific planning and decision making, would elevate national interest over the various special interests and thereby remove resource development from the realm of partisan politics, political decisions, and resource exploitation.

To effect its program, the Roosevelt administration took action within the executive branch and pressured Congress for more authority. Congress responded by passing the Reclamation Act of 1902, which established the Reclamation Service as an independent agency of experts. Conservationists hoped this new agency, by controlling the income of a revolving fund and by having power to select irrigation sites, could ignore politics. During his presidency, Roosevelt, by executive order, more than tripled the number of acres set aside as national forests.[20] Pinchot, meanwhile, devised a permit system to regulate both development of hydroelectric power and grazing within the areas that his Forest Service controlled. Similarly, the Interior Department adopted a more systematic approach toward its guardianship of the public domain. It withdrew the resources from use or sale and directed its constituent bureau, the Geological Survey, to examine and classify the lands as to their primary value, such as water power sites, oil, phosphate, and coal lands. After classification, the department restored to the category available for sale the areas suitable for agriculture and withheld the areas that contained more valuable resources. As part of this new policy, the Roosevelt administration asked Congress for legislative authority to administer the classified lands by a leasing system that recognized their diverse nature and value. The appointment of James R. Garfield as secretary in March 1907 signaled the triumph of this policy within the Interior Department. Ethan A. Hitchcock, whom Garfield replaced, had not fully accepted the Roosevelt-Pinchot conservation program. Garfield, commissioner of the Bureau of Corporations, 1903-7, on the other hand, had worked closely with Pinchot from the summer of 1906 to develop the new policy and its administrative implementation.

By the spring of 1908, Roosevelt and Pinchot, although aware of important gains they had made in conservation, realized that Congress would not enact legislation providing for either a leasing system or a commission to direct multiuse, national planning of resources. Members of Congress opposed these measures for a variety of reasons. Some considered it to their political advantage to maintain the piecemeal, log-rolling method of river and harbor improvements; others disliked, on principle, the concept of centralized planning and wished to have each state supervise the public domain within its borders; still others believed the Roosevelt-Pinchot plan would hurt economic groups within their states. Furthermore, the Army Corps of Engineers wanted to keep its jurisdiction over rivers and harbors, and used its influence to oppose congressional approval of legislation.

To pressure Congress, the administration sought to arouse public support for its conservation program. Pinchot and W. J. McGee, a major theorist of the conservation movement, organized and planned the agenda for the "Governors' Conference" on conservation that Roosevelt held in May 1908. The conference, with its dramatization of the conservation problem, did not persuade Congress to act, but it did symbolize the beginning of a new phase in the conservation movement because it brought into the ranks a new type of supporter whose chief concern was moralism rather than efficiency.

This new type of conservationist often considered commercial development exploitation and therefore wanted to save resources, not plan for their use. The new enthusiasts gave the movement a religious fervor and helped bring it into the mainstream of the progressive era. Roosevelt, Pinchot, McGee, and Garfield had fused a moral crusade and a rational plan for efficiency into an uneasy union.

When William Howard Taft became president in the spring of 1909, the conservation movement underwent further modification. The new President, while sympathetic to the objectives of the Roosevelt program, disliked many of the administrative devices the former President, Pinchot, and the Interior Secretary had employed to advance these objectives. Taft, contrary to Roosevelt, believed in a narrow interpretation of law and favored inaction unless he possessed specific legal authority to act in a given situation. His concern for legality contrasted sharply with Roosevelt's emphasis on results. Richard A. Ballinger, whom Taft named secretary of the interior, discontinued many of his predecessor's administrative policies and worked to change others, especially those that dealt with water power, the Reclamation Service, and the Forest Service.

Alarmed at the Taft administration's handling of conservation matters, Pinchot again appealed for public support to protect the nation's resources from special "interests" and "monopoly." He organized the National Conservation Association to champion his views and to dramatize the issues. His criticisms climaxed in a dispute over the Interior Department's management of coal lands in the territory of Alaska. Before the conflict ended, Taft fired Pinchot for insubordination, and a joint House-Senate committee spent four months investigating the Department of the Interior, including the Forest Service. Although the investigation provided a forum for both those who attacked and those who defended the Taft administration, it offered no constructive conclusions. The controversy, known as the Pinchot-Ballinger affair, actually obscured conservation problems because it focused on the question of public honesty rather than resource management.

In March 1911, Ballinger resigned, primarily because he and Taft did not always agree on matters of policy. The President, anxious to heal the rift within his party, appointed Walter L. Fisher as his new secretary of the interior. Fisher agreed with the Roosevelt-Pinchot conservation program and returned to the policies that Garfield had developed, but he disapproved of Pinchot's excessive zeal and moralistic crusading. Fisher failed, though, as had Pinchot, Roosevelt, and Garfield, to convince Congress to enact his legislative proposals. Nevertheless, Fisher's appointment and two years in office helped the conservationists move closer to their goal of federal control.

The conservationists, meanwhile, gained support from the Supreme Court and the voters. In July 1910, the Court upheld the Reclamation Act of 1902, under which the Secretary of the Interior acquired water sites within individual states. Less than a year later, the Court upheld the various executive regulations and procedures Pinchot had instituted in the Forest Service. After the election of 1910, Congress had fewer members who supported state administration of resources. By the spring of 1913, moreover, the political controversy over state versus federal control of resources had lost its former intensity. The demand for state control continued, but a decade of federal reclamation projects, fire and flood control, watershed protection, and equitable regulation of federal lands had convinced most voters and politicians in the western states that state control was financially inadequate and administratively difficult.

The conservation movement, therefore, had won a major victory because the country, the states, the courts, and the Congress accepted the inevitability, if not always the desirability, of federal resource control. But acceptance of the principle gave rise to a new struggle over the type and dimensions of the control. Many persons who accepted federal control still believed that states, interest groups, and localities had a right to share in the decision-making process. Other persons, echoing the philosophy of the Roosevelt administration, generally opposed this belief.

In the spring of 1913, two general issues generated debate. The first dealt with the assessment of priorities and the continuing clash between the champions of multiuse and single use of resources. Supporters of the single-use concept (waterpower, for example) attracted grass-roots participation and exerted more pressure on Congress. If a decision favored multiuse (flood control, irrigation, recreation, for example), there remained the divisive ordering of priorities among the various uses. The second issue concerned the type of opportunity to be made available to the resource developer. For over a decade, fear of monopoly and of decreasing economic opportunity for the average individual had been a widespread sentiment. Any decision or series of decisions that attempted to initiate a program of resources development under federal direction elicited hostility from certain groups and individuals, regardless of the decision made.

The ultimate arbitrator in the controversy of the type of federal control was, of course, Congress. Roosevelt, Pinchot, Garfield, and Fisher all had realized this basic fact and had requested congressional action, but with modest results. Roosevelt had advanced his program, probably to a maximum, through executive action, and Pinchot had tried to move Congress by rallying public opinion.[21]

When Lane took office, therefore, he faced the formidable challenge of playing the major role in suggesting and shaping legislation that reflected the general but vague and uneven national attitude toward the public domain. Forceful and powerful men before Lane had failed in a similar challenge, but their efforts had helped lessen congressional and public opposition to a national program. During the campaign of 1912, neither Wilson, Roosevelt, nor Taft made conservation into an issue, and their respective party platforms, with varying specificity and emphasis, all favored resource development without monopoly and without waste. Despite this vague agreement of principle, the need for enabling legislation remained. To obtain indispensable congressional action, Lane needed to work as a harmonizer, as a compromiser, and as a leader capable of communicating in a logical and understandable manner. He also had to move beyond the rhetoric of Pinchot and of Pinchot's most ardent supporters who tended to denounce publicly those with whom they disagreed. Likewise, Lane needed to pay greater attention than Pinchot had to the demands and well-being of individuals who came under, or would come under, federal programs. Finally, for Lane to generate public and congressional support, he needed to recognize and work with those persons who advocated wilderness preservation as an end in itself.

The enactment of a federal conservation program, then, constituted in terms of potential success or failure a challenge for Lane that rivaled his administration of existing policies and programs dealing with natural resources. To be certain, he directed a large and diverse department that performed a host of service functions such as handling the nation's patents, military pensions, and geological surveying, but the achievements and success of his secretaryship really depended upon his actions regarding natural resources, both from a standpoint of advancing a legislative program and of administrative policy. Fortunately for Lane, work on these two fronts demanded attributes that already had served him well. He won respect and established rapport with persons of widely divergent views. But above all, the new Secretary enjoyed the reputation of an honest and fair person.

5
Secretary Lane, His Staff, and His Department

I will give you men under you over whom you will have entire control and who will be to your liking. I will give you men to sit beside you at the table who will be of your own class.

Lane to John H. Wigmore,
March 9, 1913

I have to rely on the men below me. You can see what a frightful thing it is if I can not trust them.

Lane to Honoré Willsie,
September 1913

Is he in sympathy with progressive things, or does he in any way represent the interests?

Lane to J. H. Fleming,
November 20, 1913

I

Lane's initial chore as secretary of the interior was to recruit a top-level staff of about a dozen persons. Wilson allowed his Cabinet members free hand in selecting their subordinates, except for occasionally suggesting a candidate for a second-level position. As a recruiter of talent, Lane proved highly successful, in terms of efficiency and honesty within the department and as well as in terms of everyday politics. He gave his department leadership and left a record of sound administration.

For first assistant secretary of the interior, who supervised the bureaus and who would act as secretary in Lane's absence, he immediately sought to obtain his long-time friend John H. Wigmore, dean of Northwestern University Law School and one of the nation's foremost legal scholars. Telling Wigmore that he wanted "the largest men whom I can secure and to form a cabinet of equals," Lane outlined the challenges and opportunities, and pleaded with his friend to take the position. At $5,000 a year, the offer was just a third of the figure Wigmore had turned down eleven years earlier when Harper's Publishers offered him an editorship.[1]

When Wigmore refused to leave his legal career, Lane asked Joseph N. Teal to take the position. Teal, chairman of the Oregon Conservation Commission, and Lane were first-name friends. Seven weeks earlier, Lane had described his friend to Colonel House as "a good lawyer and a most public-spirited man," a "sane" progressive, and "a man of means . . . deeply interested in questions of conservation." After careful thought, Teal declined Lane's offer because he concluded he "could do more good . . . out of office, rather than in." Gifford Pinchot, whom Teal greatly admired, agreed because he believed Teal had too much ability and too many accomplishments for a number-two job.[2]

After this second rejection, Lane turned to Andrieus A. Jones, attorney general of New Mexico and a member of the National Democratic Committee. Jones, who used the initials A. A. rather than his first name, and Lane did not know one another but Jones had the backing of prominent Democrats. At a Cabinet meeting, Lane requested the reactions of his colleagues to the possibility of appointing Jones. Lane also asked his friend William Kent, a progressive Republican congressman from California and a conservationist, to gather information about Jones's "character and capacity." Satisfied with the evaluations he received, Lane appointed Jones. He served until August 1916, when he resigned to run, successfully, for the United States Senate. Lane praised him as "an able and faithfull assistant" and asked Wilson to write a letter of appreciation to help Jones's campaign.[3]

To replace Jones, Lane nominated Alexander T. Vogelsang who, at that time, served as solicitor for the Interior Department. Vogelsang and Lane had been friends for years. They had practiced law and been active in public affairs in San Francisco, Vogelsang serving as a member of the Board of Supervisors and as chairman of the Committee on Public Utilities. When Lane sent his friend's nomination to Wilson, he also emphasized that the appointee was "one of the most progressive Democrats on the Coast."[4]

The assistant secretary in the Interior Department dealt primarily with administrative law, or as Lane expressed it, "he is practically the supreme court on pension matters and many other things." Because the position involved much responsibility, Lane moved slowly to fill it, meanwhile keeping Republican Lewis C. Laylin, a thirty-five-year-old Ohioan, in office and gently rejecting the candidates pushed by Democratic members of Congress.[5] Finally, in May 1914, Lane selected Bo Sweeney, a tall, well-built man who had practiced law in Seattle, Washington, for the previous twenty years. Before moving to the West Coast, Sweeney, who had not solicited his new job, had served in the Colorado legislature for a decade and had been a delegate to the 1896 Democratic National Convention.[6]

On July 16, 1917, Sweeney died unexpectedly of angina pectoris and Lane immediately received advice about finding a successor. Wilson, despite heading a country at war for less than four months, told Lane that "I have been thinking a great deal recently about the chance we shall have in filling the place made vacant by Mr. Sweeney's death." The President wanted "to go out of the beaten track and select somebody from some part of the country which has hiterto been unrepresented but which is showing an inclination to take sides with us and the things we believe in." Lane did not need to be reminded of the political nature of such appointments. To an Interior official who applied for Sweeney's position, Lane replied that "Frankly, it is not possible for me to consider a Californian . . .for the reason that my First Assistant, Vogelsang, is from California, and also . . . another of my assistants." Lane responded to one senator with a note that read: "I have your letter in behalf of George H. Walker. I know him well, admire him greatly, and am very fond of him, but he can not be appointed." Walker was a Republican.[7] In the end, Lane named Seldon G. Hopkins of Cheyenne, Wyoming, who had served as state land commissioner for six years and as chairman of his state's Democratic central committee for four years. Lane told Wilson that he had "looked into the new states that are coming our way" and wanted to accommodate Senator John B. Kendrick who urged the Hopkins appointment. "There is a good chance," Lane added, of electing another United States senator from Wyoming.[8] Wilson accepted Lane's analysis. Hopkins, like Sweeney before him, carried out his responsibilities in a professional manner.

When he took office, Lane changed the title of the department's third official from special assistant to assistant to the secretary. Upgrading the position, he assigned it responsibility for direction of the national parks and "general supervision" over the territories of Alaska and Hawaii and the eight departmental investigators. To fill this policy position, Lane wrote to Adolph C. Miller, chairman of the economics department at the University of California and a friend from college days. Miller, who enjoyed a national reputation as a finance and banking expert, journeyed to Washington, conferred with Lane, and accepted the offer. Lane had found a man of recognized ability, with wealth sufficient to maintain a chauffeured limousine at Berkeley, and with a willingness to assume some of the official entertaining normally expected of Lane had he an income other than his salary.[9] During the previous winter, Lane had recommended Miller, as well as Wigmore and Teal, to Wilson for a Cabinet appointment.

Lane's good fortune in recruiting a person of Miller's ability was short-lived. During the fall and winter, Miller spent considerable time away from his office drafting what became the Federal Reserve Act and then helped organize the Federal Reserve System. In February 1914, Wilson asked Lane to recommend someone from the West Coast to serve on the newly established Federal Reserve Board. Lane logically submitted Miller's name, calling him a person who "takes a large view of questions, has abundant good sense, is progressive, and a real Democrat," but adding, "I am not desirous of parting with him."[10] Wilson named Miller to the board where he served with distinction until 1936.

Miller's successor, Stephen Mather, another of Lane's college friends, became director of the National Park Service when Congress created that agency in 1916. After that, with the most important duty of assistant to the secretary gone, that position lost some of its stature.[11]

In 1913, the Solicitor for the Interior Department held the rank of assistant attorney general of the United States and technically was a member of the Justice Department. Lane picked Preston C. West, a forty-five-year-old Oklahoma state judge, for the position. Before becoming a judge, West had practiced law in Muskogee and enjoyed a reputation of ability and honesty.[12] Between West's resignation in February 1916, to his return to practice of law in Tulsa, and the appointment of Charles D. Mahaffie in September of the same year, Alexander T. Vogelsang served as solicitor. Vogelsang, of course, ended his brief service as solicitor to become first assistant secretary.

In selecting Mahaffie, Lane followed his familiar pattern of finding a qualified westerner who had strong support within the Democratic party. Mahaffie, a 1906 Rhodes Scholar from Kingfisher College in Oklahoma, had been secretary of the Oregon Conservation Commission for several years and maintained a close friendship with Joseph N. Teal, who told Lane that Mahaffie "thinks right on public questions, and is true blue in every way." As a practicing attorney in Portland, Mahaffie had specialized in public land cases and included among his credentials a year's experience as an instructor of jurisprudence at Princeton University.[13]

II

Lane's other major appointments were the bureau chiefs, some of whom headed agencies such as the General Land Office and the Bureau of Indian Affairs known for their political patronage opportunities, and others who directed agencies such as the Geological Survey and the Patent Office respected for their nonpolitical operation.

The commissioner of the General Land Office administered a network of land offices spread across the western states and territories. Montana, for example, had ten offices. Every land office had both a register, who handled applications, and a receiver, who collected fees. But since registers and receivers were not civil service positions, the change in presidents meant changes in the land offices.

Western politicians, just as they had with regard to Wilson's appointment of a secretary of the interior, insisted that a person from their region of the country become commissioner of the General Land Office. Francis G. Newlands and Key Pittman, for example, the two Democratic senators from Nevada, both "heartily" commended to Lane a lawyer and state legislator named Clay Tallman. The Nevada legislature unanimously endorsed Tallman for the Land Office post or for the assistant secretaryship. Not knowing Tallman, Lane telegraphed his friend George S. Brown, a Reno judge, and inquired of the candidate's ability. Brown replied that Tallman was a "studious, painstaking lawyer, slow but diligent," who "might make [a] capable but not brilliant commissioner."[14] Lane followed the advice of Newlands and of Pittman, whom he knew and respected, and whose support was crucial for any legislative proposals emanating from the Interior Department. Judge Brown's evaluation of Tallman proved accurate; the Nevadan, originally a native of Michigan and a graduate of the University of Michigan Law School, served capably throughout Wilson's presidency.

For assistant commissioner of the General Land Office, Lane nominated Charles M. Bruce of Arizona and thereby satisfied another western state's petition for high-ranking representation in the Interior Department. Before making his decision, Lane had several conferences with Bruce, who had been, during Grover Cleveland's second administration, secretary of the Territory of Arizona and then acting governor for a year. Like Tallman, Bruce held his job until March 1921.[15]

During Lane's first week in office, while trying to convince John H. Wigmore to become first assistant secretary of the interior, he told Wigmore that he would have guardianship of the Indians "as his special care." Wigmore, of course, did not accept, nor did Lane's second choice, both of whom Lane had known for years. He did not know the man he eventually appointed, A. A. Jones, and despite Jones being from a state with a substantial Indian population, Lane never assigned him the degree of supervision of the Indians that he had envisioned for Wigmore. Instead, Lane himself administered whatever "special care" the Interior Department exercised above and beyond that of the Bureau of Indian Affairs.

To direct the Indian bureau, which he judged "the hardest place I have to fill,"[16] Lane chose Cato Sells, an Iowa-born banker, United States district attorney from 1894 to 1899, and member of the National Democratic Committee from Texas. On May 20, 1913, Lane requested the Cabinet's estimation of Sells, whom he did not know, and immediately heard praise from Josephus Daniels, William Jennings Bryan, and Albert S. Burleson. Before he asked Wilson to appoint Sells, Lane's special agents interviewed 188 men who knew the candidate in Iowa and Texas, and Lane himself spoke with senators from Iowa and Texas. Lane then told the President that "Mr. Sells is not a great man, but he will give wholehearted devotion to the cause of the Indians." The assessment proved correct; Sells carried out his duties with dedication and honesty.[17]

The appointment that undoubtedly required the least of Lane's time was asking George Otis Smith to continue as director of the Geological Survey. A native of Hodkdon, Maine, Smith joined the survey in 1896, the year he earned a Ph.D. from Johns Hopkins University. Eleven years later, Roosevelt named him director of the agency, whose principal activities were surveying, appraising, and classifying natural resources. The survey provided practical and scientific services in a professional manner. Lane wished to continue this policy.[18]

Lane also continued the nonpolitical posture of the Bureau of Mines by keeping John A. Holmes as director. Holmes, like Smith, was a professional. He held a Ph.D. and had headed the bureau since its establishment in 1910. Charged with investigating mining resources and operations with the intent to lessen the loss of life and increase efficiency, the bureau functioned under Holmes as an organization of trained personnel, maintaining, among other activities, ten experimental stations and nine mine safety stations. When Holmes died, Lane continued the professional tradition by promoting Van H. Manning from assistant director to director.[19]

Philander P. Claxton was the third person with a doctor's degree that Lane appointed to lead a constituent unit of the Interior Department. In 1911, President Taft had named Claxton, chairman of the department of education at the University of Tennessee, as United States commissioner of education. Lane asked Claxton to stay because the Office of Education consisted of specialists in various fields of education who collected data and carried out research, but who performed no administrative functions. Again Lane wished to keep the office a nonpolitical service unit staffed by experts.

To direct the Patent Office, Lane turned to Thomas Ewing, Jr., who possessed a distinguished family name and a reputation as one of the nation's foremost patent lawyers. Ewing's grandfather had served as the first secretary of the interior when Congress established the department in 1849. His father had been a general during the Civil War. Ewing held three degrees, had published translations of Horace and his own poetry, and had been a member of both the school board and police board of Yonkers, New York. When Ewing assumed his duties, he found a backlog of 28,709 cases awaiting action and an organization that processed only 95 percent of the annual incoming work. Four years later, when he resigned to resume private practice, Ewing left a backlog of 16,846 cases, a bureau that more than kept abreast of its day-to-day workload, and a larger revenue surplus than the Patent Office usually produced. He had accomplished this despite the failure of Congress to grant his full request for additional personnel. Lane appreciated Ewing and repeatedly thanked him.[20]

To replace Ewing in August 1917, Lane nominated James T. Newton, who had been assistant commissioner during the previous three years and to whom Ewing gave credit for "a large part of the reforms worked in the office." Newton had joined the Patent Office as a law clerk in 1891 and four years later became its principal examiner.[21]

The Pension Bureau with its six divisions and a board of review constituted the largest bureau in the Interior Department. Because of the nontechnical and well-defined work load, the Pension Brueau did not require a highly trained work force or imaginative leadership. Lane's appointment of Gaylord M. Saltzgaber as commissioner, for reasons unknown but probably political, conformed to the bureau's image. Sixty-seven years old and a Civil War veteran, Saltzgaber had practiced law for forty-four years in Van Wert, Ohio, and once had served as mayor of the town. He was Lane's least effective bureau chief.

Lane's official family blended experience, ability, and politics. To the less politically sensitive positions, he continued the practice of appointing trained experts, such as George Otis Smith, John A. Holmes, Philander P. Claxton, and Thomas Ewing, Jr. Lane staffed the highest ranking, more politically visible positions in the department, the ones that dealt with public lands and other resource policy, with men from western states: A. A. Jones of New Mexico, Bo Sweeney of Washington, Adolph C. Miller of California, Preston C. West of Oklahoma, Clay Tallman of Nevada, Charles M. Bruce of Arizona, and Cato Sells of Texas. With the exception of Miller, who was Lane's close friend, these westerners had been active Democrats and their appointments, to varying degrees, rewarded the party faithful. Before Lane recommended their appointments, however, he insisted upon knowing that they were willing and able to carry out their responsibilities.

III

Lane's filling of lesser positions within his department followed the same procedure he employed staffing his senior posts. He received the names of nominees from friends, members of Congress, and job seekers, as well as from Wilson. To assess the candidate's fitness and political acceptability, Lane checked with members of the Democratic National Committee, with members of Congress from the prospective candidate's home state, and with Cabinet members. For an appointment such as governor of Hawaii, he dispatched a special agent to investigate. At times the department's agents communicated their findings in code to the Secretary's office.

Although Lane often complied with the wishes of political friends of members of Congress, he disliked "a rank spoilsman," and on numerous occasions rejected recommendations, including those of the President. Wilson sometimes took the initiative. On August 7, 1913, for example, he wrote to Lane that "the post of Superintendent of the Hot Springs Reservation, Arkansas, has, I believe, been vacant since July," and continued that he was "anxious to have the brother of Mr. William F. McCombs appointed to this post."[22] Another time, Wilson wrote that he had "a friend in Mississippi named Kemper whom I should dearly like to provide a place for, if it were possible" and suggested perhaps an inspectorship. Two weeks later, Lane informed Wilson that both the attorney general's office and the General Land Office found Charles P. Kemper not "especially qualified for their work." The next week, Lane appointed Kemper an inspector in the Bureau of Indian Affairs.[23]

In January 1915, Wilson asked Lane to consider the appointment of Claude Weaver, former member of the House of Representatives, as counsel for the Osage Indians. Weaver, Wilson pointed out, had "rendered exceptional service in the House" and was "a man of admirable character, and, I think, abundant ability." Lane, on the other hand, found the Oklahoman unqualified for the position. Wilson did not press the matter, but wanted Lane to "keep Weaver in mind in case there is anything else to which we can turn in his behalf." Six months later, Lane again told the President that the person he recommended, this time for "some place of executive work . . . in Alaska," lacked the necessary ability and experience. Wilson replied, "I am obliged to you for being so frank about it," and inquired about a lesser position in the General Land Office.[24]

On March 1, 1921, three days before Wilson's presidency ended, Lane warned his close friend and Secretary of Commerce-designate Herbert Hoover about "hungry" politicians who "think there is no one thing as important as to satisfy some constituent." He recalled that his troubles arose from requests by officials with questionable public values such as those of Albert S. Burleson, postmaster general, Joseph P. Tumulty, Wilson's private secretary, and James C. McReynolds, attorney general and after 1914 an associate justice of the Supreme Court. Lane continued that "once a Senator gave me a man under indictment for land fraud as a land agent—another Senator got me to name an engineer for him who was crooked, drunken and lazy and he knew it.—So beware."[25] Lane's record indicated that he had tried to exercise such an awareness.

IV

As chief executive of an organization whose primary function was to provide services, Lane found himself consistently concerned about the speed with which his department carried out its responsibilities. In April 1913, when each bureau submitted its report for the previous quarter, he found the General Land Office and the Pension Bureau behind in their work, with the other bureaus and offices "practically" or "substantially current."[26]

The General Land Office faced a record volume of business, and although the office could keep abreast of incoming cases, it could not decrease the almost two-year backlog of work. Tallman, the serious, hardworking commissioner, urged his employees "to get out from under this everlasting load of old, unfinished business." By the time Lane and Tallman had been on the job two years, the number of cases awaiting action had decreased from 2,234 to 940, and the amount of time required for handling original homestead entries had dropped from six to two and one-half months. Despite such improvement, Tallman never completely eliminated the backlog of work and remained sensitive to any indication that Lane or anyone else judged his office inefficient.[27]

Whereas the Land Office had too much work for its personnel, the Pension Bureau suffered from an ineffectual work force. During his first summer as secretary, Lane ordered a study of the Pension Bureau to determine whether it needed a reorganization. He hoped to cut "a great deal of red tape," an action that "those who have been in the office but are not there now tell me . . . is possible."[28] As a consequence, Lane formulated "Orders, Instructions, and Regulations" to improve the situation. The problem, however, stemmed less from poorly conceived organizational charts and procedures than from the caliber of employees who administered the regulations at the lower levels. The 1917 annual reports submitted by two of the six division chiefs illustrated the difficulties encountered. John F. Keenan, for example, wrote that "It may not be amiss, at the moment when we approach the line demarking the old year from the new, to indulge in a brief retrospection, a cursory survey of present conditions official, and a modest hope for the times to come." In the document, he referred to his division as "the dear old Civil War Division." Acting Division Chief M. L. Dawkins opened his report with the sentence: "As the holiday season wanes and the wintry nights shorten, a momentous year passes into history." He signed it "Yours for efficiency."[29] Lane never resolved the problem of administering with civil servants of this quality.

The Pension Bureau troubled Lane periodically throughout his tenure. In August 1919, he concluded that things were "in very bad shape there" and characteristically directed Seldon G. Hopkins, the assistant secretary, to conduct an investigation. Hopkins assigned the task to Oscar W. Lange, of the Solicitor's Office, who reported finding problems regarding division of work between administrators, low morale, feelings of favoritism relating to promotion, and "discipline in minor matters." Much of the difficulty, Lange concluded, arose when new administrations replaced higher level officials with appointees of their own party affiliation. This led, Lange continued, to a widely held belief that promotion depended unduly upon political influence rather than upon the quality of work performed. The synchronized pattern of promotions and demotions, coinciding with the changes of administrations, provided grounds for such a belief. In addition, the Commissioner and Deputy Commissioner had difficulty cooperating to administer the bureau. Of the bureau's nine hundred employeed, moreover, nearly one-third were in their mid-sixties, with a corresponding absence of employees in the early years of their careers.

To improve conditions, Hopkins, Lange, and Joseph J. Cotter, Lane's administrative assistant, recommended changes in the job descriptions and duties of the commissioner, deputy commissioner, and chief clerk. Late in October, Lane directed Commissioner Saltzgaber to implement the new regulations, chief among them being the creation of a promotion personnel board and a virtual separation of the work of the bureau's top two administrators. Hopkins believed the reorganization humiliated Saltzgaber, whom Hopkins thought "desired to do the right thing," but tended to follow uncritically the advice of his subordinates. A few months later, when Lane resigned, the Pension Bureau still functioned as the least efficient bureau within the department.[30]

Throughout his years as secretary, Lane also periodically issued directives designed to improve the quality of writing within the department and the speed with which employees handled their correspondence. He believed his personnel wrote needlessly long and often unnecessary letters. Soon after he took office, for example, Lane read a letter written by a departmental lawyer explaining to an Indian the conditions of his land title. Lane later recalled the letter as "so involved and elaborately braided and beaded and fringed that I could not understand it myself." Annoyed, Lane sent back the letter with an order "that it be put in straightaway English."[31] On July 15, 1913, as a consequence of similar experiences, Lane directed the members of the Interior Department "to make their letters short, simple, and cordial." Three and one-half years later, he issued another order calling attention to his earlier one, because he had "some evidence that this request is being overlooked." In April 1919, he again told his bureau chiefs they were forgetting to insist that letters "be short and cordial. . . . Few letters should be longer than one page. . . ." and they should be "written in simple English, in Saxon rather than Latin."[32]

The seriousness with which Lane viewed his administrative responsibilities was apparent in other areas as well. When Wilson asked Lane what he thought about ending the workweek at Saturday noon, the Secretary agreed with the proposal, provided everyone worked an extra half hour on the other five days of the workweek. On another occasion, he asked the Commissioner of Education to explain why he and his assistants often were unavailable during the closing minutes of the workday. Lane, furthermore, required that either the Director of the National Park Service or his deputy be in Washington at all times, despite his complete faith in the two officials and despite their opposition to the policy.[33]

Five weeks after taking office, Lane established and publicized his work schedule. He reserved Monday, Wednesday, and Thursday mornings for appointments with members of Congress and the afternoons of those days for formal hearings and conferences within his department. From eleven-thirty to one o'clock he met with persons not covered by the above two categories. Most of Tuesday and Friday, he set aside for Cabinet meetings. When Lane's legislative proposals increased his contact with members of

Congress and congressional committees, he ordered that any communication "will be answered within five days." The communications, he commanded further, must "bear the initials of the bureau chief concerned and the particular Assistant Secretary under whose assignment the matter falls." Lane permitted bureaus only three days to prepare drafts of letters that would return to his office and go out with his signature.[34]

Lane's honesty as well as his concern for administrative detail were plainly visible the summer of 1913 when he, Adolph Miller, and their wives, made an inspection tour of the national parks. Their stay in Yellowstone lasted about a week, but when they prepared to leave, the hotel concessionaire refused to charge them. Lane insisted to no avail. This troubled him because the Interior Department granted the concession leases and he wanted no obligation or opportunity for obligation to arise. When he returned to Washington, Lane ordered that henceforth all leases state that room and board must be furnished, without charge, to any federal official in the park on government business.[35]

V

Lane's desire for an orderly personal schedule and office routine, for a department that conducted its business with efficiency, and for an organization that possessed self-pride, led him to appreciate and to guard zealously the new Interior Department building completed in June 1917. The initial planning for the building started during the Roosevelt administration, continued under Taft, and received authorization of funds on March 4, 1913. Built in the block bounded by E, F, 18th, and 19th streets, the E-shaped structure cost $2.5 million and was second in size only to the Capitol. Lane looked upon the move, among other considerations, as an opportunity to centralize the department's disbursing, purchasing, and appointments, which had been decentralized because of the bureaus' diverse functions and their locations in separate buildings spread over several blocks.[36]

When the country entered World War I in April 1917, the War and Navy departments immediately cast covetous eyes toward the Interior building then only a few weeks from completion. Lane unofficially told the departments to look elsewhere, whereupon the departments raised the question with Wilson. The President gently asked Lane his opinion and received a five-page response. "Permit me to say," Lane remarked, that "I cannot believe that after two years of alarm and preparation [,] provision of some sort has not been made for the emergency needs of these departments." After expressing his indignation, Lane explained that some of the buildings his department occupied were not fireproof and that "many of our people are working almost underground, with little sun, poor ventilation, and in quarters which the Public Health Service has repeatedly condemned officially as unsanitary." He then offered suggestions as to where the War and Navy departments could find some additional quarters. The War Department, Lane wrote, had "at least thirty rooms" of Revolutionary and Civil War records that could and should be in storage. When the Land Office moved into the new Interior building, Lane continued, the War Department could take over the old Land Office building with its 275 rooms. He also pointed out that the Navy Department could gain 98,000 square feet of space on July 1 when the Interstate Commerce Commission moved. If Navy needed emergency space, Lane offered to crowd his department and give up 100 rooms in the new building. If that did not suffice, Lane said he would leave the Land Office in its old building and release 300 rooms of the new building "at the greatest inconvenience to our work." Sensing the depth of Lane's opposition, and the logic of his comment "that the discovery [by the War and Navy Departments] of a fine new building so nearly ready and so near at hand was too great a temptation to be resisted," Wilson told Lane he could keep all of his new building.[37]

VI

Shortly after he took office, Lane held a reception for the entire department and quickly learned that the affair was the first of its kind. Bothered that most employees had neither the opportunity to meet their fellow workers in other bureaus nor the opportunity to meet him and his wife, Lane decided to organize what he named the Home Club. He wanted a social club, open to all, to help increase morale within the department and to help lessen the sense of isolation many employees experienced.[38] Reflecting Lane's wish, the Home Club held its first meeting in November 1913, and in its bylaws stated its purpose as "the mutual social improvement and enjoyment, education, literary, musical, and scientific advancement of its members, and the increase of personal interest and efficiency, with a view of promoting the public service relating to the Department of the Interior."[39] Lane also intended the club to demonstrate to "people of moderate salaries what could be done by cooperation" and took pride that there was "no caste line or snobbery in the institution."[40]

The Home Club flourished. It rented a four-story mansion in LaFayette Square, half a block from the White House, complete with billiard room, library, tea room, card rooms, and a gymnasium. Each evening, the club offered some form of entertainment such as a dance, lecture, movie, or concert. Within a year, membership, which cost $1.00 for initiation and $0.50 a month for dues, climbed to about 1,700 members, before declining to approximately 1,100 during World War I. Starting in November 1914, the club published a monthly bulletin that often ran to over twenty pages. President Wilson called the Home Club "an admirable idea which commends itself to me in every way." To underscore his support, Wilson attended a theatre party the fledgling club sponsored at the Columbia Theatre in July 1914.[41]

Lane considered his project a major success and supported it accordingly. He spoke before it, with his wife held receptions in its building, and attended some of its social activities. In the spring of 1919, Lane remarked that "we have no difficulty when we want men to work overtime . . . because they feel identified with the Department."[42]

Lane's attempt to instill a greater sense of unity among employees of his department and to facilitate his desire to see and be seen by large numbers of employees led him to schedule half-hour songfests. Years later, a former government official recalled the time he stopped at the Interior Department on business and witnessed such an activity. Before the visitor could transact his business, the Interior official he came to consult took him into the departmental auditorium where most of the department had assembled. After the singing had started, Lane entered the hall to the cheers of the audience, went to the stage, sang for ten minutes or so, waved good-bye, again received cheers, and left. The Interior official boasted to the visitor that the department had a morale that never existed before Lane's leadership and that probably did not exist in any other federal de-

partment.[43] Apparently Lane's enjoyment of family songfests prompted
him to initiate the community singing. The results, no doubt, satisfied
Lane, as did the singing itself.

Although the Home Club and occasional songfests helped employees
identify with and take pride in their department, Lane also attempted to
bring the various bureaus, which often operated as independent entities,
closer together on a professional level. In doing so, Lane intended to trim
some of the autonomy as well as encourage a broader perspective. One
of the first things he did upon taking office was to form "a Land Cabinet,"
consisting of the director of the Geological Survey, the commissioner of
the General Land Office, and the assistant secretaries. The Land Cabinet
met every Monday afternoon to discuss common problems. Similarly,
Lane organized a Reclamation Commission to consider matters common
to the bureaus responsible for the Indians, public lands, and irrigation.
The first winter in office, Lane also established "a noonday mess," where
the bureau chiefs and their assistants usually ate lunch.[44]

As he prepared to leave office, Lane laudatorily wrote that "never has
a man been better supported by those with whom he worked than have
I by the many people in its [Department of Interior] employ, and never
have I known so large a group of competent and zealous workers."[45]

From the beginning, Lane had taken firm charge of the Interior Department. He appointed conscientious officials whom he respected, improved
the department's internal efficiency, and carried out his duties according
to his own conservation and political philosophies. Years later, one of
Lane's most able and respected appointees, Horace M. Albright, recalled
that "It was a well-organized, well administered Department. Secretary
Lane was a good Secretary."[46]

6

The Reclamation Service, Alaska, Indians, and Parks

This is the initiation of a new administrative policy of direct dealing between the water users and the department, and Secretary Lane hopes that it will lead to a better understanding between all parties.

Press Release,
Department of Interior,
April 19, 1913

I would personally like to spend a few years of my life dreaming dreams about what could be done in that huge territory [Alaska].

Lane to Allan Pollock,
July 17, 1918

I

Once in office, Lane reevaluated and subsequently modified most of his department programs and responsibilities. Generally, the modifications Lane believed necessary required congressional action; often these actions instituted new programs that were modifications only in the sense they evolved from existing programs and that the Secretary of the Interior retained jurisdiction. The pressures for change came from some of the persons whose daily lives the Interior Department affected, from certain members of Congress, from interested journalists and public citizens, and from Lane's own observations. In varying degrees, interested individuals; groups; and federal officials, including Roosevelt, Taft, and Lane's predecessors, earlier had promoted the recommendations the new Secretary adopted.

The first important problem Lane confronted involved the Reclamation Service, especially the terms by which farmers paid for the service they received. Congressional passage of the Reclamation Act in 1902 represented a new direction of federal land policy. The act stipulated that the revenue from public land sales in arid states be put into a revolving fund and used for the construction of water storage reservoirs and other needed permanent irrigation works. The act authorized the Secretary of the Interior to examine, survey, locate, and construct irrigation projects; it required farmers who received benefits from the projects to repay the construction cost in not more than ten annual installments.

For the first five years, the Reclamation Service functioned as a unit within the Geological Survey, but as a result of the Interior Department's reorganization in 1907, the service became an independent bureau administered directly under the Secretary. Among the service's foremost champions were F. H. Newell, its first director; Gifford Pinchot; Representative, and later Senator, Francis Newlands of Nevada; and Theodore Roosevelt. Ideally, the original supporters believed, the Reclamation Service would base its operations on the advice of experts, would be nonpolitical, and, with the revolving fund as a source of income, would be free from the whims of Congress for its financial support. Under the leadership of Newell, the service initiated businesslike collection procedures to enforce the repayment provisions. Opposition, however, slowly mounted against the arrangements. Farmers, claiming financial insolvency, particularly demanded an extension of the ten-year payment period.

The farmers on most of the projects administered by the Reclamation Service hoped Lane would be receptive to their demands for change, and so they intensified their complaints once he took office. Their discontent had been fermenting for several years. Not only did a high percentage of the eleven thousand families settled on projects complain, but as Lane told a Montana newspaper editor in May, "ever since I came here Senators and Congressmen have been overwhelming me with curses upon the Reclamation Service."[1]

Lane listened and quickly took steps to deal with the problem. On April 19, 1913, he announced that he would hold a conference on the problem starting May 1. He asked the water users of each project to send a representative; he invited senators and representatives from western states to attend; and he directed the service to send an official from each of its projects. He also invited Gifford Pinchot. Although Lane expected the conference to last a few days, it stretched into seventeen. Most of the water users' delegates shared common grievances. They pleaded for an extension of the ten-year rule, called for an investigation of construction costs they believed to be excessive, and asked for transfer of project administration from the Service to water users' associations, and suggested federal contributions to the cost of the projects.[2]

The conference convinced Lane that the service had committed errors, that there was need for increased federal investment in reclamation, and that the Act of 1902 required modification. To Lane, the most obvious need was an extension of the repayment period, a proposal that Director Newell steadfastly opposed. Lane moved immediately. Ten days after the conference ended, he reorganized the service by creating a Reclamation Commission of five members. Although Newell served on the commission, Lane clearly had reduced the director's power. Thereafter, when Lane wanted advice, he consulted the commission rather than Newell. Lane also established the office of chief counsel, which further diluted Newell's influence, because Newell's assistant previously had handled important legal work.[3]

While western congressmen pushed to amend the 1902 act, Lane supported their efforts in a number of ways. During the summer of 1913, he sent a close friend and staff member to inspect the projects without revealing his affiliation with the department. Two weeks later, Lane himself started a public inspection trip throughout the western states to hear complaints and visit the projects. While on his summer tour, Lane also attended the public lands convention at Denver to explain his policies. In his annual report of December, he called for Congress to appropriate funds to spur development of projects. He also admitted the service had made mistakes and praised the farmers on the projects as "genuine pioneers in a new field of work."[4]

Two months after his annual report, which the *New York Times* praised in an editorial, Lane announced his sponsorship of an irrigation conference to meet in Denver on April 9, 1914. He invited the governors, senators, and congressmen from the western states, as well as businessmen and railroad officials who had an interest in irrigation. Specialists and administrators from the Agriculture and Interior departments represented the Wilson administration. Lane asked his predecessor Walter L. Fisher, with whom he maintained friendship, to serve as a delegate at large and invited Republican Senator William E. Borah to recommend three delegates at large. "My hope," Lane explained, "is that a definite program may be arrived at as to meeting the irrigation problems of the West, and practicable procedure outlined for action by the States and the Federal Government."[5] The conference, of course, served as an excellent public relations activity, dramatizing the need for state-federal cooperation.

The month after the conference, Lane authored an article in *Sunset* further publicizing his views on irrigation. He pointed out that he "could expend properly $100,000,000 in the next few years in the development of small irrigated farms" and observed that 557,000 acres of irrigation projects remained unirrigated. Lane made a direct appeal for western support. "When I assumed the Secretaryship," he wrote, "I determined that the best way to get results for the West—and most of our big problems are there—was to have Western men as officials in direct charge of Western affairs." He remarked that he was "a Western man," as were the first assistant secretary, the head of the national parks, the general counsel of the Reclamation Service, the commissioner of the General Land Office, and the commissioner of Indian Affairs. Lane's work no doubt aided the forces in Congress pushing for amendment of the 1902 Reclamation Act.[6] He was a westerner, but he had strong ties with easterners, especially Roosevelt and his supporters.

On August 13, 1914, Wilson signed the administration-backed Reclamation Extension Act of 1914. The major provisions increased the ten-year repayment period to twenty years and adopted a graduated rate of charges that required smaller payments during the first years. Congress, by the act, took from the secretary of the interior the power to appropriate money from the reclamation fund and the power to select new project locations. Despite losing these two important prerogatives, Lane considered the act a definite accomplishment. Congress, however, never did authorize funds to supplement the revenue derived from public land sales, as Lane wished. The act, furthermore, marked the beginning of a trend of financial leniency that over the years led to new and different problems.[7]

Early in December 1914, Lane took the final step in eradicating Newell's influence when he combined the positions of director and chief engineer. Removing Newell from the service's five-man commission, he gave him a three-month appointment as "Consulting Engineer," at the same salary. After the three months, however, Newell was to serve "on the same basis as other consulting engineers," which meant a per-diem basis. Lane's action brought criticisms and protests from southern and eastern papers and from Newell's friends, most notably Theodore Roosevelt and Gifford Pinchot. Lane made no explanation for his actions; Newell, to his credit, also remained silent and in May quietly resigned and accepted the chairmanship of the civil engineering department at the University of Illinois.[8]

Still not satisfied with the service, Lane established on January 20, 1915, after five months of planning, a local board for each project to review construction costs. These local boards, in accordance with Lane's plans, investigated alleged abuses, examined cost data, and submitted their reports to a central board, which in turn made recommendations to the secretary of the interior. The water users' association for each project selected one local board member; the service chose a second; and the secretary appointed an "impartial" person to chair all the projects within a general region. To direct the central board, Lane named Dr. Elwood Mead, professor at the University of California and an internationally known expert on planned land use.[9]

Next, Lane sent his newly appointed chief of construction, Sydney B. Williamson, on a general inspection tour of projects and offices. The first week in April, Williamson submitted an eighteen-page report suggesting changes for the projects. Lane accepted these recommendations and told Arthur P. Davis, who headed the service, to proceed at once with the reorganization, "eliminating such officials as will not be necessary, and making such other changes as will make for the highest efficiency and greatest saving." As a result, the executive offices of the service moved to Denver, and a small staff maintained the Washington office. In making the announcement, Lane commented that "I have felt for a long time that we were too far removed from the projects themselves."[10]

During his first twenty-six months in office, Lane moved determinedly to ease western discontent toward the Reclamation Service and in so doing improved the service's administrative efficiency and advertised his opinions

toward the federal government's role in the management of natural resources. He curtailed Newell's influence and power and eventually forced
him out of the service without creating controversy, in part because Newell
refused to challenge Lane, in part because Lane appointed one of Newell's
closest personal friends and associates as his successor, and in part because
some conservationists questioned Newell's ability. Lane's relationship with
the Reclamation Service illustrated clearly that he was a forceful administrator willing to attack a problem and determined to press his own
policies.[11]

Irrigation of arid western lands remained one of Lane's favorite programs, because it appealed to his belief that resources should be developed
to their greatest potential. In May 1914, and again the following September,
when Lane wrote magazine articles stating that his department "could expend properly $100,000,000" on irrigation, the entire federal budget
totaled $735,081,000.

Lane's enthusiasm for reclamation through irrigation led him, during
his last year in office, into a questionable position supporting irrigationists
in Idaho who wanted to use a naturally wild corner of Yellowstone Park as
part of their project. Two of Lane's most distinguished appointees, Stephen
Mather, director of the National Park Service, and Horace M. Albright,
superintendent of Yellowstone, vigorously protested, and stalled action for
months. Only Lane's own resignation stopped Mather and Albright from
resigning their positions in protest. Fortunately for the park, Lane's successor, John Barton Payne, quickly reversed the earlier ruling.[12]

The West and Lane never were able to gather enough support to satisfy
their reclamation appetites.[13] Lane's efforts, however, established and
maintained for him a reservoir of western goodwill that remained even
when some segments of western opinion criticized him and attacked his
policies.

II

In light of Lane's advocacy of resource development, evident in his
reclamation policies, his jurisdiction of the territory of Alaska became
an appealing challenge. Yet, of all the programs and policies he championed, his Alaskan plans probably provoked the least opposition, although they were comparable, at least in the minds of many Americans

at that time, in proportion to the size of the territory itself. In 1913, Alaska was a sparsely populated treasure house of natural resources, the overwhelming majority of which belonged to the federal government. Two conditions impeded development. First, the Interior Department had insufficient legislative authority to make these resources available on a planned, democratic basis, but it did have the power to keep the resources "locked up," which it did rather than violate its ideal. Second, the lack of transportation facilities within Alaska and exorbitant transportation rates to and from that northern territory made development difficult. Lane's attitude toward development in combination with his natural optimism spurred him to act.

The ideas of releasing and using Alaskan resource potential were not new to Lane or to the Wilson administration. For a number of years, various members of Congress had introduced bills on the subject but without success. The area, for some time, had captured the hopes and aroused the fears of both exploiters and guardians of the public interest. In 1911, for example, two staunch defenders of public rather than private development, Gifford Pinchot and Robert M. LaFollette, sounded dire warnings about turning Alaska over to the J. P. Morgan and Guggenheim family interests. Pinchot and LaFollette vehemently asserted that because public funds purchased Alaska, the territory's profits and advantages should benefit all citizens. To do otherwise, LaFollette declared, would be "the greatest crime of our generation."[14]

Before Lane implemented a program for Alaska to heal the public rift, he needed to appoint a territorial governor. Wilson received letters from willing candidates as early as January 1913, but by March, endorsements for John F. Strong, a Juneau editor, easily overshadowed those of all other prospects. Key Pittman, Democrat from Nevada and chairman of the Senate Committee on Territories, urged Lane to appoint Strong with whom he had been "intimately acquainted" for almost sixteen years. The territorial legislature endorsed Strong unanimously. On April 17, Lane took the obvious step and named him to the four-year post, thus rewarding another delegate to the 1912 Democratic convention who had supported Wilson from the start.[15]

The appointment illustrated, among other things, Lane's conception of sound administrative practice for his far-flung department. Simultaneously with the appointment, Lane announced that he was adopting a policy of naming no person to office who was not a bona fide resident of the territory in which the vacancy existed. A month later, when a job seeker requested Lane's intercession on behalf of his application to Strong, Lane replied that the appointment was a prerogative of the governor's and that no dictation would come from Washington in such a matter.[16]

Four years later, Strong's possible reappointment presented Lane and Wilson with a dilemma. The November 1916 Alaskan election for delegate to the United States House of Representatives, between Democrat Charles A. Sulzer and Republican incumbent James Wickersham, ended with a dispute over partial use in six precincts of "regular" but "nonofficial" ballots. The territory's Attorney General advised that all the votes in the affected precincts were void. Strong, and the other members of the territorial canvassing board, honoring what they believed to be the intent and spirit of the ballots cast, declared void only certain individual ballots. Sulzer took his case to court where Judge Robert W. Jennings ruled contrary to the canvassing board's finding and declared Sulzer the winner. Wilson remembered "how bitter and unfair" Wickersham had been in Congress and knew "of no reason" to discount Sulzer's position. Nevertheless, he confided to Lane, because of the disagreement among Alaskan Democrats, "it presents matters of a very serious nature."[17]

Strong made an impressive defense of his course of action to Lane and to Senator Pittman, denying, at the same time, the charge by some Democrats that he had failed to campaign adequately for Sulzer. Frank A. Aldrich, a Democratic member of the territorial legislature and a friend of Pittman told the senator that "the only opposition" to Strong's reappointment "comes from a class of hungry office seeking wolves." On June 14, Pittman and Montana Democrat Thomas J. Walsh, also a member of the Senate Committee on Territories, jointly wrote Lane that they had consulted with their colleagues and reported that their committee would "report favorably upon such an appointment." Dismissing the whole matter as "tribal," the two senators "most earnestly" recommended Strong's reappointment. Three weeks later, in a letter to Wilson, Pittman repeated that he was "a close personal friend" of Strong and his wife, and that the Commitee on Territories had investigated the canvassing board controversy and had found no impropriety on Strong's part. The governor, Pittman added, was "the ablest and most satisfactory" one in Alaskan history. On September 1, William C. Houston, chairman of the House Committee on Territories, sent a similar assessment of Strong's governship. Before the end of the year, Joshua W. Alexander, chairman of the House Committee on the Merchant Marine and Fisheries, joined Pittman and Houston in support of Strong.[18]

Despite the strength of support among important party leaders in Congress, Lane and Wilson moved cautiously because of the persistent opposition in Alaska of the Democratic Territorial Central Committee, the Democratic newspapers, and the majority of Democratic leaders. Lane finally recommended reappointment, but voiced no protest when Wilson did not forward it to the Senate for confirmation, preferring "to think about it a little further." The uneasy situation, with Strong serving without formal appointment, continued to the end of February 1918, when Strong resigned amid rumors, later proved correct, that he really was not an American, but a Canadian-born citizen. Lane immediately nominated Thomas Riggs, Jr., a member of the Alaskan Engineering Commission, as Strong's successor. Not until the third week of March, however, did Strong write the truth of his citizenship to Pittman, who then withdrew his opposition to Rigg's confirmation.[19]

The controversy over Strong's appointment stemmed from the political considerations of patronage and elections. Lane's major interest and effort in Alaska, however, concerned resources, not politics.

III

Central in Lane's plans to develop Alaska was a railroad built, owned, and operated by the federal government. The idea of such a railroad predated the Wilson administration and had enjoyed the ardent support of Lane's Interior predecessor, Walter L. Fisher. During the spring of 1912, the Senate Committee on Public Lands had conducted hearings on an Alaskan railroad bill. In August of that year, Congress established the Alaska Railroad Commission of four members to study transportation needs, to determine potential rail routes, and to gather information regarding costs of constructions and operation. The committee submitted its report to President Taft on January 20, 1913. When the Sixty-third Congress met for the first time the following spring, supporters and proponents of the Alaskan railroad, fortified with the commission's positive report, reintroduced their bill.[20]

In May 1913, the Senate Committee on Territories, while considering
the bill, requested Lane's opinion. The occasion afforded Lane his first
opportunity to speak publicly on the subject. He wrote to the committee's
chairman, Key Pittman, that he had high hopes that Alaska one day
would be "supporting millions of people of the hardiest and most wholesome of the race." The owners of a country's railroads, Lane explained,
"determines very largely the future of that country, the character of its
population, the kind of industries they will engage in, and ultimately the
nature of the civilization they will enjoy." Anticipating public apprehen-
sions, and at the same time expressing his political philosophy, Lane added
that a government railroad would, indeed, be "a new policy for the United
States. And policies properly change with new conditions. The one deter-
mining question in all matters of government should be, What is the wise
thing to do?" Then, with evident contempt for past abuses, Lane concluded
that a government railroad would "not suggest scandals more shameful or
political conditions more unhealthy than many we have known in new
portions of our country under private ownership." His clear-cut support of
the bill threw the full weight of the Wilson administration behind the
measure. Eighteen months later, Lane summarized, "I do not know who
drafted the Alaska Railway Bill. It was made an administration measure."[21]

Although Lane spent the summer of 1913 inspecting reclamation
projects and national parks throughout the West, and although he was ill
for six weeks in early fall, he endorsed the Alaska rail bill whenever he
could.[22] In Wilson's first State of the Union address on December 2,
1913, he recommended that the government build and operate a system
of railways in Alaska. Like Lane, Wilson wanted the territory's transportation network subordinated to the service and needs of the inhabitants. Also,
when Lane issued his first annual report in December 1913, he reiterated
his support for the railroad. In January 1914, a railway bill passed the
Senate, and in February, it passed the House.[23] On March 12, 1914, Wilson signed the bill, authorizing the expenditure of $35 million for the con-
struction of a government railroad in Alaska.

The measure empowered the President to order construction of one or
more railroads to connect inland navigable rivers with one or more Pacific
ports and to purchase and build any needed supplementary facilities such
as telephone and telegraph lines, docks, and existing rail lines. In May 1914,
Wilson created the Alaskan Engineering Commission to build the railway
under supervision by the Interior Department. Eleven months later, Wilson

announced the route of the railroad, to be known as the Susitna Route. It extended a distance of 471 miles from Seward on Resurrection Bay to Fairbanks on the Tanana River. A planned sideline ran from Matanuska Junction 38 miles to the Matanuska coal fields. Sixteen days after his announcement the first contingent of workers plus the first material landed in Alaska.

Construction of the railroad proceeded without difficulty, but slowly. The severe Alaskan winter limited the construction season; and often the funds were depleted and work stopped even before it was climatically necessary because annual appropriations came from estimates made prior to the start of the construction season. During World War I, not only did the war effort demand priority of supplies and men, but also caused a rise in prices for all materials and labor. In February 1919, the inflation forced Lane to request a supplemental appropriation of $17 million to complete the work. Nevertheless, Lane was pleased with all aspects of the railroad's construction. In December 1919, when he submitted his final annual report as secretary of the interior, he took pride in the fact that it had been built without a trace of politics or graft. The cost increase above prewar estimates, he maintained, was the least for any private or governmental construction project. Furthermore, the construction-per-mile cost was less than half that of two nongovernmental lines constructed at the same time.[24] Perhaps most important, the road was built to last. The labor force had been well paid and cared for, with medical doctors and some hospital facilities available at the work camps.

During the summer of 1923, more than three years after Lane had left office, and at the cost of another $4 million, the construction crew completed the last of the 539.9 miles of the Alaskan railway system. Lane had directed more than two-thirds of the work and had established the guidelines that served through the laying of the last rail.

IV

The second major component of Lane's Alaskan program, a leasing system for the federal coal lands, bore a close relationship to the railway. Like the railway idea, the leasing proposal originated before Lane entered the Interior Department. During the spring of 1912, for example, the Senate Committee on Public Lands designated a railway bill and

coal-leasing bill as joint measures and analyzed both at the same hearing.
In his 1912 annual report, Secretary Fisher summarized that he vigorously
had urged construction of a railroad and passage of a "carefully guarded
leasing law for the development of its [Alaska's] mineral resources and
especially its coal lands." The idea of developing the coal lands under
federal control dated from the Roosevelt administration and incorporated
the philosophy of the conservation movement. Lane sympathized with
this approach. In October 1911, he thanked Fisher for a copy of his
"address on Alaskan problems" and commented "that it is strong, sane
and statesmanlike." Gifford Pinchot likewise evaluated Fisher's views and
reported to former Secretary of the Interior James R. Garfield that
"Walter Fisher's Alaska report for the most part is good. He has simply
taken over the policy the rest of us have been following."[25]

In his December 1913 State of the Union address, Wilson asked Congress to unlock the minerals in Alaska under federal jurisdiction. Lane,
in his annual report the same month, outlined a coal-land leasing system
he hoped would insure development on a nonmonopolistic basis. To guard
against monopoly, he suggested a maximum leasing unit of 2,600 acres,
which at the time was the average size of individual coal-mining operations
in the United States. Furthermore, he suggested that the awarding of tract
leases be limited to one per person, or group of persons, and be nontrans-
ferable.

To promote immediate development, Lane wanted to collect a fixed
annual royalty in addition to a monthly per-ton royalty. Lane wanted the
leases to run for a fixed period but to be renewable under adjusted terms.
He considered an asset that the leasing system enabled an operator to put
all his capital into the development of his enterprise and nothing into the
land itself. Thus, Lane believed, it would be possible for the man of com-
paratively small means to go into the coal-mining business. As an added
incentive to the small operator, he suggested that all royalty payments
be waived for a brief initial period.[26]

Two months after Lane issued his report, Representative Scott Ferris,
chairman of the House Committee on Public Lands, announced to the
public the plans of the Wilson administration for the development of
Alaskan coal lands. The drafting of the bill, he disclosed, took place under
Secretary Lane's direction in the Department of the Interior. Lane's
December 1913 proposals formed the backbone of the bill.

The measure called for the federal government to survey all coal lands

in Alaska; to issue twenty-year leases for blocks of coal lands ranging
from 40 to 2,560 acres, which would be renewable under adjusted terms;
and to collect the type of annual and monthly royalties Lane wanted. The
income from the royalties would subsidize a special Alaskan development fund. The opportunity to participate in the program was open to
all citizens and to those who had declared their intention of becoming
citizens, but each person or corporation could lease 2,560 acres maximum.
Included in the bill was a provision that reserved almost 13,000 acres of
coal lands for use by the navy and for building and operating the then-
pending Alaskan railroad. The bill also intended that the federal coal
reserve serve as a check on monopoly; if private coal prices rose unreason-
ably, the government could market cheap coal and force down private
prices.[27] The provisions of the bill clearly indicated the danger Lane and
Wilsonian Democrats perceived in monopolistic practices and how they
hoped to use federal power to check its spread.

In addition to playing a major role in drafting the Alaska coal-leasing
bill, Lane supported it whenever he could. On February 17, 1914, he appeared before the House Committee on Public Lands and gave the bill his
hearty endorsement.[28] Also in February, Lane permitted publication of
an interview in which he discussed Alaska. In part, he declared that "Alaska
should not be regarded as a mere storehouse of resources upon which the
people of the States may draw. It has the potentialities of a state. And any
policy adopted should look toward such an Alaska." In September, Lane
published an article emphasizing his endorsement of Alaskan development.[29]

When the coal-leasing bill passed the House in mid-October, Lane
expressed delight in a press release that celebrated "the end of an eight-
year struggle"; Alaskan coal finally would "be opened to the world under
conditions that will prevent monopoly and I trust insure development."
Lane thanked Congress for accomplishing this achievement "without bitterness and practically without partisanship." Five days later, Wilson signed
the bill that incorporated every important feature Lane had recommended.
Gifford Pinchot, the National Conservation Association, and other conservation leaders had urged passage of the bill and likewise took pride in
its enactment.[30]

Passage of the coal-leasing and railroad bills owed more to the temper
of the times than to Lane's influence and efforts. By 1914, business interests, conservationists, and government officials had come to realize

that the only feasible Alaskan development program called for both federal control and for the opportunity of private profit. Most wanted to avoid the futility of another Ballinger-Pinchot affair. The West Coast was anxious to receive what it hoped would be cheap Alaskan coal. Finally, Alaska and its vast potential seemed to catch the imagination of many Americans. Nevertheless, Lane had given the railroad and leasing proposals clarity, publicity, and support and by so doing contributed toward the success of implementation that had eluded capable officials during two previous administrations.[31]

Along with the railroad and coal-leasing programs, Lane pursued other means to facilitate Alaskan development. Both in April and in September 1914, Wilson, upon Lane's recommendation, withdrew from public sale various tracts of land having natural value for townsites along several possible future railroad routes. In November 1914, following Lane's advice, Wilson withdrew forty-five additional square miles of land, this time for use by the Bureau of Education in connection with its work to improve living conditions of Eskimos. To provide for the strictly local and domestic fuel needs of Alaskans, Lane issued regulations permitting ten-year grants, without payment of royalty, for ten-acre tracts of coal lands. The Sixty-third Congress supplemented Lane's action by passing an education bill for Alaskans that provided for the setting aside of two sections of public land in every township for the benefit of public schools. The same bill included provisions granting a site for an agricultural college and for a school of mines, and included a grant of slightly over fifty thousand acres of land to help support such an institution.[32]

One Alaskan development project that particularly appealed to Lane was the nurturing of the reindeer meat industry. In 1891, a Presbyterian missionary named Sheldon Jackson, subsequently the United States general agent for education in Alaska because of his activities, purchased sixteen reindeer in Siberia and transported them to Alaska. The next year he purchased one hundred and seventy-five more from funds obtained through newspaper drives. In 1893, Congress came to his assistance and appropriated the first governmental funds to establish an Alaskan reindeer industry. Jackson's efforts helped to halt the loss of population then resulting from the declining number of available whales and walrus for use by the Eskimos. From 1893 on, Congress assumed financial and administrative responsibility for the reindeer program.[33]

When Lane took office, the Department of Interior recorded approxi-

mately 38,500 Alaskan reindeer. Seven years later, when he left office,
the count was roughly 125,000: the result of a special 1914 purchase
and of natural reproduction.[34] He maintained optimism and interest in
creating a market for reindeer meat within the United States. In July
1913, one of the reasons he gave for the desirability of a governmental
railroad in Alaska was that with proper transportation facilities, Alaska
could easily supply the country with reindeer meat, which, Lane added,
"is more tasty and nourishing than beef." From time to time, he reaffirmed
his belief that a potentially large market for reindeer meat existed in
America.[35]

V

The third part of Lane's Alaskan development plan, the only part Congress failed to enact, was his proposal to streamline, centralize, and coordinate the various federal programs and activities dealing with natural
resources in the territory. As with most of his suggestions, the plan was
not his original idea. Senator LaFollette of Wisconsin, in 1911, had called
for the establishment of a board to manage his proposed governmental
Alaskan coal leasing and to watch over resources and development to
protect the interests of conservation, consumers, and the public.[36]

In December 1913, in his first annual report, Lane outlined his plan
for an Alaskan commission, or board of directors, slated to discharge
all of the nation's responsibilities in the territory. Appointed by the
President, each commission member would operate as administrative
and residentiary head of a department, for example, a commissioner
of fisheries, a commissioner of transportation, and a commissioner of
Indian affairs. The commissioners, sitting as a group, would be able to
coordinate their individual duties and be able to advise Congress of the
territory's needs. A resident commission of public servants, Lane believed,
could advise from a firsthand knowledge of conditions, without prejudice
and in the nation's interest. In Lane's opinion, "The eye that sees the
need should be near the voice that gives the order"; laws could not be
satisfactorily administered five thousand miles from the site of action.
Lane also called for a separate federal budget for Alaska. If granted, he
believed it would show that Alaska was self-sufficient or nearly so. It

would also facilitate another of Lane's suggestions, that of using Alaskan resources, and revenues derived from them, for Alaskan development.[37]

For the next two years, Lane detailed and publicized his projected Alaskan development board. Although World War I made great demands on his time, and although Wilson displayed no enthusaism for the plan, Lane never ceased to believe in the merit of his suggestion and continued to champion its establishment. In two magazine articles in 1915, Lane amplified his request for new and simple administrative machinery to carry out the government's new policy of "opening up" Alaska. The old patchwork administrative system may have been adequate to keep the door shut, he asserted, but a new policy necessitated a new system. He pointed out that twenty-three separate offices or bureaus under nine different national departments transacted the public's business in Alaska. "Alaskan resources," he pleaded, "must be dealt with as an whole—as a single problem of large management."[38] To portray more graphically the administrative tangle, Lane pointed out that one department controlled Alaskan forests, another lands, a third fisheries, and a fourth roads. The Department of Agriculture controlled the brown bear while the Department of Commerce held jurisdiction over the black bear.[39] Over the years, Lane repeated his proposal for a development board, but he could not arouse the interests of Wilson, Congress, or the public, and his intensity and frequency of argument gradually diminished.[40]

Despite his zeal for administrative reform, Lane overlooked certain reforms that if adopted within his own Department of the Interior could have at least partially solved the maze of bureaucracy in Alaska. Of all federal departments, the Department of the Interior exercised the greatest governmental jurisdiction in Alaska; yet in the seven years of Lane's secretaryship, the Interior Department made no major administrative reforms in its handling of Alaskan affairs. In 1918, for example, the General Land Office operated in Alaska through a surveyor general, an assistant supervisor of surveys, a chief of field division, and three land offices (at Nome, Fairbanks and Juneau), each under the direction of a registrar and receiver. In his annual report of 1918, the Governor of Alaska pointed out that "All of these branches are independent of one another and deal directly with the General Land Office in Washington, frequently about the same matter, without the other being aware of what is taking place." The governor recommended the consolidation of all of these duties under one head. It would mean, he claimed, "an immediate savings in salaries, permit of the greater availability of field and office force, . . . a more economical utilization of office space, . . . [and] the keeping of one set of records instead of four,"[41] and, most important, increased efficiency. The General Land Office, as well as a number of other Interior agencies operating in Alaska, required no further authority than that exercised by Lane to retool administrative machinery.

In general, the Wilson administration paid little attention to Alaska after the passage of the coal-leasing act. After 1914, Wilson failed to mention Alaska in his messages to Congress and Lane's public criticism of government red tape dwindled to an occasional official reminder. During the last year of his administration, Wilson recognized the need of an interdepartmental committee to coordinate Alaskan affairs. On December 2, 1920, nine months after Lane had left office, Wilson approved "the formation of an Interdepartment Committee to consist of a representative of the War, the Post Office, the Navy, the Interior, Agriculture, and Commerce Departments; the Shipping Board, and the Federal Power Commission; the Governor of Alaska to be ex-officio a member." It was, however, too little and too late, and the results proved inconsequential. A bill incorporating Lane's suggestions got no further under the Harding administration than it had under Wilson's. The Alaskan administrative red tape continued to become increasingly tangled until the administration of Franklin D. Roosevelt succeded in alleviating the situation somewhat.[42]

Despite his failure to convince Wilson and Congress of the need for bureaucratic reforms, and despite his own lack of awareness of intradepartmental reform possibilities, Lane carried out his Alaskan responsibilities conscientiously and with interest. He recorded a corruption-free administration and contributed leadership in the passage of two major congressional acts.

VI

Another area of responsibility in which Lane's policies and administration elicited contemporary praise was his guardianship of the American Indians. In 1913, the Bureau of Indian Affairs employed some 6,000 persons, managed property valued at approximately $1 billion, watched over about three hundred thousand native Americans, and had the lowest budget of all the Interior bureaus.

Upon taking office, Lane judged the Indian problem and the public lands as two "of the greatest problems to meet and solve that have ever been presented to the American people."[43] The difficulty with Indians, Lane believed, was twofold. First, the Indian office needed reorganization, and for that reason when he looked for a commissioner of Indian affairs he sought primarily a person who had ability as an organizer.[44] Lane and the commissioner he appointed, Cato Sells, worked hard and successfully to bring efficiency and honesty to a bureau previously noted for neither. They were determined to suppress the Indian liquor traffic, to improve health conditions, to develop vocational training, to improve farming practices, and to protect Indian property. In November 1913, Lane told journalist Mark Sullivan that "there has already been a great improvement" in the administration of Indian affairs, in part, Lane declared, because "I have retained pretty well my old newspaper faculty of smoking things out." Interested observers found little to criticize and much to praise in this aspect of Lane's and Cato's work.[45]

Besides reorganization, the second part of the Indian problem, according to Lane, had to do with philosophy. He accepted unquestioningly the philosophy embodied in the Dawes Act of 1887 and the Burke Act of 1906. Like the sponsors of those acts, Lane believed individual Indians should receive education until they developed competencies equivalent to those of average white persons. At that point, the Interior Department would give the Indian an allotment of reservation land for his own farm and terminate its jurisdiction of and responsibility for him. Lane maintained that the Indian bureau "should be a vanishing Bureau." The problem had stemmed from officials who had inadequate perception of this philosophy and who, consequently, considered themselves caretakers. From the start, Lane expected Sells and other officials to remain sensitive to the philosophy that guided their work. One of the reasons Lane decentralized the administration of the Indian bureau, permitting field agents to exercise greater authority, was to free the commissioner of routine tasks so he could study "larger" aspects of his work.[46]

Lane believed the training and allotment process would lift Indians "into full fellowship with their civilized conquerors," a process that the Secretary found "takes hold upon the imagination and the memory, arouses dreams of the day when the Indian shall be wholly blended into our life."

Lane reasoned that the education of Indian children was crucial, because even if an adult remained a ward of the government, the children of such a person could be educated to live outside of a reservation and be similar to "all other citizens."[47]

At times, however, Lane admitted that trying to transform Indians into white persons proved "troublesome," because even after an education, "they return to the tepee, they go back to the blanket, they let their hair grow long." The Indian, Lane realized, "has a tradition of his own to which by blood and inheritance he is loyal and we have to dig that up and overturn it, and substitute a new standpoint for the one that he has, if we are going to make a new man out of him and fit him to a new life."[48]

Despite his desire to eradicate an Indian's loyalty to Indian values, Lane paradoxically wished to preserve Indian culture. During his first month in office, for instance, he assigned Geoffrey O'Hara to the Indian bureau as an instructor of music with orders "to record native Indian music and arrange it for use in the Indian schools." In appointing O'Hara, Lane stated: "I think that it is the part of wisdom to develop in the young Indian an increased respect for all those things of beauty which their fathers produced. Our effort should be to make this generation proud of their ancestors."[49] Twenty-one months later, in his second annual report, Lane labeled as enemies "those who would injustly take from him [the Indian] the heritage that is his."[50] The contradiction of these objectives, overturning Indian heritage and preserving it, apparently never occurred to Lane.

During the first four years of their service, Lane and Sells concentrated on improving the guardianship of property, education, health, and economic opportunity of Indians. Then in April 1917, they announced a shift toward emphasis and acceleration in the allotment process. At the same time, they reported a new policy of treating as competent those Indians who had "one-half or less Indian blood." At the end of 1919, Lane proudly proclaimed that in the previous three years, the Indian office has issued 10,956 allotments, compared with 9,984 allotments issued during the decade before 1916.[51]

Two months after Lane publicized these statistics, he left the Interior Department; his successor John Barton Payne quickly questioned the entire concept of granting allotments. In direct contrast to Lane's optimism, Payne concluded that it "will take generations" for Indians to gain the ability to deal on a business basis with white persons. The policy of

giving allotments of land to Indians, the new secretary warned, was
"fraught with the gravest danger and will inevitably pauperize thousands,"
because the whites would convince the Indians to sell their land "for a
wholly inadequate consideration."[52]

Payne's fears were well founded; the early 1920s witnessed a period of
muckraking exposure of the plight of the Indian. The allotment system
had always resulted in cases of landlessness and pauperization, and Lane's
firing-up process had greatly multiplied the number of incidents. The
General Leasing Act of 1920 added more grief, at least for the Navajos.
In June 1934, after over a decade of popular agitation aimed at stopping
the exploitation of Indians, the Wheeler-Howard Act ended the individual
allotment system and encouraged the restoration and revival of tribal life.

Lane's well-intentioned Indian policies, designed to develop Indian
abilities and potential, reflected his enduring concern for resource development, in this case human resources. Later generations judged Lane's
policies shortsighted, but until the twilight of the Wilson administration,
few persons voiced cirticism of them. Even then, Lane's ideas represented
the majority view. Looking back at the Indian bureau four months after
he relinquished responsibility, Lane pointed out that his tenure had "been
the only seven years in our history in which there has not been a scandal
in that very delicate department of public work." Indeed, he left a record
of efficiency and honesty.[53]

VII

Although the succeeding generation of officials rejected the allotment
policy that had guided Lane's efforts at supervision of Indians, the opposite proved true regarding his management of national parks. For three
reasons, the years from 1913 to 1920 turned out to be among the most
important in the history of the nation's parks. First, Congress established
the National Park Service in 1916; second, Lane's appointees were exceptionally dedicated and able; and third, Lane, as secretary, removed
the parks from the political arena.

The campaign to create a separate bureau to direct the parks started
during Roosevelt's presidency. J. Horace McFarland, president of the
American Civic Association, inaugurated the campaign and won the en-

dorsement of Roosevelt's successor, William Howard Taft, and Taft's
two Interior secretaries, Richard A. Ballinger and Walter L. Fisher. In
1911, Fisher called the first annual National Park Conference, but congressional and public interest increased slowly.

Once in office, Lane supported the park movement by upgrading
the position of assistant to the secretary, named Adolph C. Miller to fill
it, and directed him to improve park supervision. Never before had the
national parks received such attention. During the summer of 1914, however, Wilson appointed Miller to the Federal Reserve Board. With Miller
gone and the drive to establish a bureau of parks gaining momentum,
Lane needed an outdoor enthusiast, an organizer, a promoter, and an
administrator all rolled into one. In the autumn of 1914, with remarkably little effort, he found the ideal man.

Stephen Mather, another of Lane's college friends, was forty-seven,
a self-made millionaire, and a mountain climber. In the fall of 1914, he
wrote to Lane about the unsatisfactory conditions he had found in the
national parks. Lane replied, "If you don't like the way the national
parks are being run, come on down to Washington and run them your-
self."[54] Mather, tired of the business world, decided to accept the offer
for a year; he stayed fourteen, the rest of his working life. Once in office,
Mather decided to keep Horace M. Albright, the twenty-four-year-old
administrative assistant he inherited from Miller. The two men developed
a deep respect and affection for each other and formed a perfect team.
With the complete backing of Lane, they played the major role in the
passage of the National Park Service Act of 1916.

As a promoter, Mather had few peers. He employed journalist-editor
Robert Sterling Yard as publicity director for the parks and personally
paid Yard's $5,000 salary. Yard promoted the parks in a steady flow of
newspaper and magazine articles. The most successful of Mather's promotional schemes was a camping trip through the Sierra Mountains of
Califronia during July 1915. Among the guests were Frederick H. Gillett,
ranking Republican on the House Appropriations Committee; Henry
Fairfield Osborn, head of the American Museum of Natural History; and
Gilbert H. Grosvenor, editor of the *National Geographic.* The following
April, Grosvenor published a special issue of his well-known magazine
to focus attention on the parks. Mather, meanwhile, lobbied with congressmen on an individual basis, while the American Civic Association
and the Sierra Club intensified their efforts on behalf of a park service.

This skillful promotional drive, coordinated with the work of sympathetic members of Congress, culminated on August 25, 1916, when Wilson signed the bill creating the National Park Service. Mather, quietly and steadily assisted by Albright, had achieved an important objective of the conservation movement.[55]

The Mather-Albright team organized the new bureau, coordinated administrative policy, improved the services of park concessionaries, and carried on an aggressive campaign of publicity to get Americans to visit and appreciate their parks. Mather served as director of the National Park Service from its creation in 1916 until Albright succeeded him on January 12, 1929. Albright remained in the post until he left government service in August 1933.[56]

On the fundamental policy of removing the national parks from politics, Mather, Albright, and Lane agreed completely. All of them wanted trained professionals as administrators. Lane made this clear when he appointed Mather, a well-known Republican. At the time, most of the park superintendents owed their positions to political influence and lacked the dedication and ability for effective park work. By the time Lane's prize appointees left office, the National Park Service had become a respected agency, administered by professional conservationists.[57]

The National Park Service Act of 1916 symbolized and institutionalized acceptance of the concept of wilderness preservation as a component of the federal conservation program. Those responsible for the legislation wanted Americans to use the parks as national playgrounds, but they also intended the act to protect portions of parks in their natural state. The act, therefore, represented a victory for the aesthetic conservationists, or nature lovers, as the utilitarian conservationists often called them. Since the Roosevelt administration, these two groups of conservationists, while cooperating to advance certain programs, had clashed over the value of leaving scenic areas in their virgin condition in perpetuity.

By supporting Mather, and the National Park Service, Lane contributed significantly to the cause of preserving natural beauty as an end in itself. His contribution, however, involved a touch of irony. Although Lane was an ardent supporter of the parks, his attitude toward conservation more closely resembled the utilitarians than the preservationists. He remained a good friend of the parks until some organization or person made a demand he judged of higher use.

His position on the Hetch Hetchy controversy from 1903 to 1913 clearly exemplified his conservation philosophy years before he took his Cabinet seat. The controversy involved San Francisco's petition to Congress to dam the Tuolumne River and thereby convert Hetch Hetchy Valley into a reservoir, despite the fact that the land lay inside Yosemite National Park, an area Congress had declared a wilderness preserve in 1890. The struggle boiled down to a value judgment as to what constituted the highest or most worthy use of a valley of breathtaking grandeur. Lane, first as city attorney for San Francisco and later as secretary of the interior, favored the reservoir; in December 1913, Congress voted the same way.[58]

Mather and Albright, on the other hand, believed the parks should remain inviolable preserves. In principle, of course, so did Lane. When he announced to the public the precepts upon which the Park Service would operate, Lane declared, "first, that the national parks must be maintained in absolutely unimpaired form for the use of future generations." Lane's principle was preservationist; his operational procedure, however, revealed a utilitarian bent. For example, for several years, he served as president of the Save-the-Redwood-League and yet as secretary approved plans to build irrigation projects in Yellowstone and to graze sheep in Yosemite. When he accepted such plans, he met determined and successful opposition from his top two park administrators.[59]

Lane's tenure in the Interior Department saw, in addition to establishment of the National Park Service, the creation of six new parks, including Rocky Mountain and Mount McKinley National parks; the designation of seven national monuments, making a total of twenty-four; a 221 percent increase in visitors to the parks and an increase in appropriations of 116 percent.[60] Forces other than Lane's influence, of course, account for some of the changes the parks experienced during these years. But the imprint of his personality and policies was conspicuous on the park's administration, just as it was on the Reclamation Service, the territory of Alaska, and the Indian bureau. In these areas, Lane's record was that of a masterful and resourceful administrator. It was to be otherwise, however, in respect of waterpower and leasing of public lands. Here Lane's policies provoked one of the most bitter controversies and severe Cabinet splits that any domestic issue engendered during the Wilson years.

7
Waterpower, Leases, and Oil

We have adventured upon a new policy of administering our affairs and have not developed adequate machinery. . . . We abruptly closed opportunities to the monopolistic but did not open them to the developer.

> Lane, Report of the Secretary
> of the Interior, December 1913

[Waterpower and General Leading] these bills . . . meet the conservation demand of the East with the demand of the West for development.

> Lane to I. D. O'Donnell,
> January 26, 1915

The program of administration and legislation looking to the development of our resources, which I have suggested from time to time, is now in large part in effect, or soon will come into effect.

> Lane to Woodrow Wilson,
> February 5, 1920

I

Lane's attempt to get Congress to enact new legislation regarding regulation of natural resources within the public domain lasted throughout his years as secretary of the interior. In the end, he succeeded, but in doing so, he intensified a debate that at times became politically unpleasant for him. The broad issue concerned the type and degree of federal resource control; the specific points of contention involved leasing policies over sites suitable for waterpower development and over lands containing mineral resources, especially oil. Lane's actions harmonized with the general conservation movement that had formed during the Roosevelt administration.

Presidents Roosevelt and Taft believed that existing laws regarding natural resources did not protect adequately the public interest. Rather than make federal lands available to citizens for a fraction of their worth, Roosevelt and Taft withheld from public sale or use millions of acres. At the same time, they and their secretaries of the interior requested Congress, without success, to pass new laws recognizing the varying values of different tracts of land. The new laws, the proponents asserted, would promote a more democratic and more logical, efficient use of federal resources.

Lane continued this effort for new legislation, moving on three fronts during his first year in office. Regarding Alaska, he accomplished his objective quickly and without generating political division. He was not so successful, however, with his other two proposals, the leasing of waterpower sites and the leasing of mineral lands.

The storm over federal control of waterpower sites had been raging for years before Lane came upon the scene. Power companies wanted use of federal waterpower sites with no strings attached. Conservationists, who voiced repugnance toward the waste, dishonesty, and monopoly that too often blighted any industry not subject to some federal controls, never faltered in their demands for tight federal regulation of waterpower sites. Supporting the power companies were many congressmen from the South and West who wanted industrialization in their regions, some congressmen from states with great waterpower resources, and still other members of Congress who opposed federal regulation in general.

Between 1907 and 1909, Gifford Pinchot, as director of the Forest

Service, aroused vigorous protests when he withdrew 2,565 sites from public lands, ostensibly for use as forest ranger stations. Differing factions, furthermore, had marked the Water-Power Act of 1910, the last such legislation before Wilson took office, with a split personality. Three of the act's provisions satisfied conservationists: first, Congress could repeal or amend the act at any time without any government liability; second, no provision existed for the disposition of the properties at the expiration of a fifty-year lease; and third, Congress could direct the lessee to make undefined navigational improvements. To placate the power companies, however, the act required no payment for the privileges granted. During the latter part of the Taft administration, conservationists had defeated a bill that would have transferred ownership of the power sites from the federal government to the governments of the states within whose boundaries they lay. By 1913, the conflict over waterpower sites, with its concomitant inadequate legislation, had resulted in insufficient hydroelectric development: from an estimated 35 million available horsepower, less than 7 million had been developed. About 74 percent of the undeveloped 28 million horsepower was in the public domain, and of that, 42 percent was within government forest reserves.[1]

At first, no one knew exactly where the new Wilson administration stood on the waterpower question. In 1912, the Democratic party pledged itself to respect states' rights. Wilson, a number of his Cabinet, and Colonel House, his closest adviser, were all southerners and consequently subject to the suspicion of being sympathetic to that traditional sectional view. On the other hand, the new administration pledged itself to the nonmonopolistic development of natural resources. The country did not have to wait long, however, before Wilson's Secretary of the Interior presented his opinion on the subject and thus made known what course the administration would take.

As early as June, Lane sent a copy of his proposals to Gifford Pinchot, and then on August 23, 1913, Honoré Willsie published the first of a series of four articles about Lane in *Harper's Weekly*. In the articles, he quoted and paraphrased Lane's position in detail, including Lane's statement of broad objectives. "What I want to do," he declared, "is to develop all the available horse power in America." To accomplish this, Lane knew that Congress needed to establish a clear-cut policy and that leadership had to come from the executive branch of government. "If the States," Willsie quoted Lane, "had not been so neglectful and at times so corrupt there would be no need now for the government to step in regarding Water Power."[2]

The second article enumerated five principles that Lane believed should govern the leasing of waterpower sites: the greater the development of horsepower, the lower the government charge; the lower the consumer rate, the lower the government charge; the exemption of fees for the first five years while the power company established a market; the acceptance of state public utility jurisdiction of intrastate services and rates, and of federal jurisdiction of interstate services and rates; and the absolute prohibition of monopoly and combination, with the government having the right of revocation should either the courts or the secretary of the interior conclude that violations occurred. The philosophy supporting these principles Lane defined as "to save the country's natural resources for the people and put them where the people can get them. . . . We must not permit monopoly. We must keep the individual free."[3]

A few months later, in his first annual report, Lane enlarged on the waterpower theme. He emphasized that the existing stagnation of policy served no one, and, then, reiterating the philosophy he had articulated while a member of the Interstate Commerce Commission, he explained that the investors would not invest in waterpower development unless the government guaranteed a "fair and attractive return." But, he continued, the public must also receive reasonable rates and good service. Proper legislation was necessary. Lane also detailed his solution to the problem of how to administer the private property after the government's lease expired. At the end of the leasing period, Lane suggested, the government should purchase ownership at an appraised price. His reasoning was simple. "Within a generation I believe the people will be as alive to the value of public ownership of hydroelectric power plants as they are today of municipally-owned water works." This, to Lane, would "put these lands to their highest use." The people, Lane conceded, were not yet prepared for this, so he had offered his next best suggestion.[4] Lane's proposals, his beliefs, and his prophecy certainly did not warm the hearts of power company officials or of conservatives.

The first executive department action in the sphere of waterpower legislative proposals came, however, not from Lane, but from Secretary of War Lindley Garrison who prepared a bill subsequently introduced by William C. Adamson of Georgia, chairman of the House Interstate Com-

merce Committee. Conservationists immediately attacked the bill, which
dealt with waterpower development in navigable rivers, charging that it
made leases virtually perpetual. Meanwhile, with the help of Scott Ferris
of Oklahoma, chairman of the House Public Lands Committee, Lane
drafted a bill incorporating his principles regarding development of waterpower on nonnavigable waters in the public domain. The Ferris bill was
clear and precise exactly where the Adamson bill was vague: on the
duration of the leases and on the right of the government to purchase
all property when the leases expired. In addition to representing con-
flicting conservation views, the rivalry between the Adamson and Ferris
bills reflected a struggle within the Cabinet between Garrison and Lane
for control of waterpower policy. By precedent, the War Department
exercised jurisdiction of waterpower on navigable waters and the Interior
Department maintained jurisdiction of power on nonnavigable waters.
Garrison and Lane both hoped to stretch their jurisdiction at the other's
expense.

Conservationists, including Pinchot, William Kent, Henry Stimson,
and Theodore Roosevelt, supported Lane and the Ferris bill. At the end
of June 1914, Wilson finally stepped into the picture, called Lane, Ferris,
Garrison, and Adamson to conference, and started to make the Adamson
bill acceptable to the conservationists. For the next six weeks, the House
bitterly debated the modified Adamson bill, with the conservationists
amending it to the extent that when the House passed the bill on August
4, the waterpower interests found it unacceptable. Three weeks later, the
Lane-drafted Ferris bill passed the House. The conservationist-dominated
House had scored two victories, but the anti-conservationist Senate soon
negated them.[5]

Lane played a major role in drafting the Ferris bill, in resolving the
Adamson-Ferris impasse, and in pushing the Ferris bill through the House.
Some of the support he received for his endeavors provided a revealing index to his national popularity and to the intersectional support the Ferris
bill enjoyed. The eastern conservationists were with Lane all the way, for
his stand was a continuation of Roosevelt's position. In the midst of the
struggle, the *Chicago Evening Post* declared that "Secretary Lane always
has been a conservationist, and a good one . . . a stalwart defender of the
rights of the people to control their own property and its leasing." In
reply to his wire to a number of western governors, Lane received support from the governors of Montana, Oregon, Arizona, Oklahoma, New

Mexico, and Kansas. Governor George H. Hodges of Kansas paid Lane an uncommon political compliment when he replied that "I would be willing to accept your judgment as to whether the bill now before the Committee is a fair one." New Mexico's governor W. C. McDonald replied similarly, "I have more confidence in your judgment in this matter than in my own."[6]

In December 1914, the Senate Committee on Public Lands commenced hearings on the Ferris bill. The administration pushed the bill both in the hearings and out. During the sessions, Lane sent a statement to each member of the committee, in which he again explained why the Ferris bill fulfilled the legislative need. Lane's explanations were familiar themes of antimonopoly, public welfare, and increased possibility of development. In his annual report for 1914, Lane echoed his position once more.[7] The same month, in his annual message to Congress, Wilson called the Adamson and Ferris bills "two great measures, finely conceived," and urged "their prompt passage."[8] The efforts of the government and of the conservationists, however, proved of no avail. Walter Fisher, who worked with Gifford Pinchot and others to lobby for the bills, confided to a friend that Lane had not directed the administration's effort with the greatest possible effect. Anti-conservationists were strong enough to achieve a stalemate. In place of the Ferris bill, they substituted a bill drafted by Henry Myers of Montana, while James Shields of Tennessee introduced a bill to counter the Adamson measure. As a result, no waterpower legislation passed the Senate in 1914 or for several more years.[9]

The Shields bill produced bitter controversy. Pinchot called it "a surrender to the special interests, and its passage would be a public calamity." Lane accused the "power trust" of being behind the fight to defeat what he termed "the ultimate word of generosity on the part of the Federal government." In one of his *Harper's Weekly* editorials, Norman Hapgood called the supporters of the Shields bill "gangsters" and claimed the measure "might have been drawn by a water-power attorney." But the initial heat generated by the frustrated conservationists soon cooled.[10]

Recognizing the stalemate, Lane searched for a resolution. On January 25, 1915, he appealed to Senator Myers, chairman of the Committee on Public Lands, to cooperate in passing legislation; and, receiving no response, Lane made his letter public. Still the situation remained the same. Near the end of April, Lane announced that the conservationists planned to reintroduce their bills when the new Congress convened in December 1915.

He also called attention to the rumor that waterpower companies in five western states were about to consolidate. This consolidation, he warned, would place control of about 50 percent of the developed waterpower of the western states under one corporation. The need for legislation, Lane concluded, was obvious. In no way, Lane explained, did he wish to interfere with the rights of any states. "The sole object," he reassured, was "to secure and promote the development of the western resources, which it is self-evident would not be effected by passing them unconditionally into private ownership." During the spring and summer of 1915, Lane did what he could to keep the movement for legislation going in the right direction.[11] But while Lane and the conservationists promoted their cause, the anticonservationists were equally busy.

Early in September 1915, the Oregon legislature called a "Western States Water Power Conference" to meet in Portland from September 20 to 23. Representatives of waterpower companies and states' rights advocates dominated the conference. Although the anticonservationists drew much of their support from the western states, the same area also produced some of the stalwart defenders of federal regulation. At the Portland conference, two such westerners, Senators George Chamberlain of Oregon and Thomas Walsh of Montana, defended the provisions of the Ferris bill. The consensus of the conference, though, was never in doubt. On September 23, it resolved "that the states have the constitutional right and power to control and regulate . . . the water within their boundaries for all beneficial purposes . . ." and that it was "opposed to any policy that looks toward imposing the system of leasing generally upon the public domain." The conference resolved that leasing "is contrary to the spirit of our free institutions."[12] The anticonservationists were in no mood for compromise, and so the struggle over waterpower legislation continued.

When the Sixty-fourth Congress convened in December 1915, the conservationists again took up their cause. Lane, who worked closely with Ferris, once more endorsed the Ferris bill in a letter to the House Public Lands Committee and also in his annual report. In January 1916, as in August 1914, the House passed the Adamson and the Ferris bills. The Senate, however, approved the Shields bill on March 8, 1916. Nothing had changed substantially in the deadlock over waterpower legislation.[13]

In December 1916, when the Sixty-fourth Congress reconvened, conservationists' hopes rose when Lane suggested the establishment of a waterpower commission composed of the secretaries of agriculture, war, and interior. Lane had first suggested the idea to Wilson the previous March. Pinchot "heartily" endorsed the proposal. The commission, Lane outlined, would grant all leases pertaining to waterpower development on public lands and navigable streams. One advantage, Lane claimed, would be that each presidential administration would be responsible for the terms and conditions of the leases granted by it. During December 1916 and January 1917, Wilson and leaders of the House and Senate made progress in resolving the impasse, but negotiations again ended unsuccessfully. Lane, meanwhile, continued to withdraw waterpower sites from public sale or use under existing law and continued to regret the waste of underdevelopment.[14]

Throughout 1917, the deadlock continued. In May, Senator Walsh introduced what he hoped would be a compromise bill, but no compromise resulted. In November, conservationists again enjoyed a period of short-lived optimism. By this time, Lane, Newton Baker, who had replaced Garrison as secretary of war, and Secretary of Agriculture David F. Houston had long settled their interdepartmental squabbles and were united in their determination to secure effective and rational legislation. The anti-regulation senators, however, were able to thwart the best maneuvers of the Wilson-backed conservationists. Throughout, Lane remained a vital member of the inner circle of officials who championed regulation, along with Representatives William Kent of California and Irvine Lenroot of Wisconsin, Houston, Baker, Ferris, and, of course, Wilson.[15]

Early in 1918, Lane, Baker, and Houston sponsored a bill incorporating Lane's proposal for a single commission to regulate waterpower on navigable streams, public lands, and national forests. Once again the self-appointed watchdog of natural resources, Gifford Pinchot, sent his "hearty appreciation" for "so admirable a piece of work."[16]

For the next year, spokesmen for and against the bill presented their arguments with the critics attempting to amend the bill to their liking. Lane tried to rally support for the measure and worked with Wilson and congressional leaders to secure its passage.[17]

By the winter of 1918-19, the strength of the Senate antiregulation forces had waned. A few members had failed to win reelection in 1916 or 1918. The conservationists indicated that the resources, as far as they were concerned, could stay locked up forever, rather than to make them available without proper safeguards. With this attitude evident, some senators decided that legislation with regulation was better than an indefinite stalemate. Finally, on February 26, 1919, House and Senate conferees for a waterpower bill reached agreement. The House quickly gave its approval. But with victory in sight, the bill ran aground on the unexpected shoal of a Senate filibuster. In the last few days of the Sixty-fifth Congress, Senator Robert M. LaFollette led a small group of Republicans who wished to prevent hasty passage of a number of bills, the waterpower bill being one. They hoped that the filibuster would force Wilson to call a special session of the new Congress that was to take office on March 4. Republicans, as a result of the elections the previous November, would control the new Congress. The filibuster succeeded and the consequence for waterpower legislation was another year's delay.[18]

In July 1919, the waterpower bill passed the House again. After causing the conservationists yet a few more months of anxiety, the Senate put the bill into the hands of House-Senate conferees on January 17, 1920. Finally, in May, with neither conservationists nor anticonservationists completely pleased, Congress sent the bill to Wilson for his approval.[19]

The conservationists' battle for waterpower was not yet over when Congress sent the bill to Wilson. Although Lane strongly approved the measure, indirectly he almost forced an unexpected presidential veto. Lane had retired from the Cabinet on March 1, 1920, but one of his most important appointees, Stephen Mather, director of the National Park Service, was still on the job, and he opposed the pending measure. The bill did not exempt national parks and monuments from the leasing of dam sites, and Mather correctly saw this as a threat to their very existence. Mather took his protests to John Barton Payne, Lane's successor. Payne agreed and recommended to Wilson that he veto the bill. Park enthusiasts and wilderness preservationists, individually and through their numerous organizations, also petitioned Wilson to exercise his veto. The pressure on Wilson to sign, however, was even more intense. A compromise resulted when a group of congressional leaders promised to pass a repealer for the parks at the next session of Congress. In the meantime, the Waterpower Commission would grant no permits inside the parks. Only when Wilson had this promise did he approve the Federal Water Power Act of 1920.[20]

Lane's insensitivity to the effect of the Federal Water Power Act of 1920 on the national parks was predictable. Years earlier, his Hetch Hetchy position had illustrated his priority of values. In his commencement address at Brown University in June 1916, moreover, Lane clearly stated his philosophy of conservation applied in practice: "Every tree is a challenge to us, and every pool of water and every foot of soil. The mountains are our enemies. We must pierce them and make them serve. The sinful rivers we must curb."[21] In 1913, when Lane had asserted that he wanted to harness every available bit of hydroelectric horsepower in the country, he had meant it.

Throughout the six-year struggle for waterpower legislation, Lane played a major role. Within the Wilson administration, it was he who first spelled out the principles eventually embodied in the 1920 act, and he had drafted the initial bill incorporating these tenets. The act provided that a lease would run for fifty years, although the Power Commission could revoke it for nonfulfillment of terms. After a lease expired, the commission could renew it or take over operation of the facilities. During the long attempt to break the impasse that blocked any waterpower legislation, Lane was among the leaders.[22] The three-headed commission to grant leases followed his compromise suggestion of 1916. The two basic principles contained in the Act of 1920, those of federal control and of leasing, had been the core of Lane's proposals and the heart of the opposition to them. The act, therefore, represented a victory for him and the conservationists. Pinchot, referring to the legislation in his autobiography, exclaimed that "the people won." Some conservationists wanted the act to generate more income, but Lane always considered revenue of secondary importance. For him, the primary objectives of waterpower legislation were to promote maximum development, prevent monopoly, and ensure low consumer rates.[23] The ultimate effectiveness of the act, of course, depended on the persons who would administer it, and over this Lane had no control.

II

The struggle over waterpower legislation during the Wilson era was long and bitter, but the controversy concerning congressional passage of an act to establish a federal leasing policy governing mineral resources was just as long and even more bitter. The debate over a leasing plan for mineral resources became sidetracked by the problem of resolving what to do with private oil companies that already were at work, some with questionable legality, on public oil lands. Lane's actions toward these companies earned him greater condemnation than anything else he did or advocated while in the Cabinet. The difficulty he experienced over the oil lands, like most resource matters of 1913 through 1920, had antecedents in the Roosevelt-Taft era.

In 1909, President Taft, acting upon the recommendation of his Secretary of the Interior, Ballinger, withdrew 3 million acres of public lands containing oil deposits from all forms of disposition. Taft's action added another dimension to the conservationist movement. The anti-conservationists loudly protested the legality of the President's act. Many oil developers, with or without legal counsel, remained on their claims, filed new claims, and generally ignored the order. Under the Placer Law, which governed oil lands, oil had to be discovered before the Interior Department granted a permit to a company to use the land. To be on the safe side, Taft requested Congress to pass legislation making his 1909 action legal beyond all doubt. Congress complied with the Withdrawal Act of 1910, which granted the President authority to withdraw from sale or use any public mineral lands. The act commanded more respect from oil men, but violators persisted until the Supreme Court, in the Midwest Decision of February 1915, upheld Taft's withdrawals.

In 1912, Taft created two oil-land reserves, totaling about 68,000 acres, and set them aside for future use by the navy. Both reserves, No. 1, or Elk Hills, and No. 2, or Buena Vista Hills, were in California, and both contained considerable areas of private holdings (patents or permits already granted by the government for private development of the public lands). This was especially true in the Buena Vista reserve. In 1915, with Lane's approval, Wilson established a third naval reserve of 9,481 acres in Wyoming, known as Teapot Dome.

When Lane took office, the public oil lands, just as the public phosphate, gas, potash, and Alaskan coal lands were closed to public development. The oil lands were merely part of a much larger picture. The first significant proposals made by the Wilson administration to open the mineral lands were those Lane offered in December 1913. In his first annual report, Lane recommended that Congress adopt the same policy for the mineral lands that he simultaneously recommended for Alaskan coal lands. It called for federal control via leases issued to developers for a definite period under specific terms. Lane termed the Placer Law "an absurdity" and called for improved legislation to stimulate growth of the petroleum industry. Phosphate rock and potash deposits in the United States, he also pointed out, were rich but untapped, because no proper law existed whereby they could be developed.[24]

In April 1914, Scott Ferris of Oklahoma introduced in the House of Representatives an administration bill that called for sweeping revision of the laws applying to the disposition of oil, gas, phosphate, sodium, coal, and potassium deposits on the public lands. Lane had had the Interior Department draft the bill "after extended conferences with western Senators and Congressmen representing all shades of opinion." The intent of the legislation, Lane asseverated, was to "insure the development of the west and give to the west the full benefits of its own resources." Despite this aim, Lane recognized that "westerners" were "the chief opponents" to his proposals.[25]

The Ferris bill, commonly called the General Leasing Bill, quickly passed the House but then bogged down in the Senate. After February 1915, when the Supreme Court upheld the constitutionality of Taft's earlier withdrawals, westerners realized they would have to accept the principle of federal leasing. The "coal monopolists," Lane observed, continued to oppose the bill because it would help to develop the oil industry as a competitor. Nevertheless, Lane remained optimistic about passage.[26]

In January 1916, the House again passed the bill and the Senate conducted hearings on it during the following months. With passage a reasonable prospect, Lane became involved in a dispute over certain private claims on the naval oil reserves. Because of his emphasis on development of all kinds, he had taken a generous position toward the claims of oil companies who maintained they had started operations before the government closed the land by Taft's withdrawal orders of 1909 and 1912 and by Wilson's order of 1915. Because the Interior Department had jurisdiction to resolve these claims, only Wilson could overrule Lane's decision. Cabinet members who disagreed with Lane convinced Wilson to intervene. The resulting discord generated by the reaction to Lane's action toward the private claims on the naval reserves soon overshadowed the General Leasing Bill, delayed its passage, and cost Lane some of the support he had formerly enjoyed. Until the Wilson Cabinet and Congress resolved the problem of these private claims on the naval reserves and other federal oil lands, they could not pass legislation governing leasing of mineral lands in general.

Debate over amount of relief for oil claims and determination of qualified recipients continued until late 1919, when congressional factions finally reached agreement and passed a bill. On February 25, 1920, Wilson signed the General Leasing Act of 1920, which established a federal leasing system to develop oil shale, oil, gas, coal, sodium, and phosphate deposits. In general, it incorporated the principles Lane first expressed in his annual report of December 1913, notably acreage limitations, antimonopoly provisions, and antiwaste incentives. Provisions for claimants on withdrawn public lands were less generous than Lane originally advocated. Persons with claims on lands outside the naval reserves who based their case on activity before Taft's Withdrawal Act of 1910 could secure leases for their claims. Claimants on the naval reserves could obtain leases only if they had producing wells.[27]

Several persons who had disagreed over claimant relief during the long process of hammering out an acceptable bill expressed satisfaction with the end product. Gifford Pinchot hailed it as "a great victory for conservation." More restrained, Josephus Daniels concluded that "the bill safeguarded better than any former bill the naval reserves." Lane considered the act one of the objectives "for which we have been fighting."[28] The act constituted a major step forward in federal regulation of natural resources along lines first advanced during the Roosevelt administration.

III

The General Leasing Act of 1920 probably would have become law four years earlier had it not been, first, for the private claims on the naval oil reserves, and second, for the private claims on withdrawn oil lands.

In April 1915, the Honolulu Oil Company applied for patents to seventeen quarter-sections of land (a quarter-section is 160 acres), claiming that its discovery work had started before Taft's withdrawal order of 1909. All seventeen sections lay in the oil-rich heart of naval reserve No. 2, of

Buena Vista Hills, California. On December 15, 1915, after investigations
and reports, the Commissioner of the General Land Office Clay Tallman
approved thirteen of the seventeen patents. On December 24, after review-
ing Tallman's decision, Lane reported to Attorney General Thomas
Gregory that the commissioner's action seemed correct. Gregory was not
pleased. Since the Supreme Court ruling in the *Midwest* decision earlier
that year, his department had been diligently investigating numerous
claims for violation of law.

Secretary of the Navy Daniels similarly was unhappy because of his
concern about the naval oil reserves. He asked Lane to delay issuance
of the Honolulu patents until he could study Tallman's decision in more
detail and until the two Secretaries had a chance to confer. Lane agreed,
but asked his Cabinet colleague not to delay too long. Throughout January 1916, and the months that followed, Daniels requested additional
time to consider the situation.[29]

While Gregory and Daniels worked to check Lane's action, the Senate
seriously debated the General Leasing Bill; prospects for passage seemed
bright. During the Senate debate, Lane's friend James D. Phelan, Democrat
from California, led a successful drive to amend the bill, legitimatizing
the claims of oil developers whose rights to parts of the naval oil reserves
and to other parts of the public oil lands remained in doubt. In April,
Gregory suggested to Lane that he suspend all patents until the Justice
Department had settled through the courts the claims it had challenged.
A month later, on May 13, 1916, Daniels forcefully registered with Wilson
his protest against the oil-claimant relief provisions of the General Leasing Bill in Congress. The President, interested yet perplexed, studied the
situation.[30] Between mid-December and mid-May, reaction to Lane's
favorable opinion toward the Honolulu patents, and toward claimant
relief in general, had created a schism among important supporters of
the General Leasing Bill.

Differences between Lane and Daniels, the chief antagonists at the
start, served as the focal point of the controversy. In its broadest sense,
the feud stemmed from the clash of Lane's overzealous attitude toward
development of natural resources and Daniels's firm conviction to protect a reserve oil supply for the navy. On a narrower plane, they feuded
about a strict versus loose enforcement of laws that had produced a less-
than-clear situation. Their disagreement reached its peak early in 1916 over
the claims of the Honolulu Oil Company, the prime example of private

claims on the naval reserves. Although the official relationship between
Lane and Daniels became strained, their friendship remained intact.[31]
Supporters of Lane's position refused to act upon the General Leasing
Bill without an amendment recognizing the claimants. Daniels supporters,
on the other hand, refused to approve passage of any bill that included
such recognition.

On May 26, Wilson moved toward Daniels's position. He asked Lane
"to hold up any patents that might otherwise be issued until I can have
looked into the matter a little further." The implicit subject of Wilson's
request concerned the Honolulu Oil Company. Lane responded to Wilson
with a six-page letter: "the first letter that I have had occasion to write
you in explanation of anything that has been done by me." In his "frank
and full" reply, Lane detailed his actions and positions to the Honolulu
case, the General Leasing Bill, and the relief amendments to the bill.
Then, with obvious indignation, he asked Wilson to "tell me if you can. . . .
Why the Secretary of the Navy did not avail himself to my suggestion
made three years ago that an effort be made to develop special oil fields
for the Navy," and to create additional naval reserves "out of the two and
a half million acres of public oil lands." Lane asserted that there was
"abundant oil left in the public domain" for the navy and that Daniels,
by arguing over the legality of some private claimants, blocked passage
of the General Leasing Bill and thereby "played directly into the hands
of the great oil magnates" and others who opposed development under
a leasing system. The Navy Secretary, Lane accused, "has attempted to
create a scandal involving one of his colleagues where no scandal exists."[32]

Throughout the controversy, Lane and Daniels represented the con-
flicting approaches to the problem of the oil claimants. As Lane summarized his position, "If the full measure of the Government's right is
acted upon as a basis of our policy in dealing with these lands it will
bankrupt many oil companies and do . . . an unnecessary injustice to
those who have invested many millions of dollars under a mistake as to
the law. . . . I feel that this is one of those situations often arising in the
life of the individual and of the State when it is not wise to exact all
that the laws allow even as to those who are in the wrong."[33] Undoubtedly some persons adopted Lane's position to promote their own economic
self-interest, but nothing in Lane's actions indicated that he acted to
enhance his personal advantage. Daniels's convictions in the matter were
equally sincere. He reasoned, "About 90% of the claimants have no valid

claim whatever. . . . They will, therefore, be rewarded merely because of
their disregard of the Presidential order of withdrawal . . . and the citizens
who respected the order of withdrawal will get absolutely nothing."
Daniels, however, never questioned Lane's honesty.[34]

Others did cast doubt on Lane's character and principles. Gifford
Pinchot unleashed a fierce attack, accusing him of abandoning conservationist ideas. On July 1, the *New York Times* published an interview with Roosevelt's former forester in which he accused Lane of
favoring Phelan's amendment to the General Leasing Bill. Lane immediately demanded that Pinchot tell him "on what authority do
you make this statement?" He also commented that "our relations have
not been such as to justify me in believing that you would deliberately
falsify my record. I cannot but believe that you have been misinformed."[35]
Two days later, Lane issued a memorandum for the press stating that he
favored the Ferris bill "along the lines of the one passed by the House
twice in the last two years" and that he did not favor the Phelan amendment.[36] Pinchot replied that he would check the sources of his information, to which Lane responded, "I shall be glad to throw open to you my
official and personal file," and "to talk to you at any time about the matter."[37]

Pinchot consulted with his assistants and on August 12 issued a lengthy
open letter to Lane "concerning the Navy's oil lands." In the letter, Pinchot again accused Lane of favoring the Phelan amendment. To sub-
stantiate his charge, Pinchot used the tortured logic that since Lane had
always desired claimant relief, and since the Phelan amendment included
some of the provisions Lane had sought earlier, Lane, therefore, endorsed
the amendment. The forester also objurgated Lane for his stand on a
number of issues, either because he did not support or oppose legislative
proposals with the vigor Pinchot deemed appropriate or because the
Secretary recommended policies that would mean the "dismemberment
of our public forest reserves" and the placement of the "resources of
Alaska into the scramble of politics." He closed his letter recalling how
he had welcomed Lane's appointment to the Cabinet, but how he now
had to "oppose and condemn your action." Lane wrote to a friend that
he had "no intention of saying anything in reply to Pinchot. He wrote
me thirty pages to prove that I was a liar, and rather than read that again
I will admit the fact."[38]

Considering the absence of a responsible person to second Pinchot's

broad indictment of Lane and the inaccuracies contained therein, and in
light of Pinchot's prior and subsequent endorsements of many of Lane's
proposals and actions, Pinchot's attacks on Lane during the summer of
1916 represented the thinking of a man seeking political advantage who
was frustrated by his lack of power. Two and one-half weeks after Pinchot maligned Lane's conservation record, Joseph N. Teal, a member of
the Board of Directors of Pinchot's National Conservation Association,
still corresponded with Lane on a first-name basis, seemingly with as
much faith in Lane's conservation record as ever.[39]

During the election campaign that autumn, Pinchot continued his
strident attacks on the conservation records of Wilson and Lane. Neither
replied. On October 3, however, Norman Hapgood, a well-known editor
who had taken a prominent part in the fight against Secretary of the
Interior Richard A. Ballinger during the Taft administration, issued a
public statement. He called Pinchot "an intimate friend of mine,"
praised his character and work, and then charged that the forester had
failed "to get at the facts of what the Wilson administration has done."
Hapgood called "some of the misstatements . . . wholly outside the
domain of opinion and are demonstrably unjust." Some of Pinchot's
closest friends, in addition to Teal and Hapgood, moreover, indicated
explicitly or implicitly, that they did not agree with his critique. Republican Congressman William Kent, who opposed "the looters of the public
domain" and called Pinchot "my friend," wrote Wilson that Pinchot's
false accusation of the President's position on the Shields Waterpower
Bill "has been peculiarly irritating." Kent continued to work with Wilson
and Lane while maintaining a similar relationship with Pinchot. Late
the following winter, Walter Fisher declined Pinchot's invitation to serve
on the board of directors of the National Conservation Association, because "I have received the impression that the Association has abandoned
the effort to have any real membership and that it is only a paper organization in which you are the chief, if not the only active and responsible
factor."[40]

Lane, meanwhile, had adopted a righteous yet conciliatory attitude to
resolve the impasse regarding the Honolulu claims; his position, he hoped,
would lead to passage of the General Leasing Bill. He proposed that
Gregory either withdraw his objection to the issuance of the Honolulu
patents or submit the case to the courts for decision, despite the fact
that "the Secretary of the Interior and the Commissioner of the General
Land Office are quasi-judicial officers whose decisions are not subject

to review by the Attorney General." To Wilson, Lane defended his position by suggesting that the President "send for Mr. John W. Davis, the Solicitor General, to whom the matter was referred by the Attorney General, he will tell you that Mr. Tallman's opinion is sound; so will Mr. Lenroot, of the Public Lands Committee, one of the strongest conservationists in the country, who has taken a great interest in these oil reserves."[41]

In rebuttal, Gregory asked Lane to reopen the case within the Interior Department and permit Justice Department representatives to introduce testimony and cross-examine witnesses. Lane refused because he saw no purpose in trying the case within the Interior Department a second time before going to court. "If there are any new facts to be obtained," he reasoned, "they certainly can be brought out upon a trial of the case before the U. S. courts." To this position, Gregory replied that "it would be futile for this Department [Justice] to attempt to try this case in the courts in the face of an outstanding adjudication by your Department in favor of the applicant." The deadlock between Gregory and Lane lasted until Wilson took Gregory's side in January 1917, directed Lane to set aside Commissioner Tallman's decision, and asked for a second hearing.[42]

The next month, Virginia's Democratic Senator Claude A. Swanson offered an amendment to the General Leasing Bill that separated the Honolulu and similar claims made upon the naval oil reserves from the claims other companies made upon public oil lands. Claims upon the naval lands, Swanson contended, constituted only about a third of the total claims on all federal oil land and could be settled independently. Wilson expressed interest and asked Gregory to consult with Lane and Daniels. Both agreed with the Swanson amendment segregating claimants. With this agreement, Lane and Daniels had arrived at a working arrangement regarding naval oil lands. To be sure, they still disagreed over the Honolulu claims, but on this issue Wilson had overruled Lane and, in effect, placed the claims in limbo for the next four years. The Daniels-Lane dispute over naval oil lands no longer exerted an influence on the General Leasing Bill. In addition to the separation of claimants, Swanson's amendment offered relief to claimants on the public lands. Daniels viewed the measure as liberal but accepted it to obtain passage of the bill. Lane, on the other hand, wanted more liberal provisions. For weeks, the Senate Committee on Public Lands conducted hearings but the matter remained unresolved throughout 1917.[43]

On December 31, after reading the newest draft of the General Leasing

Bill, Wilson lamented to Lane that he was "distressed to find that it goes practically as far as was proposed the last time. . . . I cannot go an inch further than . . . the proposals of Senator Swanson." He then wished Lane to "exert your influence to get this modification of the proposed concessions adopted, not as your judgement, for I know it is not, but as my judgment, and one which must necessarily be reckoned with in the final settlement." Lane replied, "I am heartily in favor of your solution of the oil problem as set out in your letter of December 31, and shall act at once to make an effort to secure its adoption."[44] Lane conferred with a number of House and Senate leaders urging the Swanson proposals. Meanwhile, Daniels, Gregory, and Swanson drafted a bill to give the secretary of the navy control of the three naval oil reserves and authority to operate them, to make legal dispositions, and, where valid claims existed, to make adjustment offers. Throughout this foundation work in molding a settlement of the oil claims on naval lands, Lane cooperated with and supported the Daniels-Wilson-Swanson group, although he never completely agreed with their position.[45] Two years later, in December 1919, this co-operation helped produce the congressional agreement that finally resulted in the General Leasing Act of 1920.

The process of rehearing the Honolulu cases, which Wilson had ordered, consumed several years and was still unresolved when the Harding administration took office. Harding's Secretary of the Interior, Albert Fall, finally settled the claims by granting leases to all seventeen claimants, including the four Tallman and Lane had rejected.

IV

Lane's attitude and actions toward federal oil lands were consistent throughout his secretaryship. This included support of a naval oil reserve, stepped-up industrial petroleum research, and increased efficiency in the handling and use of oil resources. He also urged American exploitation of foreign sources of oil. The emphasis was on development.

His first official move regarding oil lands, in June 1913, concerned oil companies holding patents the Interior Department had granted before his tenure for tracts of oil land in areas the government later closed to private development. The closing of the land, he told his bureau chiefs, cast suspicion "upon the title of many people who at the invitation of the government and under the laws of Congress, have undertaken to put the lands of the people to use." Such suspicion, he reported, was unjust, and because of it developers could not borrow money.[46]

In 1913, when the United States followed the British lead and decided to build an oil-burning fleet, geologists estimated the American supply of oil at only twenty years. Moreover, the price the navy paid for oil had doubled during the preceding two years. Navy Secretary Daniels concluded that the government should permit the navy to enter the oil business. He wanted authorization for the navy to maintain its own oil lands, pipe-lands, and refineries. Oil interests protested the government's possible entry into a province traditionally a domain of private enterprise; Congress never gave Daniels's suggestion serious consideration. When oil prices declined in 1914 and 1915, the urgency of the proposal lessened and the idea died with few mourners. But when Daniels and the navy's General Board pushed its recommendations the hardest, they enjoyed "strong approval" from the Interior Department.[47]

Lane expressed his interest in a naval oil reserve in other ways as well. In 1914, he wrote in an article that, "In as much as the United States will need oil for its navy . . . it would seem of the highest expediency that the Government make such offers and make such legal provisions as will induce the proving of our lands, and of these proved lands retain sufficient to make our ships independent of the world for their fuel supply." The next year, when Daniels requested that Lane recommend the creation of a third naval oil reserve, Lane readily complied. Several times Lane suggested, without success, that Daniels establish additional reserves.[48]

Two months after the United States entered World War I, the Advisory Commission of the Council of National Defense wanted to turn part of the naval oil reserve No. 1 over to the Southern Pacific Railroad, a corporation that already claimed patents for more than one-fourth of the reserve. Secretary of Commerce William Redfield vigorously endorsed the idea. Daniels, of course, flatly refused. Lane remained silent.[49] Lane, as already noted, quickly accepted and worked for that part of the Swanson amendment that exempted the naval reserves from the General Leasing Bill. Although always supporting the idea of a naval oil reserve, he never offered advice regarding what policy the Navy Department should adopt in managing its reserve.[50] Lane was a real friend to the concept of a naval oil reserve.

Lane's desire to reduce waste in the oil industry took many forms. Most obvious was his broad program of withdrawing public oil lands to prevent wasteful exploitation, and his hope of enacting a more efficient and orderly leasing system. Another of his basic proposals to conserve needless consumption of oil was his effort to develop alternate sources of power.[51] He also considered industrial research a major vehicle by which oil could be conserved. The opportunity for research, he believed, was almost unlimited. "We can get three times as much energy as we do out of our oil through the use of the Diesel engine," he once asserted, "yet we are doing little to prompt development of a satisfactory type of stationary Diesel, or marine design."[52] He looked forward to the day when the production of oil from shale would be a great industry. Other areas of waste that Lane wanted improved were imperfect storage, drain-offs, pipe leakage, noncasting of wells, and nonuse of oil residues.[53] Within the Interior Department, Lane supported the Geological Survey's theoretical research and the Bureau of Mines practical-application research in oil problems. In 1915, the Bureau of Mines created a special Petroleum Division, and two years later opened a petroleum experiment station in Oklahoma.[54]

Lane supported the adoption of an aggressive overseas oil policy. By the end of 1919, he had become one of the leading exponents of meeting the expanding domestic oil needs with foreign oil. To do this effectively, he called for government assistance and regulation, and thereby became one of the "prime movers in shaping early sentiment for government action in the foreign oil fields." As a result of this changing sentiment, the United States, between 1918 and 1920, rapidly altered its attitude toward foreign sources of oil.[55]

Lane's overall grasp of the need for oil, his respect for the naval oil reserves, his attempt to reduce waste and to advance research, and his support of federal regulation support the conclusion that his attitude toward claimants on withdrawn public oil lands rested on a broad assessment of the oil situation. He believed that federal leases had to be sufficiently generous to attract private investment to search for and produce oil. In February 1919, he told journalist Albert Shaw: "I hope it will work, although our experience in Alaska has not been satisfactory because it has not attracted any development of large capital." Seven months later, he wrote that the men in the oil industry had to learn "to take the attitude of statesmen and not of selfish exploiters . . . they must tax themselves liberally . . . they must think of themselves as trustees for a Public as wide as the world."[56] Lane, with his touch of vanity, believed his attitude and actions toward oil reflected such a sentiment.

V

In his first annual report, December 1913, Lane outlined five measures he wanted Congress to enact for the development of natural resources: a government railroad in Alaska, a leasing plan for Alaskan coal, a new reclamation act, a plan for waterpower regulation, and a leasing system for minerals on public lands. The *New York Times* called the report "almost a prospectus for the development of the national resources." During the next year, Lane took pride in the fact that the first three of his proposals became law. At the end of his tenure in the Interior Department, he judged the Water Power Act of 1920 and the General Leasing Act of 1920 as direct descendants of the proposals he articulated seven years earlier. Pinchot concluded similarly. Late in 1919, with passage of the Water Power and the General Leasing bills pending, he interpreted the two measures as carrying out Roosevelt's "conservation policies."[57]

The two acts of 1920 did incorporate the principles of federal regulation through a leasing system, safeguards against monopoly, and encouragement to developers, championed by Roosevelt, Lane, and others. The descent, however, was not lineal. For example, as noted above, Lane would have permitted power companies to move into the national parks, would have included a more generous claimant relief provision on oil lands, and would have included the naval oil lands as part of that provision. In these and other areas, including the amount of revenue generated, Lane compromised because he did not consider these matters paramount. He considered the basic legislative acts fundamental and made primary contributions toward their enactment; they represented milestones of his secretaryship and of the conservation movement.[58]

8
Cabinet Meetings, Politics, and Foreign Policy, 1913-1917

> *Mr. Lane is acknowledged generally to be one of the commanding figures of this Cabinet. He would be a commanding figure in any Cabinet.*
>
> Editorial, *New York Times*
> August 24, 1916

> *There is room for only two parties in the United States, the liberal and the conservative, and ours must be the liberal party.*
>
> Lane to R. M. Fitzgerald,
> November 12, 1916

> *I don't know whether the President is an internationalist or a pacifist, he seems to be very mildly national—his patriotism is covered over with a film of philosophic humanitarianism, that certainly doesn't make for "punch" at such a time as this.*
>
> Lane to George W. Lane,
> February 25, 1917

I

Lane's range of interests and ambition drew him to matters other than those related to the Interior Department. His responsibilities as a Cabinet member, of course, included participation at regular meetings called to discuss domestic subjects and foreign policy. The insignificance of most of these meetings disappointed him because he enjoyed discussing important national and world affairs. Wilson's politics and foreign policy pleased Lane, but not completely. This trace of disappointment, combined with his characteristic restlessness, nudged Lane to welcome participation in other public activities and to consider other lines of work.

II

Wilson's failure to use consistently his Cabinet, after the early months of his administration, as a deliberative body for serious discussions of politics, problems, and policies frustrated Lane and other Cabinet members. Wilson continued to confer freely and to work with the various secretaries in matters concerning their individual departments, but quickly reduced the importance of Cabinet meetings. Instead, the President sought advice from individuals. In matters other than those relating to the Interior Department, Wilson rarely requested Lane's advice. The three most important Wilson scholars, Ray Stannard Baker, Arthur S. Link, and Arthur C. Walworth, have concluded that Lane had only himself to blame. Wilson, the historians maintain, had to abandon this vital Cabinet function because Lane talked too freely to reporters, to officials in the Washington diplomatic community, and to friends about what went on during meetings.[1] This description and analysis of Wilson's Cabinet meetings is unsatisfactory. He did at times confide in his Cabinet and use it as a forum for discussing the affairs of state, and his actions, not Lane's, determined the character of this relationship.

After the first few months, the importance of Wilson's Cabinet meetings varied widely throughout his administration. On September 6, 1913, Colonel House recorded in his diary that "As far as I can gather, he confers with none of them excepting in matters concerning their particular departments." Early in November of that year, Secretary of the Treasury William G. McAdoo told House there was a general feeling among Cabinet members that Wilson would like to eliminate the meetings entirely.[2] Throughout Wilson's administration, McAdoo, Lane, Attorney General James McReynolds, Secretary of State Robert Lansing, Secretary of Agriculture David F. Houston, and Wilson's second Attorney General Thomas W. Gregory all went to House and voiced the same criticism.[3] Looking back at the Cabinet meetings more than a decade after his resignation, Secretary of War Lindley Garrison concluded that they had been a waste of time. He had found the meetings interesting but devoted to inconsequential matters.[4] On October 23, 1918, Lane wrote in frustration that "for some weeks we have spent our time at Cabinet meetings largely in telling stories." On another occasion, Lane lamented: "Nothing talked of at Cabinet that would interest a nation, a family, or a child."[5] Cabinet members, on the other hand, left evidence that the Cabinet did discuss, at least occasionally, issues of the gravest concern.

Houston, in an analysis of Wilson, probably written in 1925, remarked that "it is not true that Wilson did not consult his Cabinet on new departures and policy, or on important matters. He did."[6] Although Lane repeatedly complained about do-nothing Cabinet sessions, he also left record of sessions that were serious. For example, on April 1, 1917, he wrote to his brother that "the meetings of the Cabinet lately have been nothing less than councils of war." On November 1, 1918, he noted that "at last week's Cabinet meeting we talked of Austria—again we talked like a Cabinet."[7] Secretary of the Navy Josephus Daniels, who in his diary often mentioned the subjects discussed at Cabinet meetings, did not dismiss them all as inconsequential. According to Daniels, on November 30, 1917, and December 11, 1917, the Cabinet discussed the rather pertinent problem of Russia.[8] Upon occasion, then, Wilson did use his Cabinet as a deliberative body. Although he may have exaggerated, Lane once commented upon the frequency of such meetings by writing that "Yesterday, at Cabinet meetings, we had the first real talk on the war in weeks, yes, in months."[9]

During an interview in 1927, former Attorney General Gregory told a historian that "one reason" Wilson stopped bringing up important subjects in Cabinet meetings was that he could not trust Lane to remain publicly silent about sensitive matters.[10] Wilson, like all previous Presidents, experienced news leaks from among his Cabinet members, advisers, and staff; Lane was one source of such leaks. Just before the December 19, 1913, meeting, Wilson, by request, conferred with Houston. The President expressed concern over "the fact that one or two members seem to be unable to refrain from telling everybody what happens in Cabinet meetings." Houston also recorded that "It was clear from what the President said to me that he knew the members who were chiefly responsible for talking on the outside about Cabinet matters."[11] Houston used the plural, not the singular, when referring to the source of leaks. He also wrote "chiefly responsible." At the minimum, then, two members talked too freely. Writing about the meeting in his 1931 autobiography, McAdoo recalled that Lane and only Lane admitted he had leaked information about Cabinet discussions.[12] Houston failed to mention any names in his diary entry. Houston did not conclude, however, that the episode resulted in the ceasing of vital Cabinet discussions. On the evening of December 22, three days after that particular Cabinet meeting, Wilson and House relaxed in the former's study and "fell to talking of the Cabinet." None of the remarks referring to the Cabinet that House later noted in his diary mentioned Lane or the problem of news leaks.[13]

In that month of December 1913, House indeed believed there was news leakage in the administration, but the person who worried him was not Lane, but Joseph Tumulty, Wilson's private secretary. House wrote in his diary that "Tumulty talks too much. I find evidence of it on every hand. Stories come to me every day of his indiscretions in this direction." Again, a year later, Wilson and House discussed a specific leak. Wilson claimed it had occurred in the State Department, despite Secretary of State Bryan's belief that Tumulty was to blame. Although he told his diary and not necessarily Wilson, House agreed with Bryan that "Tumulty had given it out."[14] Almost a decade later, Wilson, in his retirement, read the recently published *The Letters of Franklin K. Lane* and wrote to William C. Redfield, former secretary of commerce, that the volume "confirmed, namely, that the leak in the Cabinet was the Secretary of the Interior, for you will remember that nothing we said or did remained long private."[15] In 1928, former Secretary of War Newton Baker recalled Redfield as a "chatty" person who sometimes slipped and revealed information, although Baker thought Lane was the major source of indiscretion.[16]

Lane was a gossip; in company with newspapermen, he talked too
freely with government information. Through him, news of Cabinet affairs
reached the public. His colleagues, moreover, realized this; so did Wilson.
But Wilson left no record that Lane's loquaciousness caused him to curtail
Cabinet discussions. Wilson's confidential adviser and close friend, Colonel
House, kept a detailed diary throughout the period but failed to record
a word about Lane's indiscretions or of Wilson's reaction to them. On the
contrary, House, who understood and appreciated the role of presidential
adviser, held no fears about Lane keeping the secrets of state. Typical of
his respect for Lane was the diary entry: "I am sorry the President does
not consult Lane more frequently. He has real ability, perhaps the best
all around ability of any member of the Cabinet, and yet, outside of his
departmental duties, the abilities are seldom or never used."[17] The second
most conscientious diarist in the Wilson circle was Josephus Daniels, who
never accused Lane of breaking up Cabinet deliberation. In fact, none of
Lane's contemporaries asserted any relationship between his penchant
for gossip and Wilson's use or nonuse of Cabinet meetings.[18]

That Wilson's Cabinet meetings alternated between meaningful discussions and story telling did not reflect the President's periodic trust
or mistrust of Lane's ability to keep his counsel. Had Wilson seriously
wanted to use his Cabinet on a regular basis as a deliberative body, but
believed that Lane's indiscretions prevented his doing so, the President
would have paid the price of Lane's resignation to remain master of his
own meetings. Nothing in Wilson's character or actions indicated otherwise. Had Lane been the most taciturn person ever to sit in the Cabinet,
or had he never become a member of that body, there is little reason
to believe that Wilson would have consulted his Cabinet more than he
did. Wilson's ability or inability to listen to advice and to respect and
work with persons with whom he might at times disagree determined
his relationship with Cabinet members.

III

As might be expected, Lane's non-Interior Department activities
and interests during his Cabinet years, before United States entry into
World War I, were domestic politics, the European war, and the relation-

ship between the two. He had few interests other than his public life. Unlike many of his peers, Lane had no property to look after, no ties with a law firm, and no business interests. He had no real hobbies and never exercised regularly. To relax, he did two things: read and socialize. His reading was extensive—history, biography, letters, fiction, and poetry. His socializing was also extensive. The Lanes were among Washington's most delightful and popular dinner guests. Some social engagements were necessary adjuncts of his position, of course, but Lane regarded most of them as pleasure and not duty. He usually required only six hours sleep nightly, which meant he benefited from a longer day than most of his contemporaries. What time Lane had, beyond his personal schedule and the demands of the Interior Department, he spent on politics.

Lane sincerely believed the Democratic party offered the nation the most desirable political instrument for building the best of all possible societies. But partisanship did not blind him. Immediately after the Democratic victory in 1912, he congratulated Bryan for the role he had played, but added that "We shall see whether Democrats will follow a wise, aggressive, modern leadership." Two months later, he went so far as to write, "I am going to give the Democratic Party four years of honest trial, and then if it has not more precision, definiteness, and clearness of aim, am going to call myself a Progressive, or a Republican, or something else." Lane directed much of his criticism toward the South. Reconciling the conservative southern wing of the party with the progressive northern wing was, in his mind, the principal political problem facing Wilson.[19]

Lane shared the broad Democratic consensus that considered tariff, currency, and trusts the major legislative problems confronting the new administration.[20] On the more philosophical level, he lamented that Americans had "lost all traditional moorings"; they had no religion and no philosophy; they were materialists. "The ultimate problem," he concluded, "is to substitute some adequate philosophy or religion for that which we have lost." Next to moral regeneration, Lane considered the economic perfecting of "the cheapest system of distribution possible" as the most important general problem. "I have an idea," he wrote late in February 1913, "that we have too many stores, too many middlemen, too much waste motion." To help solve this broad economic problem, he considered a redistribution of wealth both necessary and inevitable.[21] Of the problems he perceived (partisan, political, legislative, moral, and economic), he anticipated progress toward solution in only the legislative sphere.

Lane's opinion of Wilson increased favorably between his election and inauguration. He especially liked Wilson's warning to the financial interests not to create an artifical panic. "That he is headstrong, arbitrary, and positive, his friends admit," Lane observed, but immediately added that "These are real virtues in this day of slackness and sloppiness."[22] The country, he thought, "will put him down as a very great President."[23]

Lane's praise of Wilson continued after the two met the day before the inauguration. On March 12, 1913, Lane wrote to his friend Albert Shaw that "The new President is a really great man and thoroughly likeable personally." On the same day, in another letter, he commented that Wilson "is the most sympathetic, cordial and considerate presiding officer that can be imagined. And he sees so clearly. He has no fog in his brain."[24] Late in July, as Lane left Washington on what turned out to be an absence of almost three months, he wrote to House that "We all work together, are united in loyalty to the Chief and vie with each other in admiration for him."[25]

Wilson reciprocated much of Lane's initial respect. On April 1, House asked Wilson to comment upon his estimation of his Cabinet members. Wilson replied that "Redfield possessed much the best analytical mind; that Lane had an analytical mind plus imagination, which Redfield lacked." Three weeks later, the University of California, Berkeley, invited Lane to receive a doctor of laws degree on May 15. Lane deemed his new duties too demanding to go. Wilson concurred, but added that the degree was an honor Lane "so richly deserve[d]."[26] One day that spring, Wilson unexpectedly stopped to visit with Lane at the Interior Department, a compliment no previous president had paid an interior secretary.[27] By the time Lane returned from his western trip in October 1913, the relations between Wilson and his Cabinet had already deteriorated. In time, Lane tempered his high opinion of Wilson with criticism.

When Associate Justice of the Supreme Court Horace H. Lurton died on July 12, 1914, newspapers mentioned Lane as a possible successor. The desire for, and possibly of, a seat on the supreme bench was not new to him. President Taft had considered appointing him in January 1912, despite Lane's Democratic party affiliation.[28] Eleven months later, Lane and Colonel House discussed Lane's ambition to be a justice.

House favored the idea, but was in no hurry, as he believed that Wilson probably would have four appointments to make during his administration.

The 1914 appointment seemed to narrow to a choice between Attorney General McReynolds and Lane. The previous winter, however, House had suggested to Wilson that McReynolds replace Lurton when the latter died or retired, since they both were from Tennessee. Lane seconded House's reasoning. "I have told every one who has approached me," the Californian told Wilson, "that under no circumstances should anyone see you to suggest or urge my appointment. My own judgment," he continued, "is that the South feels that this place belongs to it and would seriously resent the appointment of anyone excepting a Southern Democrat." The President found Lane's letter "very generous," wished him health and happiness "with all my heart," and commented that "It is a great pleasure to be associated with you." Wilson followed political custom and named McReynolds to the seat. Years later, Josephus Daniels noted that Lane had made no effort to influence Wilson's decision. If Lane were bitter about the McReynolds appointment, he gave no evidence of it.[29]

Early in January 1916, another seat, that of Justice Joseph Lamar, became vacant. Washington correspondents were almost unanimous in their approval of Lane for the position. The Bar Association of San Francisco sent its endorsement to Wilson; Daniels told Lane that "Your colleagues of the Cabinet share the high opinion so well expressed by the Bar of your city." Senators Newlands and Phelan, likewise, recommended Lane. Wilson, however, nominated the distinguished lawyer Louis Brandeis, much to the approval of ardent reformers. Although personally disappointed, Lane harbored no bitterness in losing out to such an eminently qualified person.[30]

Six months later, Wilson faced his third appointment to the Supreme Court when Charles Evans Hughes resigned to run for the presidency. Once more the press championed Lane and once more he seemed to be the prime candidate. He, however, was in an awkward position; sometime earlier, House had told him that he would be named to succeed Justice Joseph McKenna, who was seventy when Wilson took office. But Lane was impatient. He wrote to his lifelong friend Sidney Mezes, who was also House's brother-in-law, "All I want is for you, in that superlatively tactful way of yours, to find out if my chances are worth considering at this time—and if they are, will the Colonel make them something better than mere chances." Lane also reiterated the legal aspects of his record as city attorney (such as never having had a case reversed by a higher court), and interstate commerce commissioner, and as secretary of the interior. Before closing his letter, he asked Mezes to keep the letter confidential, "I wouldn't for a good right leg want Colonel E. M. to think me to be butting in." Mezes passed on Lane's information as his own. House, in turn, did the same to Wilson.[31] Once again, Lane accepted the situation without rancor; he continued to hold hope for a future appointment. As it turned out, Wilson had no further appointments to make.

Although Lane wanted to leave the Cabinet for the greener pastures of the Supreme Court, many of his California friends encouraged him to leave it to reenter politics in the Golden State. In July 1913, he replied to one of his supporters that for three reasons, he would not run for the Senate in 1914: he found his Cabinet position just as interesting as a senatorship; he believed the primary system demanded "practically a year of . . . time to make the race," which meant a candidate needed "a great deal of money"; and he thought his close friend James D. Phelan, who wanted the office, "ought to be acceptable."[32] His friends were not satisfied. In May 1914, a number of them attempted to persuade him to run for governor later that year. Lane entertained the thought, but lack of finances and his desire to help transform his Interior Department proposals into legislation caused him to reject it. That autumn, he did campaign in California but on behalf of Phelan, who made a successful bid for a Senate seat. Lane demonstrated that he still retained his popularity and campaign magic. When he spoke at Trinity Auditorium in Los Angeles, he drew a packed house. Earlier in the campaign, Phelan had filled only half the same hall.[33]

As the 1916 campaign approached, Lane's California supporters again pleaded with him to run for office, this time for California's other Senate seat, probably against Hiram Johnson. Phelan and other state Democratic leaders promised him the nomination and all the necessary campaign money. Lane was tempted, especially because of career uncertainty in Washington. Wilson was in the process of bypassing him a third time for a Supreme Court appointment. Lane also complained to his wife that "things have been made . . . uncomfortable by some of my fool colleagues who have butted into my affairs."[34]

Undoubtedly Lane referred to Gregory and Daniels, who were blocking his disposition of the Honolulu case, and perhaps to Burleson who disliked him. The chances for Lane's winning the election looked promising, and this probably added to his desire to give it a try. In July 1916, Johnson's popularity and power in California definitely seemed on the wane, even "the cards appeared to be stacked against him in the August Republican primary."[35] To his vacationing wife, Lane wrote that he "would like the excitement of the stump and to make the personal appeal once more." He also added that he would not decide until he heard from her. In general, she opposed his running for office because of the strain it placed upon his already weak heart, but she also disliked taking a positive position in such a circumstance. Her own health, however, influenced Lane's decision not to run. During the previous winter, she had suffered a serious breakdown from which she had not completely recovered.[36] Without the activity of a campaign of his own, he lent full support to Wilson.

Early in June, Lane told the President that the Democratic platform "should be one long joyful shout of exultation over the achievements of the Administration," but, he cautioned, "I can't quite see you leading the shout." Lane attested his sincerity with a $1,000 campaign contribution to the Democratic party. The sum represented six months of savings, at a time when he had neither savings nor property; he gave it without public comment.[37]

Lane could do little campaigning that fall, except for a few days in New York State near the end of the campaign, as his duties as chairman of the American-Mexican Joint Commission (to ameliorate some of the disputes between the two countries) kept him occupied. Nevertheless, he voiced and publicized opinions on all important persons and issues. He considered Hughes, for example, "a good man, honest and fine, but not a liberal." Roosevelt's trouble, he concluded, was "that he laid too much stress on the support of big business. To have Gary, and Armour, and Perkins as your chief boomers doesn't make you very popular in Kansas and Iowa." Lane suggested having Jane Addams and two or three other women send telegrams to prominent women in each state stressing Wilsonian peace and prosperity. He wired one or more papers in each of the states west of the Missouri River urging the election of Wilson. When he decided that Wilson's reaction to labor's demand of an eight-hour day was unclear, he told him so. "Your ideality and unselfishness are so rare," he wrote, "that things need to be made particularly clear to them [the people] ." In a campaign article, Lane described the Republican campaign as merely claiming, "We could have done the job better, but we decline to state how." In his only important speech, he repeated this charge and praised positive Wilsonian accomplishments such as the Underwood Tariff, the Federal Reserve Act, the Federal Trade Commission, the Seaman's Act, and the eight-hour day for railroad workers. He also defended Wilson's foreign policy. In every way, Lane backed Wilson, and at the close of the campaign, Lane and his wife went with their close friends, the Adolph Millers and the Franklin D. Roosevelts, to await election results at the Roosevelt home in Hyde Park, New York.[38]

The election returns, of course, pleased Lane. "What a splendid thing it is," he wrote to a friend, "to have our state the pivotal state!" He also emphasized that the states in which the Interior Department had major dealings voted for Wilson, and that the Joint American-Mexican Commission had kept the differences of opinion between the two countries from becoming a campaign issue. For these two particular accomplishments, Lane complimented himself.[39] The most mystifying element in the election was Lane's change of heart toward Johnson. As late as June 1914, Lane lacked respect for Republican Governor Johnson. But after his 1916 election to the Senate, Lane wrote, "Of course I am glad of Johnson's election, as he is a strong, stalwart chap, capable of tremendous things for good. He will probably be a presidential candidate four years from now, and I see no man who can beat him, nor should he be beaten unless we have a good deal better material than our run of . . . rank opportunists."[40] Lane had supported the Democrats completely, but still he was not orthodox.

IV

There was a touch of irony as well as politics in Lane's support of Wilson's foreign policy during the campaign of 1916. They had not always agreed. In a broad sense, of course, they shared similar foreign policy views, but in the past when Wilson had often moved cautiously, Lane sometimes had demanded vigorous action.

When Wilson took office, the United States had not recognized the Mexican government of Victoriano Huerta who had gained power a month earlier by means of a bloody coup. Wilson's refusal to recognize the Huerta government, internal opposition to the dictator, and United States attempts to intervene in Mexican affairs produced years of strained relations between the two countries. Lane fully supported Wilson's policies of intervention, including sending military forces onto Mexican soil on two occasions. Both men took equally as long to realize that their policies created more problems than they solved.

From the beginning of his Cabinet years, Lane showed an interest in Mexican affairs and sent the President advice regarding that country. In July 1913, he concluded that the President had "a perfectly definite and high minded policy, but" believed Wilson "long ago" should have removed the United States ambassador. The next winter, Wilson pursued a policy of watchful waiting while Lane called for stronger action. In May 1914, he canceled "at the last moment" a trip to California because of a potential crisis in Mexican relations, about which Adolph Miller determined "Lane's counsel was undispensable." In March 1916, Lane encouraged Wilson to send an army to Mexico, because, as he expounded, "I do not say that they respect only force, but like children they pile insult upon insult if they are not stopped when the first insult is given."[41] By July of that year, however, Lane had tempered his views to conform to Wilson's, and no longer considered some of the President's policies weak and vacillating. Instead, he wrote that "President Wilson's Mexican policy is one of the things which, as a member of his administration, I am most proud."[42] A continuation of Wilson's diplomacy, though, meant a war that neither country wanted.

During August, therefore, Wilson accepted the suggestion of Venustiano Carranza, leader of the Mexican Constitutionalists, who in 1915 had established a de facto government throughout most of Mexico, to create a binational commission to discuss differences between the two countries. The two heads of state asked the six-man American-Mexican Joint Commission to examine and to recommend solutions to problems that the years of political upheaval had produced: the pacification of the Mexican-American border, the protection of American life and property in Mexico, the payment for past property losses, and the withdrawal of American troops from Mexico. Because of Lane's ability, reputation, and interest in Mexico, Wilson logically placed the Californian on the commission. To serve with him, Wilson named Judge George Gray of Delaware and John Mott, secretary of the International Young Men's Christian Association. The Mexican government appointed three distinguished citizens, Luis Cabrera, Ignacio Bonillas, and Alberto Pani. Lane's appointment brought favorable comment. For example, the *New York Times* stated editorially that Lane "has the intellectual keenness and force, the strength of character, the diplomatic and personal savoir faire which a High Commissioner needs. On the economic side, too . . . he is strong."[43] Both countries wished for a peaceful settlement to their differences, so the conferences started under favorable auspices.

The commission held its first meeting, with Lane as chairman, on September 4, 1916, in New York City, and its last meeting on January 15, 1917, in the same city. In between, conferences took place at New London, Connecticut, and Atlantic City, New Jersey. The Mexican representatives insisted that before all else the commission agree to immediate withdrawal of the army contingent Wilson maintained in Mexico to capture a rebel force that had killed Americans, raided American soil, and tried to overthrow the Carranza government. Lane, Mott, and Gray rejected this procedure and pressed for accord on internal Mexican problems. On November 24, 1916, the commissioners reached a protocol agreement calling for the withdrawal of United States troops within forty days, provided the Constitutionalist forces would occupy and protect the evacuated area. After a month's delay, Carranza rejected the protocol and demanded the immediate withdrawal of American troops as prerequisite to approval of any agreement; the American commissioners would not consent. Although the commission adjourned in mid-January over this impasse, the situation did not revert to the starting point of the previous summer. Much good had been accomplished.

During the fall of 1916, while the commission met, both countries conducted national elections, after which tensions eased. By January 1917, Wilson had even less desire to become involved in a serious armed clash with Mexico than he had had six months earlier; the danger of American involvement in the European war loomed too close. Lane, Mott, and Gray recommended to Wilson that he reestablish full diplomatic relations with Mexico and urged continued negotiations. They believed a basis existed for a better understanding between the two nations. By January 18, 1917, Wilson had decided to recall his military expedition, and less than eight weeks later, the United States finally extended de jure recognition to the increasingly stable Carranza government. The American-Mexican crises abated.[44] Although the commission was not the decisive factor, it had borne some fruit.

The second major foreign concern to occur in the Wilson administration was the European war that broke out in August 1914. In broadest policy, Lane agreed with Wilson on what course the United States should take. In methods and timing to execute this policy, they were often poles apart. Initially, both wanted the United States to remain neutral, yet they both possessed ingrained pro-British biases. Lane, after all, was Canadian by birth. In time, both men championed preparedness and United States entry into the war. But whereas Wilson was often reluctant to take a step, Lane would rush forward.

Among his first reactions to the European war was a belief that the United States would gain materially. With the disruption of normal commerce, he concluded, the country would realize the value of its mineral resources and further develop them. He thought this would enhance the prospects for passage of his pending resource legislation. Six months later, he envisioned even greater benefit for the United States because the war opened new avenues of trade and new fields of investment. He expected labor to profit from the curtailment of the number of immigrants that normally flooded the labor market. The nation as a whole, he predicted, would gain prestige by remaining aloof from the smoke, din, and misery of battle. When the war prevented the exodus of Europe-bound tourists in the summer of 1915, Lane appreciated the merits of the situation: the unprecedented use of the national parks, the spending of perhaps $100 million at home instead of abroad, and the intermingling of peoples from the East and West.[45] But the war brought problems as well as material gain.

From the beginning of the war, he believed a policy of neutrality was the best course for the nation to follow. By neutrality, Lane, like most government officials and most Americans, really meant a pro-British, pro-Allies neutrality. This created a problem since Britain paid scant heed to American neutrality rights; and the problem bothered Lane. In January 1915, he noted that "I find myself from day to day feeling a

twinge or two of bitterness over England's stubbornness." A few months
later, he raised the question of whether Britain was trying to take advantage of the war to weaken United States trade.[46] As late as June 1916,
he defended the administration's policy against the charge of vacillation
by asking "Whom were we to be mad at—England, or Germany, or everybody in the world?" During the campaign that fall, he remarked that
the United States had made no friends among the belligerents because
nations at war want partisans, not judges.[47] There was no doubt, however, that Lane's sympathy lay with the Allies. Any harsh words toward
Britain for disregarding American neutrality rights ceased by January
1917. By February, he was highly critical of Wilson for not immediately
taking the nation to war. Neutrality, he observed, had failed: he called
for its abandonment.

Lane based his neutrality on the belief that war was detrimental to a
democracy and the nation's development. War and democracy, he believed,
did not mix. Equally important to him was the resource-drain that war
levied upon its participants. In July 1915, he claimed that "an amount
equal to that which we now spend upon the army and the navy would
put under cultivation at least 40,000,000 acres of new land now arid in
the West and Southwest." The war, he added, would deter European advancement for at least two generations. If the United States maintained
its neutrality, it would hold an immense advantage when the war ended.
"We have no time for war," Lane told the Brown University graduates
in June 1916, "We are doing something so much more important. We
are at work."[48] His concept of conservation influenced his attitudes
toward World War I.

Although Lane did not want to corrupt democracy and squander resources upon war, he ardently believed that to remain neutral, a nation
had to be prepared for war and ready to fight for its interests and rights.
This belief initiated his criticism of British violation of United States
rights on the seas. Only his pro-British sympathies kept him from as-
suming a more pugnacious posture toward that nation. Lane's willingness to defend national rights with force motivated his early desire
for an aggressive Mexican policy; it finally led to his demand for war
against Germany, as well as to differences of opinion with Wilson.

From the early months of the European war, Lane championed
increased military spending. As late as May 5, 1915, though, Wilson
and the rest of the Cabinet opposed the spending Lane and Secretary

of War Lindley Garrison sought. Eventually Wilson and Garrison parted company over this issue. Lane concurred with Garrison, but was less dogmatic and more patient than his colleague.[49] Still, Lane never wavered in his support of preparedness. He not only wanted to carry a big stick, he wanted to speak out loudly and clearly. If United States rights were not respected, the nation should make it plain that it would fight. To make this understook, "Princetonian English" and diplomatic jargon were a handicap. They created, Lane surmised, the impression of a bluff, insincerity, and hesitation.[50]

Although Lane wanted to mince no words in making clear the United States' position, although he was one of the original proponents of preparedness, and although he demanded aggressive action even if it meant war, he hoped that such a firm policy would maintain the peace. He recognized the difficulty of this approach. Throughout the summer of 1915, he admitted that the course was a hard one. In December 1915, he explained to a good friend that, considering the circumstances, there was nothing to do but be patient. A few months later, he defended diplomatic means over use of force to enforce American rights by concluding in an article that "The good lawyer settles his case out of court if he can."[51] During the campaign in October 1916, Lane declared that "We are at peace when, if we had been intemperate, we should have been at war. . . . We have made the seas safe to travel for Americans." Lane never wanted war if neutrality were a feasible alternative. But when German submarines periodically made neutrality seem a hopeless policy, he quickly switched to a more aggressive policy.[52] His faith in neutrality fluctuated with German submarine policy.

From January 1917, until the United States entered the war in April, Lane was openly belligerent in favor of war whenever the subject came up at Cabinet meetings.[53] Wilson, Lane complained in his letters, was "dead wrong" in his lack of sympathy with preparedness; he moved toward war "slower than a glacier"; and, when he finally made his decision to fight, he did so "unwillingly."[54] Lane did not appreciate his President's reluctance.

As Wilson launched his second administration, the relationship Lane maintained with the President and the feelings he expressed toward him differed from what they had been four years earlier. He still respected and praised Wilson, but he did so much more sparingly than before. Similarly, by the spring of 1917, his nondepartmental activities and interests had produced neither brilliant success nor abject failure. The country had given the Democrats and Wilson a vote of confidence, but Lane remained wary about the future prospects of his party. His fondest professional desire, a seat on the Supreme Court, had eluded him, although he nursed hopes of a future appointment. Cabinet meetings had lost much of their original deliberative vitality, but Lane continued to enjoy the complete confidence of House; and, to the country at large, he was an unusually popular Cabinet member. His enduring interest in foreign affairs focused on Mexico, where the United States avoided armed conflict, and on the European war, in which, soon after Wilson's second inauguration, the United States became a participant.

9

The War Years,
1917-1918

*These are great days. . . . This is a combina-
tion of the Democracies of the world against
feudalism and autocracy.*

Lane to George W. Lane,
May 3, 1917

*Unquestionably the ownership of property
has a tendency to develop patriotism. . . .
There is no property, moreover, that carries
with it this characteristic more strongly than
does land.*

Lane to R. L. Watts,
April 10, 1919

I

Firmly convinced that the war was a crusade for righteousness, Lane wil-
lingly did everything in his power to support it, both within and outside
of the Interior Department. He served on commissions and committees
that helped to keep the homefront machinery of war oiled; he promoted
the sale of Liberty Bonds; and he fostered patriotism. To lend assistance
to returning servicemen, he suggested a program to provide farms for

veterans. This farm plan, plus a campaign to promote American values, he believed, would result in a better postwar nation. Although his work was far from indispensable, he did make several noteworthy contributions, and he longed to do more. Colonel House had wanted him to head the War Department rather than the Interior Department; during the war years, Lane shared House's wish.

Intellectually, Lane demanded war because he concluded that Germany violated his country's neutral rights, but once the United States became a belligerent, he interpreted the war as a struggle over a difference of moral and political philosophy. Until the United States entered the war, he had based his mild criticisms of Britain as well as his more severe criticisms of Germany on those nations' violations of American neutrality. After April 1917, however, he dramatized the conflict as a struggle for principle and for democracy, a war against war, and a war against feudalism.[1] The seed of neutral rights suddenly blossomed into the flower of civilization and Christianity. He seemed oblivious to the transmutation; on May 1, 1917, though, he explained his change of attitude with the simple remark that "It has taken us a long time to learn the meaning of this war."[2]

Lane perceived the meaning of the war as "a combination of the Democracies of the world against feudalism and autocracy."[3] He considered Britain, France, and the United States "democracies"; sometimes he included Russia. He judged Germany, on the other hand, feudalistic and determined to master the world: a nation that understood only the language of force. Thus he believed the war was one of self-defense to make safe the reign of democracy in the world. "We are at war, when the last word is said," he explained in July 1918, "for the preservation of what we call Christian civilization." Next to his family, Lane deemed nothing more important than fighting for principle and for civilization. "These are great days," he exclaimed, during the first month of the war, when British and French commissions visited the United States. A few weeks after the war's end, he reflected that the war had been the nation's "greatest adventure."[4] Although he viewed the war in terms of a righteous crusade, he sometimes was mindful of the undesirable side effects that war left in its wake.

War, Lane thought, degraded all people, including the victors. He tried, therefore, to minimize the degradation. In December 1917, he refused to be interviewed on the moral benefits of the war. "That," he replied to the request, "would be sheer camouflage," and elaborated that the

war would "make sheer brutes out of us, because we will have to descend
to the methods that the Germans employ."[5] Although he upheld the
American practice of pressing into service German and Austrian ships
that happened to be in the nation's ports at the outbreak of war, he was
against confiscation. The acquired ships should be treated exactly as if
they were American vessels, he asserted, and at the war's end, the government should pay their owners for the services rendered. "This spirit of
fairness," he noted, "is to animate us throughout the war."[6] Although
he believed the United States fought for principle, he would accept nego-
tiated peace terms. Practicality often tempered his judgments. For example, he disliked the Russian Bolsheviks who forceably seized power
in November, 1917, but he recorded that "My single word of caution
was to so act that Russia, when she 'came back,' should not hate us."[7]
He stood ready to act on matters of principle, but he often realized that
he had to accept less than ideal.

Lane acknowledged war's complex situations sometimes demanded
more sophisticated analysis than simply the good-versus-evil approach
he usually employed, but he still overlooked much of significance. He
admitted that both he and the United States had been slow in realizing
the meaning of the war, that it really was a crusade for democracy. But
the thought never occurred to him that his and the nation's post-1917
thinking may have been as faulty as their earlier reasoning. Also, more
countries were at war than Britain, France, Russia, Germany, and the
United States, and they did not fit into Lane's democratic-versus-
autocratic dichotomy. Moreover, for the first two-and-one-half years
of the war, the British and French democracies allied themselves with
a most autocratic European nation, Czarist Russia. Neither this, nor
the British disregard of American neutral rights were of sufficient influence to balance the weight of Lane's simplistic concept of the war.

On the homefront, Lane's belief in a "spirit of fairness" did not extend to those who did not share his views. He branded as "pro-German"
the pacifists and other citizens who earnestly believed that only volunteers should be sent to fight in Europe. According to Josephus Daniels,
Lane was willing to support George L. Bell, executive officer of the
California Commission of Immigration, and Housing, who, as representative of eight western governors, wanted the federal government to
intern without trial all members of the Industrial Workers of the World
who agitated against the war effort. Wilson rejected Bell's position.

Lane's commitment to the war sometimes clouded his thought process; the same commitment spurred him to devote countless hours to the war effort.[8]

II

On August 29, 1916, as part of the preparedness program, Congress created the Council of National Defense. Lane's membership on this body permitted him to play an important role in the war effort, his performance, however, lessened the confidence Wilson placed in Lane's judgment.

The other members were the secretaries of war, navy, agriculture, commerce, and labor. To assist the council, its members nominated, and the President appointed, an Advisory Commission of seven citizens who served without compensation.[9] The Council of National Defense had two chief functions. First, it coordinated all forms of transportation and ascertained additional facilities required to meet the commercial, military, and industrial transportation needs of the nation; and second, it surveyed the industrial resources of the country to determine how they might be adapted to the demands of war. The council and its Advisory Commission possessed little real power; it exercised no administrative jurisdiction or controls; it made no purchases. Primarily, the council conducted investigations and made recommendations to the President and to the heads of executive departments. Its contribution to the war effort was, however, of fundamental importance.[10]

Initially the council and its Advisory Commission organized slowly and ineffectively. In February 1917, Lane submitted a comprehensive organizational suggestion to divide the commission into seven committees with each original member a committee chairman. The council adopted his suggestion and established the committees: for example, transportation, labor, and munitions. During the early months of the war, no other mobilization machinery existed except the council and its Advisory Commission. Years later, Bernard Baruch wrote that "What the Commission did do ... was to chart the course for much that was accomplished later."[11] From the start, though, the council and the commission realized they were inadequate to plan and direct the nation's economy. On July

28, 1917, therefore, the Council of National Defense created the War Industries Board. In time, under the direction of Baruch, the board harnessed the industrial machinery of the United States to work efficiently for the war effort. Its organizational pattern followed that of the original seven committees of the Advisory Commission. The board's Railroad Administration, for example, evolved from the earlier Committee on Transportation. Lane's detailed administrative plan for the council, although no panacea, constituted a vital early step in the right direction.[12]

Although the War Industries Board and various other war boards diluted the original responsibility of the Council of National Defense, the council nevertheless provided important services throughout the war. Lane, too, continued to make his contribution. When the head of the Women's Committee of the Council threatened to quit in protest unless women received a greater allotment of war work to do and increased recognition for what they did accomplish, the council appointed Lane to placate her. The "prince of diplomats," as Daniels called him, helped effect desired harmony. Toward the end of the war, Lane served as chairman of the Field Division of the council. This body directed and coordinated the activities of 184,000 community, municipal, county, and state councils of defense, as well as those of the women's committees.[13]

Membership on the council involved him in several controversies. In the late summer of 1916, Wilson recommended that Congress enact a measure providing for an obligatory eight-hour day for railroad employees, including provisions for overtime pay. Congress complied by passing the Adamson Eight-Hour Law, to become effective January 1, 1917. The railroads contended that the act was unconstitutional and turned to the courts for what they believed would be a favorable ruling. When the first of the year arrived, and the Supreme Court had not yet heard the appeal from a lower court's decision, the railroads refused to abide by the Adamson law. The four railroad brotherhoods decided not to strike to gain compliance until the Supreme Court rendered its decision. Several months passed with no action. By March, the brotherhoods had lost patience and announced that if the railroads did not obey the law by seven o'clock on the evening of March 17, they would strike.

On March 16, the Council of National Defense, with Wilson's approval, appointed a commission to attempt to avert the strike. With war iminent, a nationwide rail strike would have serious consequences. The council designated Lane and Secretary of Labor William Wilson to represent the

government along with Daniel Willard, president of the Baltimore and
Ohio Railroad, and Samuel Gompers, president of the American Federation of Labor, both of whom were members of the council's Advisory
Commission. At 9:00 p.m. on that Friday, March 16, the government
representatives met at the Hotel Baltimore in New York with the representatives of the brotherhoods and the railroad executives.[14] Their first
meeting lasted until 3:45 a.m. At 10:00 a.m., Saturday, the meeting reconvened and continued until 3:30 p.m. that afternoon. At the close of
that session, a spokesman for the group announced that both sides had
agreed to postpone strike action forty-eight hours until the Supreme
Court would render its traditional Monday decisions. The disputants and
the four representatives of government hoped the Court would announce
its verdict on the Adamson Act. Actually, Lane and Willard already knew
what the Court's decision would be because on the way to Washington's
Union Station, Lane had stopped at the home of Chief Justice Edward
White. The Secretary's smile upon emerging a few minutes later con-
veyed a disheartening message to Willard who had waited in the car. Besides gaining a two days' strike delay, the conference had reached agreement upon the action to be taken if the act were upheld.

On Sunday afternoon of that same weekend, a new factor entered the
deliberations when news reached the hotel that German submarines had
sunk three American ships. Lane telephoned Wilson, who declared that
he would not tolerate a strike. That evening Lane delivered a long speech
to the group appealing to the patriotism of the railroad executives. "In
such a time, gentlemen," he exhorted, "there is something bigger than
what this will cost you—there is the good of our country."[15] After an
extended session among themselves, the railroad executives sent their
surrender to Lane. By dawn on Monday, March 19, the conference had
ready a final agreement. Later that day, the Supreme Court upheld the
Adamson Act.

Lane's plea for patriotism had not solely produced the settlement,
although the *New York Times* editorialized as though it did.[16] But from
his arrival in New York, he had served as unofficial chairman of the negotiations. Although sympathetic to the unions in this case, he was the only
one of the four government representatives without an official association with either labor or the railroads. Nevertheless, more persuasive than
Lane were the brotherhood's firm demand for compliance to the act,
Wilson's implied threat of government action, potential adverse public

opinion with war pending, and Willard's knowledge of how the Supreme Court would rule.[17]

Wilson's good feeling toward Lane, as a result of his contribution in averting the strike, did not last long. By May 1, Lane concluded that Americans had not received the real facts regarding the losses of American ships to German U-boats. The first week in May, when governors and other state representatives met with the Council of National Defense to discuss the war, Lane recognized an opportunity to alert the country to the magnitude of the U-boat threat. He released council information that German submarines had sunk four hundred thousand tons of shipping the previous week. The situation, he warned, teemed with peril. His speech had the desired effect; the country considered it the story of the day. Wilson's annoyance at Lane's action negated much of the goodwill he had established six weeks earlier.[18]

Even more annoying to Wilson than his Secretary's submarine speech was Lane's participation in a coal-pricing incident. The country's move toward war during the spring of 1917 brought rising coal prices and anxiety about the adequacy of supply of that resource. In March of 1917, he urged Wilson to direct the Federal Trade Commission to investigate an expected increase in the price of bituminous coal. Wilson thought it a good idea and contacted the chairman of the Federal Trade Commission William J. Harris, who replied that his commission already was investigating the matter under a resolution passed by the House of Representatives in August 1916. He added that the commission also was investigating the price of anthracite coal under a similar resolution passed by the Senate in June 1916.[19]

Late in April 1917, the Council of National Defense took direct action and established a Committee on Coal Production. On May 7, the new committee held its first meeting, chaired by Francis S. Peabody, president of the Peabody Coal Company. The committee soon decided to ask all the nation's coal producers to meet in Washington late in June. Lane followed the work of the Peabody Committee and kept in close touch with its chairman.[20]

On June 26, Lane, Daniels, T. L. Lewis, assistant to Gregory, and John F. Fort of the Federal Trade Commission addressed a meeting of the coal producers. In turn, each of the four government officials stated explicitly that unless the producers freely established a fair selling price for their product the government would step in and control the industry.

Lane's speech highlighted the gathering. He appealed again to patriotism. "You are not living for today," he told them, "and you are not living for yourselves. You are living for the United States—indeed you are living for the people of the world. . . . The life of the nation is at stake, and there are greater things than making money." His speech ended amid tumultuous cheering.[21] Two days later, the four hundred coal producers adopted two resolutions. The first granted authority to the secretary of the interior, the Federal Trade Commission, and the Committee on Coal Production, consulting with the producers, to set a tentative maximum selling price of coal until a thorough investigation of production costs would be made. The group established the temporary price of bituminous coal at $3 a ton at the mine.[22]

Reaction to the price setting varied drastically. Lane and Peabody believed the group had reduced coal prices. Lane called the action of the producers "an inspiration to the people of the country," and Peabody estimated that the price meant a reduction of $1 to $3 per ton. The government's power costs, he added, would drop approximately $2 million in the coming year and the American consumers would save about $200 million. Fort, although without comment upon whether the set coal price was a reduction, concluded that the price set was high, but proposed that "the motive was to increase production and throw a large amount of coal on the market as rapidly as possible." After that, he maintained, the principle of supply and demand would reduce the artificially established maximum selling price.[23]

Wilson, Gregory, Daniels, and Baker, on the other hand, were displeased, not only because Lane had failed to keep them informed, but also because they considered the price set intolerably high. At a hastily called conference, President Wilson told Gregory, Secretary of Labor Wilson, and Baker that he was about to repudiate the agreement publicly. Baker suggested that the President allow him to do so in his capacity as president of the Council of National Defense; that way the President would not force Lane's resignation. Baker, in a public letter to the director of the Advisory Commission, denounced the price setting and termed the figures agreed upon "exorbitant, unjust, and oppressive." He also stated that the Council of National Defense had no authority to fix the price of coal. Furthermore, he pointed out, the Committee on Coal Production functioned in a purely advisory capacity to the council. Baker's letter settled the immediate issue; the aftereffects lingered.[24]

Lane emerged from the incident tarnished, although neither he nor Fort regretted their actions. Lane's neglect of communications with the White House and within the Council of National Defense itself was obvious and inexcusable. Baker and Daniels believed the coal producers had misled Lane to fleece the government and the consumer. The price of coal, however, differed markedly according to mining areas, types of coal, and methods of sale. In some cases, the price setting did mean a reduction in price, but, undoubtedly, the producers had taken advantage of Lane, who had placed too much faith in their patriotism. A few days after the Baker repudiation, Lane commented that he had acted "on the theory that the business men of the United States were not all scoundrels," and the following day, in another letter, wrote that "If we cannot get co-operation out of our businessmen, we are going to fail."[25]

Subsequent events partially vindicated Lane's position. In August, Congress passed the Lever Act granting the President power to set certain prices. With this authority, Wilson established the Fuel Administration, which, in turn, quickly raised the price of coal to encourage greater production.[26] Although on July 2, Wilson told Fort that he was "not in the least inclined to criticize" the part Fort had played in the price-setting episode, toward Lane the President expressed a different feeling. In mid-August, House recorded in his diary that Frank Polk, counselor of the State Department, believed that Lane had lost Wilson's confidence entirely, and Polk wondered why. The President, of course, still judged Lane a useful member of his administration, but he no longer accepted his Secretary's judgment as readily as he once had. Wilson's displeasure and Baker's letter almost caused Lane to submit his resignation. The war and the Interior Department, however, kept him busy so the momentary bitterness soon weakened.[27]

III

In January 1918, Lane became a member of another committee, the Railroad Wage Commission. Unlike some of his work on the Council of National Defense, his participation in this commission provoked no ill feelings. The immediate impetus for establishment of the commission came from an Interstate Commerce Commission report of December

1917 that recommended the government either assume operation of the railroads or remove the legal restrictions to pooling. Wilson had to act because the railroads operated with intolerable inefficiency. The Army Appropriations Act of August 1916 empowered the President to take possession of any and all systems of transportation in time of war. Daniels, Gregory, Burleson, and McAdoo favored this approach to the problem while Lane led the opposition. The railroad brotherhoods shared Lane's apprehension about governmental control. Wilson decided, however, that the government would operate the railroads.[28]

On December 26, 1917, Wilson issued a proclamation effective January 1, 1918, announcing nationalization of the railroads and the appointment of McAdoo as director-general of them. Of all the names mentioned for the post of directing the Railroad Administration, Lane's perhaps met with the most favor among both railroad management and labor. His years on the Interstate Commerce Commission had given him a knowledge of railroad affairs possessed by few men. His ability and fairness were above question. The brotherhoods, furthermore, respected him for the role he had played in their successful attempt to force compliance with the Adamson law. Wilson apparently never considered him for the appointment, despite the logic of such a choice. Wilson had not forgotten Lane's submarine speech or his action in the coal pricing or his position on the Honolulu oil case. By December, according to House, Wilson had "cooled considerably toward Lane."[29]

To gain acceptance of nationalization, the government guaranteed railroad owners and managers profits based on those of 1916. Workers' wages posed a more difficult problem. By almost any standard, the workers were grossly underpaid. On January 18, 1918, McAdoo appointed an impartial commission to investigate and report on wages, relative to wages in other industries, the economy in general, and among the different categories of railroad jobs. He named to the four-man commission Lane, Charles C. McChord of the Interstate Commerce Commission, J. Harry Covington, chief justice of the Supreme Court of the District of Columbia, and William R. Willcox, who resigned as chairman of the Republican National Committee to accept the post. At the commission's first meeting, the members elected Lane as chairman. For the next three and one half months the commission conducted hearings, collected data, analyzed both, and finally wrote its report.[30]

On April 30, 1918, the commission submitted its report. McAdoo termed it "a remarkably thorough and informative study of wages and economic conditions," and ordered into effect immediately its wage-increase recommendations (under which some workers received as much as a 43 percent pay raise). The report helped ameliorate a potentially dangerous situation.[31] Three weeks after the report, Wilson agreed with House's suggestion to appoint Lane as successor to McAdoo, if McAdoo resigned as he had threatened. The following December, McAdoo did resign, and although rumors reported that Lane would assume the position, Wilson followed McAdoo's recommendation and named Walker D. Hines.[32]

One of Lane's wartime activities, speaking on behalf of Liberty Bond drives, especially suited his talents. The government conducted four such campaigns during the war and a fifth drive, the Victory Liberty Loan, in December 1918. Lane's oratory was captivating and persuasive wherever and whenever he spoke. He made a three-week tour for the second drive in the autumn of 1917, speaking his way from Louisiana through Oklahoma, Kansas, Colorado, Wyoming, Utah, and Idaho, to Oregon. Often he made two or more speeches a day and upon his return to Washington, he immediately took to the platform in the East. In May 1918, the audience at the Commonwealth Club of California at San Francisco interrupted his eleven-page speech with applause twenty-eight times and gave him a prolonged standing ovation at the end.[33]

Another illustration of Lane's talent with words took place in April 1917, when Wilson summoned twenty-four men to Washington to help initiate an American Red Cross fund-raising drive. One of the men, Henry Morgenthau, suggested that the best way to start the drive would be to have the President issue a proclamation commending the campaign to the nation. Everyone agreed but feared that Wilson was too busy. Morgenthau commented that Franklin Lane could easily phrase an idea in Wilson's style and the President would then only have to sign it. Lane agreed and Wilson approved the result. Morgenthau later concluded that the proclamation "thrilled the country and made easy the path of the Red Cross campaign."[34]

Lane believed deeply in the war. Shortly after the United States entered the war, his only son, nineteen-year-old Ned (Franklin K. Lane, Jr.) received an army commission and with it the distinction of being the youngest lieutenant in the army. When Secretary of War Baker asked Lane whether he wanted his son to go overseas, Lane replied that he did. In fact, the next day, in a letter to his brother George, Lane wrote that "It was the most momentous decision that I have made in the war."[35] Before young Lane got overseas, he transferred to the navy. Subsequently, he served in France as a naval aviator, had a number of "narrow escapes," and returned home to a proud father. Had Lane been younger, he eagerly would have volunteered to go himself. At Cabinet meetings, to the displeasure of Wilson, Lane supported Theodore Roosevelt's request to raise and command a division of volunteers for duty in France. During the summer of 1918, when Lane learned about the combat death of Roosevelt's son Quentin, he sent the former President a four-page handwritten message "in the effort to make stout your heart." Lane wrote that the nation "must get used to death" and stressed the importance of making "the sacrifice generously, with exaltation, nobly." In that spirit, he continued, "you will lead the country." The Secretary recognized, of course, that "it might have been my boy." As did Roosevelt, Lane placed military service in defense of one's country among the highest of man's duties and privileges.[36]

Within the Interior Department, Lane worked to the limit of his jurisdiction to advance the cause of the war. In his eagerness to help, however, he approved proposals for the National Park System that would damage the parks. Under the guise of increasing war production, cattle and sheep men pressured the Interior Department to permit grazing in the parks. A California national defense committee, headed by his longtime friend Benjamin Ide Wheeler, approved a request to pasture fifty thousand sheep in Yosemite. The request was actually a get-rich-quick scheme rather than a display of patriotism, but Wheeler, an embarrassed friend of the German Kaiser, was too anxious to be pro-American to realize it. When Lane gave his final approval, Horace Albright, acting director of the National Park Service in place of an ailing Stephen Mather, protested with all his might. Lane snapped that the country was at war and the sheep were to enter the park. The Sierra Club, some congressmen, and California's Senator Johnson spread alarm of the pending ruination of Yosemite. Lane yielded to the pressure and withdrew the order. The wildflower meadows and slopes of Glacier National Park came equally close to disaster. Lane decided to allow the Penwell Sheep Company to graze its herds in the park and turned the details over to Albright. Albright's own dedication to the nation's parks, and a large measure of good fortune, enabled him to devise a plan that subsequently circumvented Lane's directives without disobeying them. The sheep did not enter the park.

In addition to the herders, there were other interests hoping to reap large profits that brought pressure to bear upon the National Park Service. Most used the emotional appeal of the war to gain entry into the parks. Herbert Hoover, director of the Food Administration, quickly and effectively squelched a plan, which Lane had approved, to kill the elk in Yellowstone for their meat. The efforts of Mather, Albright, Hoover, and other enthusiasts of park preservation protected the parks from Lane's enthusiastic support of the war effort.[37]

In all other activities of the Interior Department, Lane's work during the war was commendable. He displayed intense pride in the department members who donned military uniforms and marched off to fight. Through the Bureau of Education, he encouraged the nation's teachers to arouse in their students a desire to cultivate home gardens. Grosvenor Clarkson, director of the Council of National Defense, concluded that "Lane might be styled the great mobilizer of the subterranean war resources of America. . . . The cooperation of the Department of the Interior was invaluable to the War Industries Board as the great purveyor of raw materials."[38]

IV

During the last six months of the war, and well into the postwar period, Lane expended much of his thought and energy to his plan to provide farms for returning veterans and to his desire to "Americanize" his fellow countrymen. He introduced his farm plan in a letter to Wilson on May 31, 1918, and then sent copies to all members of Congress. The problem of relocating a surplus army at the onset of peace, Lane noted, was ageless but could be solved simply. "The experience of wars points out the lesson," he concluded, "that our servicemen, because of army life, with its openness and activity, will largely seek out-of-doors vocations and occupations." Allied nations had already adopted a back-to-the-soil policy, he added, and the United States had previously done so with the Homestead Law of 1862. He admitted that the nation no longer enjoyed bountiful public domain of the Civil War era, but he averred that the country still did contain millions of acres of undeveloped land. These acres were the cutover, swamp, and arid lands then lying fallow throughout the country. The era of cheap or free land was past, but he believed a new policy applied to the new conditions would provide similar opportunity.

The plan he suggested attempted to replace speculation with security. It called for the Interior Department to conduct surveys and studies to determine the usefulness of swamp, arid, and cutover lands. The discharged servicemen would then have a variety of prospective farm lands from which to choose. Under his proposal the government would plan the farms and direct the construction of homes, the clearing of land, and the building of dams and irrigation projects. The veteran who wanted the farm would supply the muscle power. Under no condition, Lane insisted, would the farms be "turned over as the prairies were—unbroken, unfenced, without accommodations for men or animals." The government would meet the cost of development, which the veteran would repay over a period of "perhaps 30 or 40 years." He considered his plan practical, and "it is," he wrote, "with slight variations, a policy which other countries are pursuing successfully."[39]

Lane's proposal was not original. Other countries did have similar plans in various stages of operation. The Reclamation Service had established the principle of government assistance to the settler with repayment provisions. As secretary of the interior, he had consistently championed the development of unused resources, especially land. Shortly after the United States entered the war, for example, he tried unsuccessfully to get the Council of National Defense to endorse as a war measure a bill to appropriate $5 million to reclaim western land. Even his combination of government training and financial aid for a program of farm colonization to help alleviate surplus labor was not new. Secretary of Labor Wilson had suggested a program incorporating similar principles in his annual report of 1915.[40] These same ideas also long had been basic tenets in the thought and work of Professor Elwood Mead of the University of California, who in March 1917 published a twenty-seven page article titled "Government Aid and Direction in Land Settlement." Mead had lived in Australia and had studied that nation's land colony projects. He was influential in the passage of the California Land Settlement Act of 1918, a blueprint for experimental, planned agricultural settlement. In 1916, Robert Crosser of Ohio had introduced a national colonization bill in Congress embodying

Mead's proposals. Lane was well acquainted with Mead and his work. Early in 1915, he had appointed him chairman of a central board to review the construction costs of reclamation projects.[41] Without a doubt, the plan that Lane suggested to Wilson had been in the public domain of ideas for some time.[42]

Some of the impetus for Lane's letter to Wilson stemmed from interdepartmental rivalry. Before May 1918, the Agriculture and Labor departments, as well as the Interior Department, had planned and promoted postwar land settlements. For example, Tariff Commissioner William Kent, a former Republican congressman from California with a strong interest in conservation, wrote to the President four days before Lane regarding the same subject. Kent, whom Wilson respected, suggested the establishment of a commission under the Department of Labor to coordinate all work being done in land settlement by the various departments. On the day Lane wrote to Wilson, the President replied to Kent's letter with a request for more information about the suggestion. Kent complied, and repeated his belief that the Department of Labor should have jurisdiction of the program.[43] When Lane wrote to Wilson, the Interior Secretary knew about Kent's unofficial lobbying for the Department of Labor. Lane's letter to Wilson, which reminded the President that the Interior Department had handled similar programs in the past, seemed well timed.[44] Kent, meanwhile, continued to keep Wilson informed about the considerable work already done by the Department of Labor. On July 1, 1918, Congress settled the question of jurisdiction by appropriating $100,000 for an Interior Department investigation of the costs and feasibility of preparing swamp and cutover lands for cultivation.

With the exception of his letter to Wilson, Lane did nothing to promote land settlement until after Congress appropriated the modest sum on July 1. After that, however, he championed his plan in speeches and articles. He also elaborated upon his original suggestion and upon his motivation. He had many reasons for promoting a farms-for-veterans program. First, he sincerely believed that such a program would be a show of gratitude to the servicemen he admired. The plan also would help ease inevitable postwar unemployment, develop the nation's resources, reduce farm tenancy, and stop the national trend toward urbanization. All of these measures, he believed, would have a stabilizing effect on the nation.[45] Many persons, of course, shared his concern about the country's political and social stability. His colleague Secretary of Labor

Wilson, for example, predicted that "if there is any serious unemployment, there will be a period of industrial unrest which may lead us to a repetition of the French or the Russian revolution."[46] Lane saw in his land scheme a counter to Wilson's stated fears because he believed that "the happiest people, the best farms, and the soundest political conditions are found where the farmer owns the home and the farm lands." Since Lane considered the veteran a proven American, he also judged him as the best of citizens to put on the land. "There can be no surer insurance for the Nation," he pronounced, "than to put its men on the soil."[47]

Lane soon explained for the public and for congress the details of the plan he had suggested to the President. He proposed copying the centuries-old European pattern of grouping about one hundred small farms around a farm village, and providing "a good schoolhouse, not a one-story affair," churches, "a good moving-picture house," stores, and a town hall. This arrangement would provide a full social life, he maintained, and, furthermore, adequate roads, the automobile, post office, and the telephone would eliminate traditional rural isolation. "Our insane asylums in the West are filled with the wives of farmers," Lane lamented, "who have gone crazy in the dreary isolation of farm life." To carry out his program, Lane recognized that small farming communities had to be attractive, something they had not been in the past. Workmen must build the communities, he contended, at the same time veterans prepared their land for cultivation.[48]

Most Americans wanted the increased patriotism and stability, the reward for veterans, the lessening of unemployment, and the improvement in the quality of rural life that Lane promised his plan would produce, although some doubted that his plan was the best way to effect those particular ends. Nevertheless, he drew considerable support for his project. In his annual message to Congress in December 1918, Wilson heartily endorsed the plan. The *New York Times* praised it in editorials. The last article Theodore Roosevelt wrote before he died was a magazine editorial supporting the proposal. In March 1919, Frederic Howe, lawyer, professor, and reformer, published *The Land and the Soldier,* a book that treated in detail the principles and ideas embodied in the Mead-Lane social approach to organized land settlement. A year later, Mead published his own book, *Helping Men Own Farms: A Practical Discussion of Government Aid in Land Settlement.* When Lane appeared before the

House Committee on Public Lands in May 1919, he disclosed that some 52,000 veterans had expressed an interest in his farm lands proposal; ten months later, the figure stood at 166,161. Forty states and numerous commercial and industrial organizations also endorsed the project. Lane stressed the state-federal cooperation involved and the fact that the program in time would pay for itself. Eventually both the House and Senate committees on public lands favorably reported bills incorporating his suggestions. In the spring of 1919, he reported that "it seems to be the general consensus of opinion that Congress during the coming session will provide the necessary legislation." This assessment proved wrong.[49]

Decisive opposition to his plan came from the commercial farmers and their allies in the Department of Agriculture, farm organizations, farm journals, and agricultural colleges. Fear of overproduction and of depressed prices for farm produce motivated this strong opposition. Lesser opposition derived from fear that land speculators would reap profits from land previously judged useless but which, if Congress approved the plan, would gain new value. Lukewarm support from veteran organizations, who were busy promoting their own proposals, and the fact that the Republican Congress had no desire to grant Wilson his legislative wishes, also hurt Lane's farm bill. A sense of urgency, moreover, never developed because mass unemployment never became a reality.[50]

Lane's concept of the farmer as the most virtuous citizen, his faith in the power of government to create a better society, and his emphasis upon land use fit within the framework of his previous thought and action. In 1911, while an Interstate Commerce commissioner, for example, he expounded in a speech in Chicago that "No man can do a greater service than to turn men from our cities and lead them to the fertile lands of the West. We brag and boast of the size of our cities, but the better boast would be that they were small in size and many in number."[51] He always had championed government action as a positive force; the theme of his Interior Department work, of course, was resource development under federal regulation. His inclination toward practicality rather than adherence to a well-defined political ideology, a trait apparent during the 1890s, remained evident during his attempt to win congressional adoption of his farm plan. Referring to his proposal in September 1918, Lane remarked that "This is not social-

ism, it is common sense applied to a condition, and if it were socialism
and was necessary, I would not be feared by the word."[52]

V

Two of the strongest feelings Lane experienced throughout his life
were his love for the United States and his desire to use the full potential
of the nation's resources. Curiously, it took the impact of the World War I
for the two feelings to combine into a single theme in his thinking. He
termed his love of the United States "Americanism," and he called the
blending of his patriotism with his conservation philosophy by the same
name. His definitions became ambiguous. Among the ways he expressed
his Americanism during his prewar years in the Cabinet was making annual Flag Day observances in the Interior Department major events. Lane
regularly invited all the members of Congress, the Supreme Court justices,
and the President to attend. In 1914, Lane's short Flag Day address, titled
"Makers of the Flag," quickly became a classic of its kind. Wilson praised
it as "rich in patriotism and inspiration." House wrote to Lane predicting
that "You have done something that will live." The next month, a *Review
of Reviews* editorial commented that "A finer expression of this sentiment
has perhaps never been given." The following year, the New York State
Commissioner of Education Dr. John H. Finley requested that "Makers of
the Flag" be read in every classroom.[53]

Lane's patriotism encompassed more than a love of his country; it included admiration of national character, or American spirit. National
character meant many things to him: desire to help the world, a fondness
of adventure, taking advantage of an opportunity to get ahead, believing
in fair play, and a devotion to justice and liberty.[54] Someone born in any
country, Lane maintained, could have the essence of the American spirit,
but Americans possessed this spirit with sufficient strength to elevate it to
the level of national character.

Although he had recognized the relationship between Americanism and
education before the spring of 1917,[55] it took American participation
in the war for him to crystallize the meaning of the relationship and to act
accordingly. The war made him conscious of the dual need for education,
first, to reduce the large percentage of adult illiteracy brought to national
attention by the draft; and second, to make the United States a showplace

of democracy, because he sincerely believed that the United States fought the war to promote worldwide democracy. Once Lane had defined the problem, he worked to solve it.

In the spring of 1918, he started a campaign through his Bureau of Education to educate the native and foreign-born persons who could not read or write. He asked President Wilson to support a bill to provide a modest appropriation for this work. Lane buttressed his request with several arguments: that in the last census (1910), there were 5.5 million Americans over ten years of age who were illiterate, 700,000 of them single males suitable for military service; that illiterates represented an economic loss to the nation's manpower resources; and that an illiterate citizenry lacks access to the mediums of public opinion and the acts of government. "An uninformed democracy," he told Wilson, "is not a democracy."[56] In April, he published an article calling for a greater spirit of Americanism, a deeper insight into the nation's problems, and a firmer sense of purpose. He wanted to make America more "worthwhile to Americans and of higher service to the world."[57] Freedom, responsibility, Americanism, and education were, to Lane, inseparable. He used Russia as an example to illustrate the result of illiteracy. Eighty percent of the Russian people, he pointed out, were illiterate, and this mass ignorance made possible the Bolshevik seizure of power. Throughout the summer and fall of 1918, he wrote, spoke, and lobbied to advance his campaign against illiteracy and for Americanism. In August, although still believing that everyone had in his soul a "mystical quantity which represents . . . Americanism," he wrote that "We want to give a new significance" to the term "Americanism." "We want it to mean help; . . . sympathy; . . . understanding; . . . largeness of view . . . [and] the largest human fellowship. We want that word to be translated into terms of wages for men, of living conditions for men, of justice for those who work for us."[58]

Perhaps he developed the fullest expression of his conception of Americanism in his annual Interior Department report of 1918. In the report, he pleaded to give the tools of Americanism, the ability to read and to write, to all persons living in America. The war had placed upon the United States, he concluded, "a greater burden of national responsibility and a larger sense of the meaning of America—America as a leader of a world of democracies, if not a world of democracy."[59] The United States, he believed, had to be the exemplar of democracy; but, without the means of communication, this was impossible. What kind of a democracy, he demanded to know, allows 10 percent of its adults to remain illiterate, has millions of citizens who can read only foreign newspapers, spends twice as much annually for chewing gum as for schoolbooks, has one state that spends only $6 a year per child for public education, and permits the average teacher to earn less than the average day laborer? The native-born white in less developed areas of the country, the Negro, and the foreign-born were the groups Lane believed most needed help. Education, he recognized, was not an end-all, it was but a beginning. Americanism was many things, both tangible and intangible; it was, moreover, a never-ending process of becoming. Lane ended his 1918 report with these lines: "To be useful is the essence of Americanism, and against the undeveloped resources, whether it be land or man, the spirit of this country makes protest."[60] By late 1918, his conception of Americanism seemed less abstract than it had been earlier. Accordingly, his suggestions for promoting Americanism were more specific.

The war's conclusion did not terminate his concern for eradicating illiteracy or his constant praise of America. He continued to want additional federal funds for the Bureau of Education and championed an improved teaching profession with higher salaries.[61] Education, he asserted, was not solely a matter for individual states; it was a national concern, and he eloquently and consistently called for help from the federal government. Neither Congress nor Wilson answered his call.

Lane believed the United States fought World War I to make the world safe for democracy, and he did everything possible to expedite that war. By the spring of 1918, he had started to think about the reconstruction period. His farms-for-veterans proposal, his campaign against illiteracy, and his praise of Americanism were attempts to improve the United States, much as the United States was attempting to improve the world. He summarized it in this way: "We must not only at this time make the world safe for democracy but we must make democracy safe for the world."[62] Although his thoughts and actions fell short of his idealistic expression, the parallel themes of improving democracy at home and abroad keynoted Lane's war years.

10
Collapsed Hopes and Retirement, 1918-1921

I find myself at fifty-five without a dollar,
in debt, and with no assurances as to the future.
I assure you that it is with the deepest regret
that I leave public life for I like it, and the
public has treated me handsomely. . . .

Lane to Frank W. Mondell,
February 13, 1920

The end has come. We were identified with
an historic period, one of the great days of the
world. . . . I look back over the eight years with
some personal satisfaction.

Lane to Alexander Vogelsang,
March 4, 1921

I

Starting during the war, and symbolized by the election of a Republican
Congress in November 1918 and by the inauguration of a Republican
President in March 1921, the Wilson administration and the country
turned from reform, first at home and then abroad, to accept and even
embrace intolerance and to establish a benevolent stance toward the
business community. The decline of the Wilson administration, the Senate's

refusal to ratify the Treaty of Versailles, and the death of Theodore Roosevelt appeared to Lane as signs of the end of an era. Some of the events that took place during these transitional months, especially the failure of the 1919 Industrial Conference, the bitter labor strikes, the Red scare, and the drift of national politics, troubled him. Although concerned, Lane decided to abandon his career as a public official and instead to seek personal wealth. Once retired from public service, however, his health quickly declined; he died in May 1921 at age fifty-seven.

II

Because of the war, Lane took no active part in the congressional election campaigns of 1918. The most controversial aspect of the elections came on October 25 when Wilson appealed to the country to return Democratic majorities to Congress so he might continue in office unembarrassed. Lane and other Cabinet members opposed Wilson's making the plea, but the President followed the contrary advice of Postmaster General Burleson. A few days later, Lane issued a public statement asking Americans to vote so Wilson would "not be discredited, weakened, or worried by an apparent hesitation on the part of the people to generously support him."[1] All Cabinet members issued similar statements, with the exception of Secretary of War Baker, who declined on the grounds that he wanted to keep the army out of politics.

Lane believed that Wilson had made a "mistake," but he expected the Democrats to maintain their congressional majorities nevertheless. When they did not, he was surprised and thought it "a slap in the face" to Wilson. In addition to Wilson's ill-advised appeal to the nation, Lane attributed the Democrats' defeat to a feeling in the North and West that the administration was pro-southern and also to the fact that the Republicans enjoyed their greatest unity since 1908. The loss of congressional control did not seem to bother Lane, who believed that the end of the war and the subsequent hope of a permanent peace for the world made the elections at home appear ephemeral. The election result, he concluded, "means nothing, so far as international questions are concerned." History would judge the Wilson administration, Lane believed, "by the great things that he has done—the unparallelled things—and the election . . . will get but a line . . .

while the Versailles conference and the Fourteen Points . . . will have books written about them for a century to come."[2] Although the nation's joy over the Armistice and forthcoming peace conference did overshadow the elections, the country continued to suffer from the pernicious forces the war had released.

Perhaps the worst evil the war helped to spawn was an increase of intolerance. Many Americans forgot compassion and mercy, and respect for personal differences. The hatred, hysterias, and brutality of the war years, moreover, continued into the postwar period, bequeathing a legacy that spent itself slowly. The responsibility for the prevalence of this intolerance and its corresponding denials of civil liberties rested with the Wilson administration, which, rather than acting to mitigate the situation, increased its severity. The Espionage Act of June 1917, the Trading-with-the Enemy Act of October 1917, and the Sedition Act of May 1918 provided the legal guise for federal officials to inflict actions born of biases upon other Americans.

Because of his inertia, Lane shared some of the responsibility for this blemished page of the Wilson administration. In some instances, Lane took positive steps to counter intolerance, but his efforts were minor compared to what the situation demanded. For instance, one of the countless loyal Americans to suffer from the oppressive censorship maintained by Postmaster General Burleson was Oswald Villard, editor of the *Nation*. On September 13, 1918, Burleson banned from the mails that week's issue of the *Nation* on the grounds that it contained an unfavorable view of Gompers, who had rendered considerable services to the war effort. Villard took the night train from New York to Washington and immediately called upon his good friend Lane. He advised Villard to "Go straight to the White House and demand to see the President . . . your constitutional rights have been infringed . . . this is an extremely important matter—of vital interest to the press and the country." Lane, House, and Tumulty all intervened on Villard's behalf, with the result that Wilson overruled Burleson and reversed the ban, one of the two times Wilson interferred with Burleson's censorship. In both cases, Wilson knew the victims personally. Indignant though Lane was about Villard's case, he never explored the possibility that other Americans might be in similar unjust situations. Actually there were countless persons who suffered more than Villard.[3]

The hatred of anything German and the shock of the Bolshevik revolution created a domestic hysteria that Americans turned loose on "Reds," radicals, Negroes, Catholics, Jews, foreigners, and dissenters. Although Lane shared with most Americans a revulsion of the Bolsheviks, and although he feared that anarchy threatened America, he never followed fellow Americans in venting his fears upon numerous minority groups. To be sure, he remained alarmed during 1919 over what he considered disloyalty, irresponsible labor, "wild" Negroes, and Red anarchy; but his fears took constructive rather than destructive channels of expression.[4]

Lane's fears prompted him to reflect over the broad questions of social, economic, and political change. Throughout his life, he liked to believe he welcomed change. New conditions, he maintained, necessitated new thinking, new policies, and new programs; he placed little value, therefore, in theoretical models, whether religious, economic, or political. The Bolshevik revolution reaffirmed his views. In the spring of 1918, he analyzed the American "system of life" as too conservative and estimated that it must change within a few years. He believed the question, "What is property?" needed reevaluation. Rhetorically he answered, property belongs "not [to] the man, necessarily, who has it, but the man who can use it to good purpose." Other changes Lane believed the nation would have to adopt to prevent future trouble were national women's suffrage, increased inheritance and income taxes, national life insurance, and tighter control of railroad finances and operation. Further, he predicted that if industry did not introduce profit sharing, it would be nationalized. He believed that his "kind of socialism" was "to have its fling."[5]

Despite his vocabulary, Lane's practicing philosophy never approached the theoretical position of the American socialists of his day. He did endorse a number of proposals that socialists advocated, but he believed that no socialistic scheme provided adequate incentives for the managerial class. He would accept democratic socialism if it came as a result of the ordinary processes of the law, but he much preferred his eclectic, non-doctrinaire approach to government. "The way to beat wild-eyed schemes is to show that they are impractical," Lane wrote to a friend in the summer of 1918. To do this, he advised the application of pragmatic tests. "We are not going to destroy socialism, or prevent it from coming strong," he wrote the following year, "by refusing to answer it." His response to Bolshevistic totalitarian socialism was to advocate the end of illiteracy, to provide greater opportunity, and to encourage change. In an article published in March 1919, he encouraged Congress to assume the responsibility so "that no man who is willing to work shall be without a job."

Eighteen months later he warned presidential candidate James Cox that
"we cannot stand pat and let things drift without their drifting not to the
'good old days' but to bad new days."[6] Lane realized that his view of
democracy and his belief in continual change involved the dangers of
charting new courses without the benefit of landmarks, but he saw no
alternatives. He judged the postwar period a momentous time, and he
concluded that if democracy did not act constructively a dangerous radical
reaction would inevitably follow.[7]

To meet what people called the "Red" challenge, he offered a constructive antidote. Paradoxically, in his attempt to help to bring about
the needed alterations, he may have fanned flames of intolerance while
accomplishing little else. He called for a greater understanding and appreciation of things American. The casual hearer and reader, the superficial
thinker, or the bigot looking for a weapon could distort or misinterpret his
call for Americanism as a demand for conformity and a crusade against
anything foreign; yet, he wanted just the opposite.

Lane did not want to deport or persecute native and foreign-born minority groups; he wanted to blend, not mold, them into the mainstream of
American civilization. "Let them," he wrote in an April 1919, article,
"bring their music, bring their art, bring all their soulfulness, their ancient
experience to the melting pot and let it enrich our mettle. We welcome
every spiritual influence, every cultural urge and in turn we want them to
love America as we love it because it is holy ground—because it serves the
world." This was Lane at his antidogmatic best. In *World Outlook* the
next autumn, he reiterated his belief that America was a blend of sympathies and heritages and called for each citizen annually to "interpret America sympathetically to at least one foreign-born person." The country must
recognize, he counseled, "that there are defects in our land and lacks in
our system; that our programs are not perfect; that our institutions can be
bettered"; but cooperation, he added, would help make the United States
"a land in which there will be a minimum of fear and a maximum of
hope." To help build such a land of hope, he welcomed diversity. In a
speech he delivered in June 1920, when Harvard University conferred
upon him an honorary doctor of laws degree, he accused businessmen
of being carried away with industrial standardization. Urbanization and
standardization, he warned, deny individual expression. "We cannot continue to make great individuals," he lamented, "if we build all men alike
and mould them in common grooves."[8]

Although he repeatedly expressed deep concern for American society
during the last three years of his life, he took little action to correct the
unwelcome trends and abuses he saw. He knew the Wilson administration
suppressed newspapers and denied some citizens their constitutional
rights; he knew self-appointed groups and organizations harried other
Americans;[9] yet he never lashed out or worked directly against the ex-
cesses of some of his associates who were responsible. In his articles,
speeches, and letters, he publicly praised tolerance, justice, and democracy, but he never censured an individual or group directly perverting
the meaning of those ideals. Part of his silence came from his reluctance
to criticize individual actions and motives, and part derived from his
fears of encouraging anarchy. Nevertheless, when the country needed
a popular, respected official to speak out against officials and vigilantes
who corrupted democracy, Lane did not step forward.

His failure to speak out decisively against the perpetrators of intolerance during the war and postwar years served him no credit; his postwar
stand and activities on behalf of Senate ratification of the Treaty of Versailles, on the other hand, deserved praise.

III

Less than a month after the Armistice of November 1918 ended World
War I, Wilson appointed an American peace commission and together with
the members sailed for France to draft a formal peace treaty. By the end
of June, the Peace Conference finished drafting the Treaty of Versailles.
Wilson made certain that the covenant of his proposed League of Nations
was an integral part of the treaty; acceptance or rejection of the treaty
meant acceptance or rejection of the covenant, and vice versa. Long before the Peace Conference ended, however, most observers envisioned
serious difficulty in getting the United States Senate to ratify the treaty
if it incorporated the league's covenant. When the Peace Conference concluded, the struggle between Wilson and those, led by Massachusetts
Senator Henry Cabot Lodge, who opposed American participation in the
league, increased in intensity. The battle continued until the end of May
1920, when hope of Senate ratification died.

Irresponsible political leadership led to Senate rejection of the treaty, with acceptance of the League of Nations charter constituting the base of contention. By July 1919, thirty-two state legislatures and thirty-three governors had endorsed the league. The necessary two-thirds of the Senate also favored ratification, provided the covenant included some mild amendments or reservations. All the situation needed was responsible leadership, which neither Republican Chairman of the Senate Committee on Foreign Relations Lodge nor President Wilson provided. Responsibility for Senate rejection of the treaty (and thus the league) also rested with the small group of irreconcilable senators who opposed ratification and with the Democratic senators who voted against the amended treaty out of fear of Wilson's displeasure. Throughout this sad episode in American political life, Lane acted meritoriously.

At the close of the war, he emphatically agreed with Wilson's conception of an international League of Nations. He also believed, along with Wilson, that the success of the Peace Conference depended upon the President's going to Paris. In January 1919, as the Peace Conference got underway, Lane publicly announced that he strongly favored a League of Nations. Such a league, he proposed, should consist of two bodies, a council to formulate a body of international law and a court to decide upon violations of the law. To enforce adherence to the law, he suggested three steps. First, he wanted the pressure of world disapproval; second, he recommended the stoppage of all imports, exports, and communications to and from the offending nation; and third, he advised mobilizing assistance from all nations to defend any nation that suffered from a breach of international law.[10]

In Lane's opinion, the league would not be a certain cure but "a serious effort to get at the disease"; it would be, he believed, an attempt to fulfill the aspiration of civilized man to make the world a better place in which to live. It would serve as a watchful eye and a warning bell against uncivilized actions. He hoped that in time, the moral effect of the league would help to bring about disarmament. But in 1919, he saw the league as merely a first step in that direction that just as easily could have been taken in 1910 when Theodore Roosevelt suggested it. Until early August 1919, Lane expected Senate ratification of the Treaty of Versailles.

By early August, the display of personal and partisan prejudices made clear to him that Wilson could not expect to secure passage of the treaty without reservations of some kind. Lane considered reservations unnecessary because he sincerely believed that the nation "might, even selfishly, surrender more than this covenant calls for, if only that such an experiment might have its chance!" Nevertheless, he would have accepted reservations gladly to gain ratification. In October 1919, he put his finger directly upon the problem when he complained that "The whole damn thing has gotten into the maelstrom of politics, of the nastiest partisanship, when it ought to have been lifted up into the clearer air of good sense and national dignity."[12] Unfortunately for the country, neither Wilson nor Lodge, nor many other senators, shared Lane's view.

He did his utmost to back the league. He enthusiastically supported the activities of the League to Enforce Peace, a public nongovernmental organization that endorsed ratification; and after the Senate voted against ratification in November 1919, Lane, along with many Democratic leaders, urged Wilson to adopt a more conciliatory position. In January 1920, a number of Democratic senators held a series of conferences with some of their Republican peers to work out a bipartisan solution to the deadlock. As a result of these conferences, Tumulty, Lansing, Baker, Houston, and Lane composed a letter they wanted Wilson to send to Democratic Senator Gilbert M. Hitchcock. The letter, conciliatory in tone, was a masterful attempt of compromise. Lansing and Houston both claimed the treaty would have been ratified quickly had Wilson used the letter. But Wilson, recovering from a debilitating stroke, never even acknowledged he received the document. With Wilson's position frozen, there was little the more responsible Democratic leaders such as Lane could do. As the chances for American participation in the league ebbed away, he blamed Wilson for failing to reach an obtainable common ground with the Republican-controlled Congress.[13]

The restlessness of labor during the postwar era also saddened Lane. Throughout his life, he sympathized with labor's objectives because he considered them democratic and just. In 1916, for example, he concluded that "the American Federation of Labor has for a quarter of a century led in a movement that will make our national life more nearly approach those classic standards of liberty, equality, and fraternity." His feelings toward labor, and his worry about the disruptive effects upon the nation's work force that inevitably would come with the end of the war, had prompted him in May 1918 to introduce his farms-for-veterans program. The following January, with the Armistice two months old, he expressed his concern by cabling Wilson at the Paris Peace Conference, urging the

President to open European markets to American copper exports for "our own internal industrial peace." Seven months later, Lane still was reminding Wilson of the benefits to the economy that would accrue from increased American exports to European nations, especially to Germany.[14] By the late summer of 1919, however, as the number of strikes mounted, Lane feared that labor might go to extremes in an attempt to satisfy their demands. At the same time, he concluded that employers moved too slowly in passing on to labor a greater share of industrial profit. He did not like the prospects of a labor-capital economic split in American society. Fixed classes, he maintained, had no place in a democracy in which there was opportunity for upward mobility. Instead, he believed in a community of interest between labor, capital, management, and the public. This emphasis upon cooperation and responsibility seemed to him the best solution to the economic tangle that he observed approaching a climax.

On August 28, 1919, Lane repeating an idea he had set forth several weeks earlier, declared in a prepared press statement that Wilson without delay should call a conference of representatives of labor, capital, management, and the public to meet in Washington for a discussion of the serious economic problems facing the nation.[15] Six days later, Wilson followed Lane's suggestion and summoned a conference to meet in October. He asked for voluntary cooperation among capitalists, managers, and workmen, and promised to fight for federal legislation if it would help. "The object of all reform in this essential matter," Wilson declared, reflecting some of his prewar progressivism, "must be a genuine democratization of industry based upon the full recognition of the rights of those who work, in whatever rank, to participate in some organic way in every decision which directly affects their welfare or the part they play in industry." To help bring about the voluntary cooperation he desired, Wilson suggested that Chamber of Commerce of the United States of America, the American Federation of Labor, the farm organizations, the National Industrial Conference, the investment bankers, and the President himself all choose conferees. By the time the conference met, the expanded list of delegates included selections from the Railroad Brotherhoods, railroad managers, and women's organizations. The conferees represented three groups: labor, capital, and the public, with Wilson selecting the representatives for the public. Secretary of Labor Wilson, presiding as temporary chairman, opened the Industrial Conference on October 6, 1919, in the Pan American Union Building.[16]

From the start, President Wilson wanted the conference to organize itself, establish its own rules, and find its own methods of facing its formidable challenge. The conference immediately selected Lane as its permanent chairman because representatives of both the business community and labor respected him. Samuel Gompers, for example, seconded the nomination of his long-time friend with a glowing tribute.[17] Lane aimed his opening speech at what he hoped would be a common middle ground. "We will draft here," he announced, "a declaration of dependence, not of independence; a declaration that we are united with one another . . . that we must join hands together, not just for our sake alone, but for greater sake of our country and of the world." He also reiterated a number of his familiar themes, including his belief that democracy was a continuing process, not a fixed condition, and that the United States required no class interests because opportunity flourished unlimitedly. The solution to the current economic problems, he reasoned, was not to aim for some distant goal, but to take a first step toward it. He spoke optimistically, but the conference had little chance for success.[18]

While the conference met, the steel industry maneuvered to break an industry-wide strike, organized labor's most important postwar effort to advance the concept and practice of collective bargaining. Violence increased. Newspaper headlines on the second day of the conference read "Federal Troops Now Guard Gary. Martial Law Declared."[19] Reverberations of the steel strike constantly echoed in the Pan American Union Building's "Hall of Americas."

The representatives of labor firmly maintained the conference could get nowhere unless capital recognized labor's right to collective bargaining. At the same time, the employers' group adamantly refused to grant this recognition. On October 21, the conference decisively voted down Gompers' plan for arbitration of the steel strike and his proposal for recognition of the right of collective bargaining. Only labor representatives supported his proposals. The next day the employers' group refused to accept labor's final resolution, which stated that "The right of wage earners to organize without discrimination by representatives of their own choosing in negotiations and adjustments with employers in respect to wages, hours of labor, and relations and conditions of employment is recognized."[20] Following the rejection of this resolution, the labor representatives walked out of the conference.

Lane worked to prevent labor's walkout. On October 19, he wrote

to the President, who was gravely ill at the time, requesting a letter from
him to the conference to be used as a last appeal. With his request, he
enclosed a suggested letter. Wilson complied with Lane's suggestion,
but even a letter from the President did not bring the disputing factions
of the conference any closer together. The conference failed, Lane concluded, "because we got into the steel strike at first, and people talked
about their rights instead of their duties." He wanted the contingent
of public representatives to remain in conference, but on October 24,
the group submitted its report to Wilson with the recommendation he
call another industrial conference; Lane concurred with the recommendation. Almost all conferees agreed that none of the participants
of the first conference should take part in the second. On December 1,
1919, the President convened the Second Industrial Conference which,
like its predecessor, proved unsuccessful.[21]

The failure of the two industrial conferences and management's
victory in the steel and other strikes during 1919 doomed Lane's hope
of establishing a concert of labor-management interests. He persisted
in his concern for labor, however. Late in July 1920, when Democratic
presidential nominee James M. Cox invited him to express his opinions
on public questions, Lane advised working "toward a condition in which
Labor will have recognition and be more certainly insured against the
perils of non-occupation and old age, and capital become entitled to a
sure return." Instead of a cooperative labor-capital advance, after the
election that autumn, he lamented that "nothing constructive is opened
by the world for men to think upon, as a means of bettering their lot."[22]

During the postwar period, the country's failure to ratify the treaty,
the Democratic party's failure to enlist effective leadership, and the failure of labor and management to come to agreement (even within the
Industrial Conference) disappointed him, but the event that moved him
most was the death of Theodore Roosevelt in January 1919. During the
Wilson administration, Lane criticized some of Roosevelt's less temperate
remarks and positions, although these chidings never lessened his esteem
for the former Rough Rider. In December 1915, Lane commented to his
friend John Wigmore that Roosevelt "hates Wilson so, that he has lost
his mind." During the campaign of 1916, Lane and Roosevelt publicly
exchanged letters of opposing views concerning the latter's criticism of
diplomatic note sending.[23] However, shortly after Roosevelt's death,
Lane summarized that the former President's major fault was "that he

took defeat too hard. He had a sort of 'divine right' idea," Lane analyzed, "but he was a bully fighter." Lane added, "Of course . . . he said a lot of things that were unjust and unjustifiable, but if a fellow doesn't make a damned fool of himself once in a while he wouldn't be human." Although aware of his faults, Lane revered Roosevelt more than any other public figure. He was, Lane believed, "a great and good man, a man's man, always playing his game in the open."[24]

Following Roosevelt's death, Lane worked to honor the former President. He attended the funeral and a few days later helped to initiate a drive to establish a lasting memorial to Roosevelt in the creation of a national park in California. Lane became a charter member and a trustee of the Roosevelt Memorial Association, an organization dedicated to erecting a memorial in Washington comparable to the Washington Monument and the Lincoln Memorial; to improving Roosevelt's land in Oyster Bay, donated by the family as a memorial park; and to perpetuating Roosevelt's ideals by spreading the knowledge of his career and character. When the House Pensions Committee considered granting an annual pension to Mrs. Roosevelt, Lane endorsed the proposal in a letter to the committee. The committee found his letter "one of the most beautiful, fair, and just tributes" to Roosevelt it received. Consequently, the committee adopted Lane's letter as part of its favorable report on the pension bill.[25]

During his lifetime, Roosevelt had returned the respect Lane paid him. In 1914, for instance, Roosevelt told him that "I hear nothing but good of you—but if I did hear anything else I should not pay any heed to it." The summer of 1918, Roosevelt remarked to Lane that "you know how strong my feeling for you has always been." Six weeks before his death, the former President described Lane to William Allen White as "not only the best, but the only good man in Wilson's Cabinet."[26] Roosevelt's death on January 6, 1919, marked a sad beginning to a year that included disappointments for Lane regarding Wilson's leadership, Senate nonratification of the league, a national mood of intolerance, and the Industrial Conference; the year ended, however, on a happier note.

IV

On December 17, 1919, Lane confirmed reports that he intended to resign from the Cabinet in the near future. The praise for him that ensued in newspaper editorials across the country gave him a sense of profound satisfaction. Despite his western orientation, many of the expressions of praise for his abilities, and of regret over his resignation, originated in the East. The *New York Times* commented that he "would be a Presidential probability," were he native-born. "There has been," the editorial continued, "no more useful public servant than Franklin K. Lane." The *New York World* voiced its opinion he was "one of the ablest men now in public life." Another of New York City's major papers, the *New York Tribune,* added that Lane, unlike many persons in the Wilson administration, had grown steadily in the public's respect. "A good many things would be better," its editorial continued, "it he had been more called into counsel." Part way across the continent, the *Sioux City Journal* expressed similar sentiment, and added he was the "most capable, efficient, and . . . best balanced Cabinet member." At the eastern edge of the Rockies, the *Denver News* claimed no other man in the Wilson administration "stands higher in public regard and confidence. . . . We have had from him enlightenment and inspiration." Editorial acclaim also appeared in other cities, such as Baltimore, Richmond, Chattanooga, and Sacramento.[27]

After February 7, 1920, when Wilson formally accepted Lane's resignation, newspapers published another laudatory round. The *Portland Telegram* declared it doubted "if in the history of public service in this country any man ever relinquished a public trust that was generally acknowledged to have been so well administered as that which has been under Mr. Lane's direction during the past seven years." Had he been born in the United States, the editorial continued, "he today would be, pre-eminently, the available candidate for president on the Democratic ticket." Also on the West Coast, the official paper of the local and state building-trades councils of California mourned the trade unions' loss of "a staunch friend," praised his public record, and wished him well. Perhaps the editorial best summarizing public attitude toward him at this time was the February 9, 1920, editorial of the *Washington Post.* "Mr. Lane is recognized," it read, "as one of the best equipped men identified with the Wilson administration, in fact, one whose equipment has been far superior to the tasks assigned him, whose ability the President has not availed himself to the full. . . . Were Mr. Lane of American birth there is little doubt that he now would be seriously considered for the leadership of his party in the approaching campaign. . . . He leaves the Cabinet with a fine record of accomplishment . . . and with the respect and gratitude of his countrymen."[28]

Lane enjoyed the commendation that accompanied him throughout his public career, and he disliked relinquishing the rewards of public service. But in 1919, he was fifty-five years old and in debt.[29] With the prospect of perhaps only ten years of employment before him, and a wife who was far from well, he decided to accept one of the many attractive business positions he had previously rejected. Lane did not resign because of a strained relationship with Wilson. Although he admitted that it was "hard for him [Wilson] to get on with anyone who had any will or independent judgment," he repeatedly stated he was leaving the Cabinet "without a grouch, without a complaint or a criticism—with a great admiration for Wilson and with a thorough knowledge of his defects."[30] Had Lane not had financial worries,[31] he would have remained in the Cabinet until the end of Wilson's administration.

In September, he planned to submit his resignation to Wilson as soon as the President returned from his trip west to enlist support for the ratification of the Versailles Treaty. Lane wanted to leave office on November 1. In the middle of the trip, however, Wilson's health failed; his doctor canceled the speaking schedule and rushed the President back to Washington. On October 4, Lane and Lansing discussed their mutual desires to retire from the Cabinet, but both agreed they should wait until Wilson recovered. By early February 1920, Wilson's doctor decided the time was opportune, and Lane finally submitted his resignation, effective March 1.[32]

Employment opportunities were plentiful for Lane had much to offer. An experienced lawyer, journalist-editor, and administrator, he was articulate on paper, captivating on a speaker's platform, and likeable on an individual basis. Moreover, he had friends the country over. During the war, a well-known New York law firm had offered him a position that guaranteed $30,000 annually plus contingent profits. In November 1919, Lane wrote to his brother that he had been "offered two fifty thousand a year places, and another even more." Two months later, he declined a salaried position with the Pan Pacific Union while he seriously considered assuming the presidency of the Fidelity and Deposit Company of Maryland. Late in 1920, this company hired one of Lane's best friends, Franklin D. Roosevelt, as vice-president at $25,000 per year. On February 17, ten days after Wilson accepted Lane's resignation, President Edward J. Doheny of the Pan American Petroleum and Transport Company and the Mexican Petroleum Company, announced Lane's decision to accept a vice-presidency of the two companies, at a salary of $50,000 annually. His new salary represented an increase of $38,000 over what he earned as secretary of the interior.[33]

Although Lane left the Cabinet, he maintained his interest in politics. Two days before he left the Interior building for the last time, he wrote to Wilson urging him to consider a number of changes to make the federal government more efficient. The government, in Lane's opinion, was "honest beyond any commercial standard"; moreover, federal officials wanted to promote the public good and possessed the ability to do so, but they lacked the organizational tools. Infinite details, he complained, inundated public servants while many officials were unwilling to take responsibility. "Everyone seems to be afraid of everyone," he observed, and there were too many checks upon public servants. He called for more authority and responsibility residing in the lower levels of the government and more planning, engineering, and statesmanship emanating from those in higher positions. Lane believed that employing a system of either rapid promotions or early discharge, along with doubling salaries for top administrative officials, would improve governmental administration.[34] His assessment no doubt evolved, in part, from his own financial situation and from his affinity for efficient use of resources. After he left, he continued, as a private citizen, to voice opinions and proposals about improvement of government operations.[35]

Lane also accepted three appointments that reflected his continuous interest in public service. In May 1920, he served as national chairman of the Salvation Army's Second Home Appeal. The following November, he became treasurer of the European Relief Council, a merger of eight large relief organizations, under the chairmanship of Herbert Hoover. Four months later, Lane won election to the board of trustees of John D. Rockefeller's General Education Board.[36]

As the 1920 elections drew near, Lane doubted that the Democrats had much chance for success. His pessimism centered on Wilson himself. At least as early as 1916, Lane had been highly critical of Wilson's lack of interest in party organization. He would "leave a mere shadow of a party," Lane ventured, "Unless he takes an interest in reorganizing it."[37] During the campaign of 1920, Lane predicted defeat and placed the blame squarely upon Wilson. "The little Wilson (as distinguished from the Great Wilson)," Lane wrote in September, "is now having his day." He believed Wilson could have helped the situation if he had been frank about his illness. People might then have been sympathetic enough to excuse some of his dogmatic actions. Cox would lose, Lane asserted, not because of his campaign, but because of anti-Wilson feeling. On November 1, 1920, Lane gloomily wrote that the Democrats were "to be badly smashed nationally."[38] After the election, he continued to be pessimistic about the Democratic party. For the previous eight years, he remarked, "all possible leaders have been submerged, squelched, [and] drowned out." The party, he rued a few days later, had "no force, no will, [and] no self-confidence."[39]

Although he saw little to cheer about in either party in 1920, he judged that Herbert Hoover possessed qualities of leadership the country needed desperately. Hoover had impressed Lane favorably at their first meeting in 1915. In January 1917, Hoover reluctantly declined Lane's offer to become assistant secretary of the interior. Their friendship deepened during World War I while Hoover served as food administrator and occasionally sought professional advice from Lane.[40] By October 1919, Lane considered Hoover a prime presidential candidate. "Hoover can be elected," he told a friend, and added that the country needed him. A few months later, he told another friend that Hoover was neither a Democrat nor a Republican, having "voted for Wilson, Roosevelt, and McKinley. But he is sane, progressive, competent." Hoover's knowledge of European and American affairs, his administrative ability, and his grasp of economics, particularly impressed Lane. "It would not surprise me to see him nominated on either ticket," Lane declared, "and I believe I will vote for him now as against anybody else."[41] The Democrats might have nominated Hoover in 1920, had he not ended that possibility by announcing he was a Republican. Hoover's announcement, however, did not diminish Lane's hope of seeing him in the White House. Until the end of his life, he viewed Hoover as the man who could best carry out progressive ideals and constructive statesmanship in the 1920s.[42]

On various occasions during 1920 and 1921, Lane explained his conception of the progressive ideals he believed Hoover represented. "We want. . . ," he wrote to candidate Cox, "better schools, better roads, . . . better means of distribution of products, . . . more men with garden homes instead of tenement houses, . . . more stored water for irrigation, more hydro-electric plants, . . . electric lights upon the farm, . . . streams controlled, . . . [and] our unused lands put to use." Lane believed the nation needed to eliminate illiteracy, to dignify the teaching profession, and to give all boys and girls as nearly an equal opportunity as possible. To accomplish the latter, he advocated an increasingly heavier inheritance tax. "There must come to society," he explained, "an increasingly large portion of the wealth created by each generation. . . . Thus all boys and girls will start the race of life more nearly at the scratch." Lane's final words expressed a concern for "the negroes being lynched, the miners' civil war, labor's hold ups, employers' ruthlessness, the subordination of humanity to industry." Although his progressive ideals prompted him to want "to help in any way I can to make this administration [Harding's] a success," his activity in public affairs since leaving the Cabinet had changed from occupation to avocation. Four days before he died, however, he wrote to a friend, "I feel a faith growing in me, and I may yet draw my sword in some good fight."[43]

Actually, the concern that dominated his capabilities after his Cabinet resignation was health. During the summer of 1920, his health began to fail. Early in September, his doctors ordered him to take a complete rest because he suffered from angina pectoris and internal gases. After two weeks in Katonah, New York, he went to Bethel, Maine for a longer rest. About December 1, 1920, he returned to New York and, after a brief stay, traveled to Washington to see his married daughter and to visit friends. On December 31, Lane arrived at the Mayo Clinic in Rochester, Minnesota.

During the summer and fall of 1920, he had seen a number of doctors, who disagreed in their diagnoses of the nature of his illness. The Mayo Clinic doctors, however, confirmed the conclusions of his last New York doctors that his gall bladder needed to be removed, but they did not want to operate during the winter for fear of his contracting pneumonia. Instead, they removed his tonsils and told him to rest in the California sun until warm weather. Lane followed the doctors' instructions. In the spring, he left California to attend his son's wedding, on April 23, 1921, near Lake City, Minnesota. From there he returned to the Mayo Clinic for his operation. On May 6, Dr. Will Mayo removed Lane's stone-filled gall bladder and his seriously infected appendix. Dr. Mayo and other hospital doctors hoped the operation would result in the easing of the severity of Lane's heart condition; it did not. Twelve days later, on May 18, his heart failed.[44]

One of the many persons who followed the course of Lane's health was Hoover, who returned his friend's affection and respect. In March

1921, while Lane rested in the California sun, Hoover wrote to him that "not a day goes by that your name is not mentioned in our household." After Lane's operation, Hoover requested Dr. Mayo to telegraph to him news of his friend's condition.[45]

Eulogies to Lane indicated that the idealism he often expressed found sympathetic ears in the newspaper world as well as among his friends. The *New York Times* commented, "it would be hard to find a . . . man . . . who illustrated better the best qualities of American character and public service than Franklin K. Lane." Editorially, the *World's Work* remarked, "the country has lost one of its most wholesome national characters." The *Washington Post* editorialized, "if he had been born in the United States, he probably would have been nominated for the Presidency by the Democratic party, and if nominated he probably would have been elected." Oswald Villard, in the *Nation,* made the same assertion. Lane received praise for having been the strongest and the most able man in the Wilson Cabinet. Americans from coast to coast believed they had lost a friend.[46]

Individuals and organizations honored Lane's memory by giving his name to a peak in Mount Rainier National Park, to a redwood grove in California, and to a high school in Brooklyn, New York. During World War II, the United States Maritime Commission christened a liberty ship with Lane's name, a tribute extended to only one other Interior Secretary, Carl Schurz.[47]

Several friends honored him in an unusual fashion. Stephen T. Mather and Adolph C. Miller, friends who had first known Lane in California, quietly endowed a trust fund to provide a lifelong income for his widow. By personal letter, they asked for additional contributions from other friends, including Hoover, and Franklin D. Roosevelt, with whom Lane had developed close friendships during the Cabinet years. Within four months, his friends donated almost $100,000 to augment his original estate of less than $10,000. In September 1921, news of the fund spread to the press, and as a consequence, the general public also contributed. Hoover, Miller, and Roosevelt served as trustees for the fund, which, they decided, should go to the University of California, Berkeley, after the death of Anne Lane.[48]

A few years after Lane's death, when the Teapot Dome oil scandal seriously involved his former employer, Edward L. Doheny and splashed suspicion on some Democrats as well as Republicans, Lane's friends and associates stood ready to disclaim any wrongdoing on his part. In April

1924, following a winter of corruption disclosures, Mark Sullivan, one of the decade's most successful journalists, in writing about "Public Men and Big Business," insisted, "Lane would never have done anything questionable for his new employer, or for anybody else." Four years later, Teapot Dome was still in the news because of the trials stemming from Senate investigations. During a Senate discussion, Republican Senator Arthur Robinson of Indiana asked an insinuating question about Lane. "Quick as a flash," the *New York Times* reported, "Senators [David A.] Reid of Pennsylvania and [Hiram] Johnson of California, Republicans, and Senators [Carter] Glass of Virginia and [Thomas J.] Walsh of Montana, Democrats, resented the implication against Mr. Lane." Walsh, who headed the Senate investigation of Teapot Dome, and Johnson were progressive westerners, while Glass and Reid were political conservatives from the South and East. The four senators represented a broad range within American politics; yet they shared similar respect for Lane.[49]

Lane left a legacy that was easy for his friends to defend and to respect. He had been an honest, fair-minded person, with "a genius for friendship," as Josephus Daniels remembered. Lane's accomplishments included reform activities, issue-oriented election campaigns, efficient administration, and influence on legislation that earned him widespread national praise. The areas of his interests—political reform, railroad regulation, and federal control and development of natural resources— were major public concerns of his generation. Because of this, and because of his personality, Lane was able to use his positions, first as a local politician, then as an interstate commerce commissioner, and, finally, as a Cabinet member, to promote his career and reputation. The fact that he gained greater recognition than usually accrued to persons holding similar offices attested to his ability. Perhaps the most remarkable aspect of his life, however, was not his ability or his achievements, but his consistency. Lane, the outgoing teenager with a Christian ethic and a commitment to reform, grew older and worked at an increasingly greater level of responsibility, but his values and attitudes remained the same. The success he enjoyed resulted from the extent to which his contemporary Americans shared these values and attitudes.

Notes

INTRODUCTION

1. Three recent historiographical essays dealing with progressivism are Robert H. Wiebe, "The Progressive Years, 1900-1917," in *The Reinterpretation of American History and Culture,* ed. William H. Cartwright and Richard L. Watson (Washington, D.C.: National Council for the Social Studies, 1973), pp. 425-42; David M. Kennedy, "Overview: The Progressive Era," *The Historian* XXXVII (May 1975): 453-68; and Gerald N. Grob and George Athan Billas, "The Progressive Movement: Liberal or Conservative?" *Interpretations of American History,* vol. II (New York: The Free Press, 1978), pp. 215-31. For a useful collection of readings, see Arthur Mann, ed. *The Progressive Era* (Hinsdale, Ill.: The Dryden Press, 1975). Syntheses of the Progressive Era are plentiful. Three of the newest are William L. O'Neill, *The Progressive Era* (New York: Dodd, Mead and Company, 1975); J. Leonard Bates, *The United States: 1898-1928* (New York: McGraw-Hill Book Company, 1976); and Richard L. Watson, Jr., *The Development of National Power: The United States, 1900-1919* (Boston: Houghton Mifflin Company, 1976).

2. My classifications are taken from Kennedy, "Overview: The Progressive Era," especially p. 454.

3. Richard Hofstadter, *The Age of Reform* (New York: Vintage, 1960; originally published by Alfred A. Knopf, in 1955), p. 135.

4. Gabriel Kolko, *The Triumph of Conservativism* (New York: The Free Press, 1963), pp. 2-3.

5. Professional historians who disagreed with Kolko have handled the matter in various ways. In researching their prize-winning book, *The Republican Command, 1897-1913* (Lexington: The University Press of Kentucky, 1971), Horace Samuel Merrill and Marion Galbraith Merrill

found the Kolko assertions without basis and remained silent, letting
their work tell a different story. Richard H. K. Vietor, on the other hand,
directly challenged Kolko in an article, "Businessmen and the Political
Economy: The Railroad Rate Controversy of 1905," *The Journal of
American History* LXIV (June 1977). With convincing documentation,
Vietor concluded that "Big business, and particularly the railroads, did
not initiate expanded governmental involvement in the market economy"
(p. 66).

6. Wiebe, "The Progressive Years, 1900-1919," pp. 425, 439.

7. *Mississippi Valley Historical Review* XLIV (June 1957): 29-57.

CHAPTER 1

1. My summary of Lane's early years rests upon the "Introduction"
in Anne Wintermute Lane and Louise Herrick Wall, eds., *The Letters of
Franklin K. Lane* (Boston: Houghton Mifflin Company, 1922), pp. 1-8;
and upon Henry W. Wiens, "The Career of Franklin K. Lane in California
Politics" (m.a. thesis, University of California, Berkeley, 1936), pp. 1-5.
For this portion of Lane's life, Wiens relied heavily upon interviews with
Lane's sister and brother, Maude Lane Anderson and George W. Lane.

2. Quoted in "Introduction," Lane and Wall, *Letters*, p. 10.

3. Lane and Wall, commentary, pp. 17-18; and "Introduction," pp.
9-12; Lane to Charles McClatchy, n.d. January 1912, p. 83; and Lane to
John H. Wigmore, 27 February 1888, p. 18; all Lane and Wall, *Letters;*
Walton Bean, *Boss Ruef's San Francisco* (Berkeley: The University of
California Press, 1952), pp. 1-2; Wiens, "Lane in California," pp. 7-12,
19; and Oscar T. Shuck, ed., *History of the Bench and Bar in California*
(Los Angeles: The Commerical Printing House, 1901), p. 1078.

4. Lane to Wigmore, 27 February 1888, 9 May 1888, Lane and Wall,
Letters, pp. 18-20. For a memoir description of Lane and his work by
a fellow reporter, see Lawrence F. Abbott, "A Passionate American,"
The Outlook CXXVIII (1 June 1921): 205-6.

5. For the league and the fight for ballot reform, see Lane to Wigmore, 20 September 1888, p. 20, 2 December 1888, pp. 20-21, 29 January
1889, p. 22, and 17 February 1889, pp. 22-23, all Lane and Wall, *Letters;*
Robert E. Hennings, "James D. Phelan and the Wilson Progressives in
California" (Ph.D. diss., University of California, Berkeley, 1961), pp. 18-
19, 21; and Wiens, "Lane in California," pp. 14-18.

6. Lane and Wall, commentary, pp. 24-27; and Lane to John W. Hal-

lowell, 9 December 1920, p. 375; both Lane and Wall, *Letters;* Lane to Henry George, 14 August 1891, Henry George Papers; and "Lane, the White Hope of the Wilson Cabinet," *Current Opinion* LV (September 1912): 163.

7. *Tacoma Daily News,* 7 July and 11 July 1892, both p. 4. Unless otherwise cited, all references to the *Tacoma Daily News* will be editorials. Although the editorials were unsigned, Lane obviously wrote them. Some, for example, 15 November 1892 and 28 February 1894, reflected a knowledge of San Francisco possible only by a one-time resident. The editorials, moreover, are consistent in prose, content, and opinion with Lane's known pre- and post-Tacoma sentiment and writing. One of the reasons Lane purchased the paper, of course, was to express his views.

8. For labor views, see 13 July, 24 August, and 12 October 1892, all p. 4.

9. Ibid., 22 July, 27 September, and 12 November 1892, all p. 4; 7 July and 10 July 1893, both p. 4.

10. The tariff issue was of vital concern to Lane at least as early as 1888; see Lane to John H. Wigmore, 2 December 1888, Lane and Wall, *Letters,* p. 21. For antitariff sentiment, See *Tacoma Daily News,* 8, 9, 12, and 15 July, 2 September and 12 and 22 November 1892, all p. 4; 19 September and 13 December 1893, both p. 2; and 16 April and 14 and 25 May 1894, all p. 2.

11. *Tacoma Daily News,* 5 July 1892, p. 4.

12. Ibid., 5 and 15 July, 22 October, and 10, 12, 14, 15, and 18 November 1892, all p. 4; 19 September and 27 December 1893, both p. 2; and 13 January, 16 April, 12 May, and 12 June 1894, all p. 2.

13. Ibid., 6 March and 12 June 1894, both p. 2; Wiens, "Lane in California," pp. 25-27, Lane and Wall, commentary, pp. 28-31; and Lane to John H. Wigmore, 25 October 1894, Lane and Wall, *Letters,* p. 30.

CHAPTER 2

1. *Arthur McEwen's Letter,* 17 February 1894, pp. 1 and 2, and 3 March 1894, p. 1.

2. *Tacoma Daily News,* 28 February 1894, p. 2.

3. *Arthur McEwen's Letter,* 5 May 1894, p. 1; for glimpses of McEwen, see W. A. Swanberg, *Citizen Hearst* (New York: Charles Scribner's Sons, 1961), pp. 52, 59, 73-75, 197; Henry W. Wiens, "The Career of

Franklin K. Lane in California Politics" (M.A. thesis, University of California, Berkeley, 1936), pp. 28, 30; and Will Irwin, "Franklin K. Lane: The Story of a Presidential Impossibility," *Collier's* LIV (26 February 1916): 12.

4. A notable example of one of the friends Lane made during these years was Ernest Lister. While in Tacoma, Lane helped nominate and elect Lister, then a young foundry worker, to the city council. Lister went on to become governor of Washington from 1913 to his death in 1918. See press memo of the speech Lane gave at the unveiling of the Washington State memorial tablet in the Washington Monument, 1 October 1914, Franklin K. Lane Papers.

5. George Mowry, *The California Progressives* (Berkeley: The University of California Press, 1951), p. 9; Walton Bean, *Boss Ruef's San Francisco* (Berkeley: The University of California Press, 1952), pp. 8-10; Robert E. Hennings, "James D. Phelan and the Wilson Progressives in California" (Ph.D. diss., University of California, Berkeley, 1961); Wiens, "Lane in California," pp. 31-32; Fremont Older, *My Own Story* (New York: The Macmillan Company, 1926), pp. 14-24; and Alexander Callow, Jr., "San Francisco's Blind Boss," *Pacific Historical Review* XXV (August 1956): 262.

6. Wiens, "Lane in California," pp. 32-34; Hennings, "James D. Phelan," pp. 27-28; Older, *My Own Story,* p. 24; James D. Hay, Jr., "The Fighting Commissioner," *Cosmopolitan Magazine* L (March 1911): 570.

7. Lane to John H. Wigmore, 14 November 1898, in Anne Wintermute Lane and Louise Herrick Wall, eds., *The Letters of Franklin K. Lane* (Boston: Houghton Mifflin Company, 1922), p. 34.

8. Wiens, "Lane in California," pp. 34-40; Hennings, "James D. Phelan," p. 28; Irwin, "Franklin K. Lane: The Story of a Presidential Impossibility," p. 13; Lane to Wigmore, 14 November 1898, pp. 33-34, and Lane to P. T. Spurgeon, 30 December 1913, pp. 32-33, both Lane and Wall, *Letters;* Lane, "The Present Political Outlook," *Overland Monthly* XXXII (August 1898): 145-49.

9. Lane to P. T. Spurgeon, 30 December 1913, Lane and Wall, *Letters,* p. 33.

10. Lane to Wigmore, 10 November 1901, ibid., p. 36.

11. Commentary, pp. 31-32, and Lane to Wigmore, 10 November 1901, pp. 35-36, both ibid.; Hennings, "James D. Phelan," p. 29; Wiens, "Lane in California," pp. 41-44; Oscar T. Shuck, *History of the Bench and Bar of California* (Los Angeles: The Commercial Printing House, 1901), p. 1038; and *Official Opinions and Communications of Franklin K. Lane* (San Francisco: The City and County of San Francisco, 1902).

12. Lane to Wigmore, 14 November 1898, Lane and Wall, *Letters,* p. 34; Wiens, "Lane in California," p. 49.

13. My account of Lane's nomination is based upon Wiens, "Lane in California," pp. 50-62; and upon Edward Fawsitt Staniford, "Governor in the Middle: The Administration of George C. Pardee, Governor of California, 1903-1907" (Ph.D. diss., University of California, Berkeley, 1955), pp. 73-75.

14. For an assessment of Pardee, see Staniford, "Governor in the Middle"; and H. Brett Melendy and Benjamin F. Gilbert, *The Governors of California* (Georgetown, Calif.: The Talisman Press, 1965), pp. 274, 286.

15. Both quotations in this paragraph are from an undated campaign speech found in the Lane Papers.

16. Lane to Woodrow Wilson, 3 July 1912, series 2, The Woodrow Wilson Papers.

17. For Lane's campaign, see Staniford, "Governor in the Middle," chap. 4; Wiens, "Lane in California," pp. 65-80; Irwin, "Franklin K. Lane: The Story of a Presidential Impossibility," p. 13; Benjamin Ide Wheeler to Theodore Roosevelt, 10 March 1903, The Benjamin Ide Wheeler Papers.

18. Pardee to Lane, 4 September 1902, and Lane to Pardee, 8 September 1902, both quoted on p. 78 of Staniford, "Governor in the Middle." For Pardee's campaign, see ibid., chap. 4.

19. *California Blue Book: 1903,* p. 332.

20. *San Francisco Star,* 8 November 1902, p. 1, quoted in Wiens, "Lane in California," p. 82.

21. Lane to Wigmore, 26 January 1904, Lane and Wall, *Letters,* p. 44.

22. *San Francisco Bulletin,* 1 October 1903, p. 14; Wiens, "Lane in California," p. 106.

23. *San Francisco Bulletin,* 8 October 1903, p. 2.

24. Ibid., 21 October, p. 1; 22 October, p. 1; 23 October, p. 2; 28 October, p. 1; and 30 October, p. 2; all 1903.

25. In the election of other city offices, the Democrats did well. They elected ten of eighteen supervisors, both police judges, and seven of the other twelve officials.

26. Lane to Wigmore, 26 January 1904, Lane and Wall, *Letters,* pp. 43-44. For Lane's campaign, see Wiens, "Lane in California," pp. 94, 114-15, 118-26, 130, 132, and 137-50; Bean, *Boss Ruef's San Francisco,* pp. 37-41; *San Francisco Bulletin* and *Chronicle,* 1 October to 5 November 1903; Lane to William R. Wheeler, November 1903, Lane and Wall, *Letters,* p. 45; Benjamin Ide Wheeler to Theodore Roosevelt, 10 October 1903, series 1, Roosevelt Papers; for election results, see *San Francisco Chronicle,* 5 November 1903, p. 16.

27. Wiens, "Lane in California," pp. 85, 163-65; Lane to Wigmore, 26 January 1904, Lane and Wall, *Letters,* p. 44.

28. *Tacoma Daily News,* 12 December 1892, p. 4, and 25 July 1893, p. 2.

CHAPTER 3

1. For example, see Roosevelt to Wheeler, 17 October 1903, series 2; Wheeler to Roosevelt, 2 March 1904, series 1; Wheeler to Roosevelt, 13 June 1904, series 1; Roosevelt to Lyman Abbott, 14 December 1905, series 2; and Roosevelt to Wheeler, 14 December 1905, 13 August 1906, 26 August 1907, 27 September 1907, and 31 January 1909, all series 2; all in Roosevelt Papers.

2. The case involved the Hetch Hetchy Valley, part of Yosemite National Park. See Elmo R. Richardson, "The Struggle for the Valley," *California Historical Society Quarterly* XXXVIII (September 1959).

3. Wheeler to Roosevelt, 10 March 1903, Benjamin Ide Wheeler Papers.

4. *San Francisco Bulletin,* 22 March 1903, p. 15; Roosevelt to Wheeler, 17 October 1903, series 2, Roosevelt Papers.

5. Roosevelt to Wheeler, 2 December 1904, Elting E. Morison, ed., *The Letters of Theodore Roosevelt* vol. IV (Cambridge: Harvard University Press, 1954), pp. 1056-57; Roosevelt to Wheeler, 27 November 1905, series 2, Roosevelt Papers; Lane to Edward B. Whitney, 13 November 1905, in Anne Wintermute Lane and Louise Herrick Wall, eds., *The Letters of Franklin K. Lane* (Boston: Houghton Mifflin Company, 1922), p. 52.

6. Roosevelt to Lyman Abbott, 14 December 1905; Roosevelt to Wheeler, 14 December 1905; Roosevelt to Lane, 16 December 1905; Roosevelt to Abbott, 19 December 1905; and Roosevelt to Wheeler, 6 and 18 January 1906; all series 2, Roosevelt Papers.

7. "The Progress of the World," *Review of Reviews* XXXIII (February 1906): 132.

8. Lane to Edward B. Whitney, 13 November 1905, Lane and Wall, *Letters,* p. 53.

9. Roosevelt to Lane, 16 December 1905, series 2, Roosevelt Papers; also see Roosevelt to Wheeler, 14 December 1905, ibid.

10. For support for Lane, see Lane to William E. Smythe, 15 December 1905, pp. 55-56; and Lane to John H. Wigmore, 27 June 1906, pp. 61-62; both Lane and Wall, *Letters;* Roosevelt to Wigmore, 15 October

1905; and Lane to Wigmore, 21 December 1905; both Wigmore Papers; Roosevelt to Wheeler, 30 April 1906, series 2; and Albert Shaw to Roosevelt, 26 May 1906, series 1; both Roosevelt Papers; Lane to James D. Phelan, II May 1906, James D. Phelan Papers. For Senate confirmation, see Lane to Phelan, 13 July 1906, Phelan Papers. Roosevelt's incoming correspondence from mid-November 1905 until early July 1906 is void of criticism of Lane.

11. My division is that of I. L. Sharfman, *The Interstate Commerce Commission*, four parts (New York: The Commonwealth Fund, 1931-1937), part 4, pp. 362-63. In his prize-winning book, *Enterprise Denied* (New York: Columbia University Press, 1971), Albro Martin recognizes the same division.

12. My information and conclusions are those of Sharfman, *The Interstate Commerce Commission*, part 1, pp. 19-33, and part 4, p. 365; for a convenient one-volume history of the ICC, see Ari and Olive Hoogenboom, *A History of the ICC: From Panacea to Palliative* (New York: W. W. Norton, 1976).

13. Sharfman, *The Interstate Commerce Commission*, part 1, pp. 34-39, and part 4, pp. 362-63; Hoogenboom, *A History of the ICC*, pp. 44-45.

14. Horace Samuel Merrill and Marion Galbraith Merrill, *The Republican Command 1897-1913* (Lexington: The University Press of Kentucky, 1971), pp. 205-6, 213-16; John Morton Blum, *The Republican Roosevelt* (New York: Atheneum edition, 1972), pp. 73-105.

15. Sharfman, *The Interstate Commerce Commission*, part 1, pp. 40-52, and part 4, p. 363; Hoogenboom, *A History of the ICC*, pp. 52-54.

16. Lane, "Arlington Heights Fruit Exchange vs. Southern Pacific Company," *Interstate Commerce Commission Reports* XXII (Washington, D.C.: Government Printing Office, 1912), p. 158; Lane, "The Interstate Commerce Commission—To Date," *The City Club Bulletin* II (23 December 1908): 218, 220.

17. Lane, "Arlington Heights Fruit Exchange vs. Southern Pacific Company," pp. 157-58; *Twenty-Second Annual Report of the Interstate Commerce Commission* (Washington, D.C.: Government Printing Office, 1909), p. 95; Roosevelt to Lane, 27 November 1908, series 2, Roosevelt Papers.

18. Lane, "The Railroad Commission of Louisiana v. St. Louis Southwestern Railway Company Et Al.," *Interstate Commerce Commission Reports* XXIII (Washington, D.C.: Government Printing Office, 1912), pp. 31-68, especially pp. 46-48. Also see Allan P. Matthew, "Franklin K. Lane," *Interstate Commerce Commission Practitioners' Journal* II (June 1935): 363.

19. Lane, "In Re-Investigation of Advances in Rates by Carriers in

Western Trunk Line, Trans-Missouri, and Illinois Freight Committee Territories," *Interstate Commerce Commission Reports* XX (Washington, D.C.: Government Printing Office, 1911), pp. 379, 309-10. In *Enterprise Denied,* Martin argues that the ICC's unwillingness to permit general rate increases prevented railroads from obtaining investment capital and, therefore, along with other ICC rulings after passage of the Hepburn Act contributed to the deterioration of United States railroads.

20. Lane, "Success of Federal Railroad Legislation," *Journal of Commerce and Commercial Bulletin,* 3 January 1912, p. 4.

21. Lane to Roosevelt, 28 March 1907, series 1, Roosevelt Papers.

22. Lane, "Railroad Capitalization and Federal Regulation," *The American Review of Reviews* XXXVII (June 1908): 711-14; also see Lane, "A Remedy for Overcapitalization," typed manuscript, dated 1908, Lane Papers.

23. Lane to Taft, 2 October 1909, series 5, William Howard Taft Papers; *Twenty-Third Annual Report of the Interstate Commerce Commission* (Washington, D.C. Government Printing Office, 1909), p. 8; Oscar King Davis, *Released for Publication* (Boston: Houghton-Mifflin Company, 1925), pp. 237-41.

24. Lane to Benjamin Ide Wheeler, 31 July 1912, Lane and Wall, *Letters,* p. 102.

25. James S. Harlan quoted in commentary, ibid., p. 101.

26. The leading historian of the history of the commission has concluded that as a result of the investigations of the express companies, the commission issued "one of the most sweeping constructive determinations in its entire history." See Sharfman, *The Interstate Commerce Commission,* part 2, fn. 114, p. 60.

27. For the express companies case, see Lane to William R. Wheeler, 22 June 1911, p. 79; Lane to George W. Lane, 2 July 1912, p. 99; Lane to Benjamin Ide Wheeler, 31 July 1912, p. 102; Lane and Wall, commentary, pp. 100-101; all in Lane and Wall, *Letters;* Lane reporting for the commission, "Memphis Freight Bureau vs. Adams Express Company," *Interstate Commerce Commission Reports* XXIV (Washington, D.C.: Government Printing Office, 1913), pp. 381-541, but especially pp. 432-34; Sharfman, *The Interstate Commerce Commission,* pp. 2, 59-82; Lane, "The Federal Hand on Express Business," *The Independent* LXIV (9 January 1913): 95-98.

28. Lane, "Consolidations and Combinations of Carriers" (abbreviated title), *Interstate Commerce Commission Reports* XII (Washington, D.C': Government Printing Office, 1908), p. 281.

29. Felix Frankfurter to W. Averell Harriman, 3 February 1969, box 66, The Felix Frankfurter Papers; *New York Times,* 19 December 1919, p. 14.

30. Lane, "The Interstate Commerce Commission—To Date," p. 220; Lane, "H.S. Gile and Company Et. Al. vs. Southern Pacific Company Et. Al.," *Interstate Commerce Commission Reports* XXII (Washington, D.C.: Government Printing Office, 1912), p. 302.

31. Lane interview by unnamed person, dated "1908-1909," Lane Papers; Lane to Lawrence F. Abbott, 22 September 1909, Lane and Wall, *Letters,* p. 72.

32. Lane to John H. Wigmore, 20 January 1913, Lane and Wall, *Letters,* p. 124.

33. Lane, "What I Am Trying to Do," *The World's Work* XXV (March 1913): 563; for Lane's view on the willingness of people to invest in railway securities, see Lane, "The Average Man's Money," *Collier's Weekly* XLVII (25 March 1911): 25.

34. Sharfman, *The Interstate Commerce Commission,* part 1, fn. 40, p. 41; for Lane's comment about the volume of work, see Lane to E. B. Beard, 19 December 1908, Lane and Wall, *Letters,* pp. 67-68.

35. Lane to Joseph N. Teal, 20 January 1913, Lane and Wall, *Letters,* p. 124; *Twenty-Second Annual Report of the Interstate Commerce Commission,* p. 83; *Twenty-Sixth Annual Report of the Interstate Commerce Commission* (Washington, D.C.: Government Printing Office, 1913), p. 70.

36. Lane to Lawrence F. Abbott, 22 September 1909, p. 71; Lane to Carol Snyder, 6 March 1912, p. 90; both Lane and Wall, *Letters.*

37. Roosevelt to each of the men mentioned and to his Cabinet, 23 May 1908, series 2, Roosevelt Papers; Roosevelt, *Theodore Roosevelt* (New York: Charles Scribner's Sons, 1920 edition), p. 437.

38. Before the mid-1930s, three-fourths of the aggregate membership of the commission received reappointment when their terms expired. See Sharfman, *The Interstate Commerce Commission,* part 4, pp. 39-40. For samples of Lane-Taft friendship, see Lane to Taft, 27 September 1910, series 5; Lane to Taft, 2 December 1910, series 6; Taft to Lane, 28 October 1914, series 8; and Lane to Taft, 29 July 1916, series 3; all William Howard Taft Papers.

39. *La Follette's Weekly* V (15 March 1913): 1.

40. "Two Prominent Men," *The World's Work* XIII (March 1907): 8602; "Commissioner Franklin K. Lane," *The Independent* LXXIV (9 January 1913): 93-94; also see "A Railroad Regulator," *The Outlook* CIII (25 January 1913): 228-29; and James C. Hamphill, "Franklin K. Lane," *The North American Review* CCVI (August 1917): 252-54; for Lane's articles, see fns. 16, 20, 22, 27, and 33.

41. *New York Times,* 19 May 1921, p. 14; *Washington Evening Star,* 18 May 1921, p. 2.

42. Lane to Hugo K. Asher, 22 October 1912, Lane and Wall, *Letters,* p. 108.

43. The Hoogenbooms support this general conclusion. See Hoogenboom, *A History of the ICC,* pp. 63, 66, 69, 187, and 189.

CHAPTER 4

1. Lane to George W. Lane, 2 July, p. 99; Lane to Benjamin Ide Wheeler, 31 July, p. 102; Lane to John H. Wigmore, 21 September, p. 104; Lane to Timothy Spellacy, 30 September, pp. 104-5; and Lane to Francis G. Newlands, 28 October, pp. 109-10; all 1912; all in Anne Wintermute Lane and Louise Herrick Wall, eds., *The Letters of Franklin K. Lane* (Boston: Houghton-Mifflin Company, 1922).,

2. Lane to William F. McCombs, 19 October 1912, pp. 106-7, ibid.

3. Ibid., p. 106.

4. Lane to Hugo K. Asher, 22 October 1912, ibid.. p. 108.

5. For examples, see Lane to James D. Phelan, 19 July and 6 August 1912, Phelan Papers.

6. Arthur S. Link, *Wilson: The New Freedom* (Princeton: Princeton University Press, 1956), pp. 5-6; Link, *Woodrow Wilson and the Progressive Era* (New York: Harper and Row, 1954), p. 26.

7. Arthur D. Howden Smith, *Mr. House of Texas* (New York: Funk and Wagnalls Company, 1940), pp. 66-67; Ray S. Baker interview with Thomas Gregory, 14 and 15 March 1927, Ray S. Baker Papers. Lane and Houston became members of Wilson's Cabinet, as did two other dinner guests that evening, Albert S. Burleson and Thomas Gregory.

8. Lane to Hugo K. Asher, 22 October 1912, p. 108; and Lane to Francis G. Newlands, 28 October 1912, pp. 109-10; both Lane and Wall, *Letters;* Lane to James D. Phelan, 6 November 1912, Phelan Papers.

9. Lane to Hugo K. Asher, 22 October 1912, pp. 107-9; Lane to Timothy Spellacy, 30 September 1921, p. 104; Lane to Charles K. McClatchy, 25 November 1912, p. 114; and Lane to Adolph C. Miller, 4 December 1912, p. 117; all Lane and Wall, *Letters; San Francisco Call,* 15 November 1912, p. 1.

10. House to Lane, undated; House to Lane, 6 December, 1912; House to Lane, 23 January 1913; and House Diary, 20 November 1912 and 16 February 1913, all Edward M. House Papers.

11. Lane to House, 13 December 1912, pp. 118-19; Lane to Benjamin Ide Wheeler, 23 December 1912, p. 120; and Lane to House, 22 January 1913, pp. 124-25; all Lane and Wall, *Letters*; Lane to House, 5 December 1912; Lane to House, 4 January 1913; House to Wilson, 27 and 29 January 1913; and House Diary, 6 and 26 January 1913; all in House Papers; Lane to James D. Phelan, 3 and 20 January 1913, Phelan Papers.

12. House to Wilson, 22 November 1912, House Papers; and Lane to Charles K. McClatchy, 25 November 1912, p. 113, Lane and Wall, *Letters*.

13. House Diary, 8 January 1913; House to Lane, 23 January 1913; and House to Wilson, 27 January 1913; all House Papers; Lane to House, 22 January 1913, pp. 124-25, Lane and Wall, *Letters*.

14. House Diary, 14, 16, and 21 February 1913, House Papers.

15. Ibid., 22 and 23 February 1913.

16. Lane to James D. Phelan, 12 March 1913, Phelan Papers; Lane to Edwin Alderman, 17 March 1913, p. 134, Lane and Wall, *Letters;* Judson C. Welliner, "The New Cabinet," *Munsey's Magazine* XLIX (May 1913): 168; *New York Times,* 3 March 1913, p. 2.

17. Albert Shaw to Wilson, 5 March 1913, series 4, Wilson Papers; James M. Head to Josephus Daniels, 10 March 1913, box 49, Josephus Daniels Papers; Lane to House, 29 March 1913, House Papers; Lane to Roosevelt, 24 March 1913, pp. 134-35, Lane and Wall, *Letters;* Roy Robbins, *Our Landed Heritage* (Princeton: Princeton University Press, 1942), p. 381; "Lane, The White Hope of the Wilson Cabinet," *Current Opinion* LV (September 1913): 163; Burton J. Hendrick, "The American 'Home Secretary,'" *The World's Work* XXVI (August 1913): 396; and House Diary, 15 March 1913, House Papers.

18. Department of Interior Records, Record Group 48, File Symbol 1-125; also see "Memorandum History of the Department of the Interior" (Washington, D.C.: Government Printing Office, 1913), pp. 14-20.

19. For an informal description of the Interior Department as it existed in 1913, see Horace M. Albright, "The Reminiscences of Horace M. Albright" (Columbia University, Oral History Research Office, 1962), pp. 21-26.

20. Roosevelt increased the total from 46,410,209 acres to 150,832,665 acres.

21. I based my outline of the conservation movement before 1913 on: Samuel P. Hays, *Conservation and the Gospel of Efficiency* (New York: Atheneum, 1969; originally published by Harvard University Press in 1959), especially pp. 25-26, 46-48, 64-65, 70-91, 102-5, 121-74, and 261-76; Elmo R. Richardson, *The Politics of Conservation* (Berkeley: The University of California Press, 1962), especially pp. 155-59; and the sum-

mary provided by Donald C. Swain, *Federal Conservation Policy, 1921-1933* (Berkeley: University of California Press, 1963), pp. 1-5.

CHAPTER 5

1. Lane to Wigmore, 9 March 1913, in Anne Wintermute Lane and Louise Herrick Wall, eds., *The Letters of Franklin K. Lane* (Boston: Houghton Mifflin Company, 1922), pp. 131-3; Lane to Wigmore, 9 May 1902, John H. Wigmore Papers.

2. Lane to Edward M. House, 22 January 1913, Lane and Wall, *Letters*, p. 125; Joseph N. Teal to Gifford Pinchot, 14 March 1914; and Pinchot to Teal, 21 March 1913; both box 172, Gifford Pinchot Papers.

3. Lane to Wilson, 29 August 1916, FS 22-4, RG 48, Department of Interior Records; William Kent to Gifford Pinchot, 21 May 1913, box 477, Pinchot Papers.

4. Lane to Wilson, 29 August 1916, FS 22-4, RG-48, Interior Records.

5. Lane to J. H. Fleming, 20 November 1913; and Lane to John Sharp Williams, 3 December 1913; both FS 24-1-3, RG 48, Interior Records.

6. Lane to Wilson, 16 May 1914, FS 22-2, RG 48, Interior Records.

7. Wilson to Lane, 28 July 1917, series 3, Wilson Papers; Lane to Henry P. Andrews, 28 July 1917; and Lane to Miles Poindexter, 27 July 1917; both FS 24-1-3, RG 48, Interior Records.

8. Lane to Wilson, 8 August 1917, FS 22-2, RG 48, Interior Records.

9. Donald C. Swain, *Wilderness Defender* (Chicago: The University of Chicago Press, 1970), pp. 19, 21-22, 23, 26-27, and 32-33; Horace M. Albright, "The Reminiscences of Horace M. Albright" (Columbia University, Oral History Research Office, 1962), pp. 1-9.

10. Lane to Wilson, 25 February 1914, series 2, Wilson Papers.

11. For a discussion of Mather and the National Park Service, see chapter 6.

12. D.N. Fink to Lane, 23 July 1913, FS 22-60, RG 48, Interior Records.

13. Teal to Lane, 30 August 1916; Lane to Thomas W. Gregory, 1 September 1916, both ibid.

14. George S. Brown to Lane, 15 March; C. H. McIntosh to William F. McCombs, 19 March; and Lane to Francis G. Newlands, 25 March; all 1913 and in FS 22-5, RG 48, Interior Records; Newlands to Lane, 14 March 1913, series 2, Wilson Papers.

15. Lane to Wilson, 26 May 1913, FS 22-6, RG 48, Interior Records.

16. Lane to Theodore Roosevelt, 24 March 1913, Lane and Wall, *Letters,* p. 135.

17. Lane to Wilson, 22 May 1913, FS 22-3, RG 48, Interior Records; E. David Cronon, ed., *The Cabinet Diaries of Josephus Daniels, 1913-1921* (Lincoln: University of Nebraska Press, 1963), p. 73.

18. FS 22-8, RG 48, Interior Records.

19. Lane to Wilson, 25 August 1915, series 4, Wilson Papers.

20. Lane to Ewing, 17 July 1914; Ewing to Lane, 31 May 1917; both FS 3-1, RG 48, Interior Records; *New York Times,* 8 December 1942, p. 25.

21. Lane to Wilson, 8 August 1917, FS 22-2, RG 48, Interior Records.

22. Wilson to Lane, 7 August 1913, series 3, Wilson Papers.

23. Wilson to Lane, 21 April, series 3; Lane to Wilson, 2 May, series 2; and Wilson to Lane, 12 May, series 3; all 1914 and all Wilson Papers. See also Wilson to Lane, 14 April, 12 June, and 25 July, all 1913; and Wilson to Lane, 17 June 1914; all series 3 and all Wilson Papers.

24. Wilson to Lane, 7 January, 20 January, 2 July, and 28 August; all 1915 and all series 3, Wilson Papers. For journalistic awareness of Lane's attitude toward patronage, see Honoré Willsie, "Mr. Lane and the Public Domain," *Harper's Weekly* LVIII (23 August 1913): 6-8.

25. Lane to Herbert Hoover, 1 March 1921, Papers of Herbert Hoover.

26. Lane to Wilson, 29 April 1913, series 2, Wilson Papers.

27. Clay Tallman, "Open Letter to All Employees of the General Land Office," 13 December 1913, FS 2-15, RG 48, Interior Records; Press memo, 29 April 1915, Lane Papers; Lane to Tallman, 17 April 1919, FS 1-1, RG 48; and Tallman to Lane, 24 April 1919, FS 2-15, RG 48; both Interior Records.

28. Lane to Gaylord M. Saltzgaber, 16 July 1913, FS 4-10, RG 48, Interior Records. The source of Lane's information probably was former Secretary of the Interior Walter L. Fisher.

29. Keeman to Chief Clerk, Dr. F. D. Byington, 27 December 1917; and Dawkins to Byington, 29 December 1917; both FS 4-10, RG 48, Interior Records.

30. Lane to Hopkins, 22 August; Lange to Hopkins, 27 September; Hopkins to Lane, 29 September; Lange to Hopkins, 20 October; Hopkins to Cotter, 22 October; and Lane to Saltzgaber, 29 October; all 1919 and all FS 4-10, RG 48, Interior Records.

31. Lane to William M. Bole, 29 December 1915, Lane and Wall, *Letters,* p. 196.

32. Lane orders, 15 July 1913, 2 December 1916, and 11 April 1919, all FS 1-12, RG 48, Interior Records.

33. Lane to Wilson, 21 October 1916, series 2, Wilson Papers; Lane to P. P. Claxton, 30 April 1915, FS 1-12, RG 48, Interior Records; Horace M. Albright to Stephen T. Mather, 11 March 1919, FS 201-03, RG 79, Interior Records.

34. Lane to Members of Congress, 10 April 1913, FS 1-84; E. J. Ayers to All Bureau Chiefs, 2 and 21 December 1913; and Lane to Cato Sells, 4 May 1916; FS 1-12; all RG 48, Interior Records.

35. Interview with Horace M. Albright, 3 April 1963.

36. Lane to Bureau Chiefs, 14 June 1917, FS 1-187, RG 48, Interior Records; see also Lane, *Interior Reports,* 1918, pp. 175-77.

37. Cronon, *Cabinet Diaries,* 3 April 1917, p. 128; Lane to Wilson, 11 April 1917, series 2, Wilson Papers.

38. Lane to Wilson, 5 November 1913, series 3, Wilson Papers.

39. "Articles of Incorporation and By-Laws of THE HOME CLUB," p. 5, FS 1-167, RG 48, Interior Records.

40. Lane to Albert Shaw, 8 April 1914, Lane and Wall, *Letters,* p. 149.

41. Wilson to Lane, 6 November 1913; and Wilson to Lane, 8 July 1914; both series 3, Wilson Papers.

42. Lane remarks at a luncheon at the Department of Interior, 26 March 1919, Lane Papers; for records and correspondence relating to the Home Club, see FS 1-167, RG 48, Interior Records.

43. Interviews with M. L. Wilson, 4 and 5 April 1963.

44. Lane to Albert Shaw, 8 April 1914, Lane and Wall, *Letters,* pp. 148-9.

45. Lane to each field agent of the Department of Interior, 28 February 1920, FS 22-44, RG 48, Interior Records.

46. Albright, "The Reminiscences of Horace M. Albright," p. 77.

CHAPTER 6

1. Lane to William M. Bole, 26 May 1913, in Anne Wintermute Lane and Louise Herrick Wall, eds., *The Letters of Franklin K. Lane* (Boston: Houghton Mifflin Company, 1922), p. 137; also see Peggy Heim, "Financing the Federal Reclamation Program, 1902-1919: The Development of Repayment Policy" (Ph.D. diss., Columbia University, 1953), pp. xx-xxi, 156.

2. A. P. Davis to Lane, 8 April 1913, FS 8-64, RG 48, Interior Records; Lane to Pinchot, 19 April 1913, box 167, Pinchot Papers; Honoré Willsie, "Mr. Lane the Public Domain," *Harper's Weekly* LVIII (30 August 1913):

7-8; press memo, 19 April 1913, FS 1-127, RG 48, Interior Records; Heim, "Financing Reclamation," pp. 158-59.

3. Press memo, 27 May 1913, FS 1-127, RG 48, Interior Records; Heim, "Financing Reclamation," pp. 161-70; Lane, *Interior Reports,* 1913, p. 20.

4. Lane, *Interior Reports,* 1913, pp. 20-21; Elmo Richardson, *The Politics of Conservation* (Berkeley: The University of California Press, 1962), p. 153.

5. Lane to Fisher, 18 March 1914, box 2, Walter L. Fisher Papers; Lane to Borah, 23 March 1914, box 114, William E. Borah Papers; press memo, 27 February 1914, FS 1-127, RG 48, Interior Records; *New York Times,* 24 December 1912, p. 10.

6. Lane, "Uncle Sam, Contractor and Builder of Western Homes," *Sunset* XXXII (May 1914): 1018, 1022.

7. In 1924, for example, Congress extended the repayment period to forty years. Heim, "Financing Reclamation," pp. 174-86, 195-97, and 271; Lane, *Interior Records,* 1914, pp. 15-16; Lane to Frank C. Page, 21 January 1916, FS 2-194, RG 48, Interior Records.

8. Lane to Newell, 3 December 1914, box 512, Pinchot Papers; Heim, "Financing Reclamation," pp. 163-65; for a scrap book clipping coverage of Newell's removal, see box 22, F. H. Newell Papers.

9. Heim, "Financing Reclamation," pp. 209-21.

10. Williamson to Lane, 7 April; Lane to Davis, 19 April; press memos, 27 April and 6 May; all 1915 and all FS 1-1, RG 48, Interior Records.

11. William Kent to Walter L. Fisher, 21 March 1911 and 28 February 1913, box 12, Fisher Papers; for another example of Lane publicizing his views, see Lane, "Our Paternal Uncle," *Sunset* XXXIII (September 1914): 512-18; House Diary, 26 November 1915, House Papers.

12. Robert Shankland, *Steve Mather of the National Parks* (New York: Alfred A. Knopf, 1954), pp. 212-14; Horace M. Albright, "The Reminiscences of Horace M. Albright" (Columbia University, Oral History Research Office, 1962), pp. 79-82.

13. For an example of the criticism on this subject from a newspaper that admired Lane, see *New York Times,* 16 October 1913, p. 10.

14. *Congressional Record,* 62nd Cong., 1st sess. (21 August 1911), pp. 4262-67; Gifford Pinchot, "Who Shall Own Alaska?" *Saturday Evening Post* CLXXXIV (16 December 1911): 3-4, 50-52.

15. Pittman to Lane, 19 March; Z. R. Chenny to Lane, 20 March; both 1913 and both FS 22-9, RG 48, Interior Records.

16. *New York Times,* 18 April, p. 1; 22 May, p. 6; both 1913.

17. Wilson to Lane, 1 May; Sulzer to Joseph P. Tumulty, 23 April;

Sulzer to Lane, 21 May; and John W. Troy to Lane, 19 May; all 1917 and all FS 22-9, RG 48, Interior Records.

18. Aldrich to Pittman, 20 June 1917, series 4, Wilson Papers; Strong to Lane, 28 April; Strong to Pittman, 11 June; Walsh and Pittman to Lane, 14 June; Pittman to Wilson, 6 July; Houston to Wilson, 1 September; and Alexander to Wilson, 21 December; all 1917 and all FS 22-9, RG 48, Interior Records.

19. Lane to Wilson, 18 June 1917, series 2; Wilson to Lane, 7 August 1917, series 3; and Lane to Wilson, 28 February and 22 March, both 1918 and both series 4; all Wilson Papers. In a letter to Wilson, 20 March 1913, Strong wrote "I am a native of the State of Kentucky." FS 22-9, RG 48, Interior Records.

20. See reports, documents, and correspondence in box 33, Fisher Papers.

21. Lane to Key Pittman, 15 May 1913, FS 1-127, RG 48, Interior Records; *New York Times* 16 May 1913, p. 2; Lane to C. E. S. Wood, 9 October 1914, series 2, Wilson Papers.

22. *New York Times,* 23 July 1913, p. 4; Willsie, "Mr. Lane and the Public Domain," pp. 7-8.

23. *Congressional Record,* 63rd Cong., 2nd sess. (2 December 1913), p. 45; Lane, *Interior Reports,* 1913, pp. 10-11.

24. Press memos, 10 April, 22 June, and 20 July, all 1915 and all Lane Papers; Lane, "Alaska's New Railway," *The National Geographic Magazine* XVIII (December 1915): 567-89; Lane to Wilson, 28 April 1915, series 2, Wilson Papers; Lane to Wilson, 21 September 1917, Lane and Wall, *Letters,* pp. 258-9; Lane to Wilson, 9 March 1918, series 2, Wilson Papers; Lane, *Interior Reports,* 1919, pp. 33-34; Lane to Herbert Hoover, Hoover Papers; Department of the Interior, *General Information Regarding the Territory of Alaska* (Washington, D.C.: Government Printing Office, 1923), pp. 49-51.

25. Fisher, *Interior Reports,* 1912, p. 12; Lane to Fisher, 30 October 1911, box 14, Fisher Papers; Pinchot to Garfield, 22 November 1911, box 145, Pinchot Papers.

26. Lane, *Interior Reports,* 1913, pp. 11-13.

27. *New York Times,* 10 February 1914, p. 2.

28. Press memo, 17 February 1914, FS 1-127, RG 48, Interior Records.

29. Arthur Dunn, "Tomorrow," *Sunset* XXXII (February 1914): 414; Lane, "Our Paternal Uncle."

30. Press memo, 15 October 1914, Lane Papers; *San Francisco Star,* editorial, 31 October 1914. For this editorial as well as an excellent clipping coverage of the Alaskan coal-leasing bill, see FS 2-24, RG 48, Interior Records.

31. For example, see *New York Times,* editorial, 28 May 1914, p. 12.

32. Ibid., 25 April 1914, p. 6; press memos, 8 October, 24 November, and 31 December, all 1914 and all Lane Papers; Lane, *Interior Reports,* 1914, p. 14; Ernest Gruening, *The State of Alaska* (New York: Random House, 1954), pp. 188-90.

33. Karl Ward, "A Study of the Introduction of Reindeer into Alaska," *Journal of the Presbyterian Historical Society* XXXIII (December 1955): 229-38 and XXXIV (December 1956): 245-56; Dorothy Jean Ray, "Sheldon Jackson and the Reindeer Industry of Alaska," *Journal of the Presbyterian Historical Society* XLIII (June 1965): 71-99; for correspondence and additional details of reindeer in Alaska, see FS 6-4, RG 48, Interior Records; and *Rules and Regulations regarding the United States Reindeer Service in Alaska* (Washington, D.C.: Government Printing Office, 1911).

34. Lane, *Interior Reports,* 1913, p. 78, and 1919, p. 166.

35. *New York Times,* 23 July 1913, p. 4; Lane, *Interior Reports,* 1915, p. 98, and 1916, p. 68; Lane, "A Mind's Eye Map of America," *The National Geographic Magazine* XXXVII (June 1920): 482-83.

36. *Congressional Record,* 62nd Cong., 1st sess. (21 August 1911), pp. 4266-67.

37. Lane, *Interior Reports,* 1913, pp. 6-9.

38. Lane, "Red Tape in Alaska," *Outlook* XIC (20 January 1915): 140.

39. Ibid., pp. 135-41; Lane, "Freeing Alaska from Red Tape," *The North American Review* CCI (June 1915): 841-52; Lane, *Interior Reports* 1913, p. 8; *New York Times,* 22 March 1914, sec. 5, p. 3, and 1 June 1914, p. 3.

40. Lane, *Interior Reports,* 1918, p. 141, and 1919, pp. 153-54; Lane to Wilson, 28 February 1920, FS 22-44, RG 48, Interior Records.

41. Thomas Riggs, Jr., "Report of the Governor of Alaska," *Reports of the Department of the Interior,* 1918, pp. 569-70.

42. Wilson to John Barton Payne, 2 December 1920; Payne to Josephus Daniels, 24 March 1920, both box 48, Daniels Papers; Gruening, *The State of Alaska,* pp. 200-206.

43. Lane to John H. Wigmore, 9 March 1913, Lane and Wall, *Letters,* p. 131.

44. Lane to Woodrow Wilson, 22 May 1913, FS 22-33, RG 48, Interior Records.

45. Lane to Sullivan, 6 November 1913, Lane and Wall, *Letters,* p. 141; *New York Times,* 24 July 1913, p. 6, 11 December 1914, p. 12, and 11 July 1920, p. 2; Josephus Daniels, *The Wilson Era: Years of Peace* (Chapel Hill: The University of North Carolina press, 1944), p. 116; press memo, 21 April 1913, FS 1-127, RG 48, Interior Records; Lane to Walter L.

Fisher, 19 December 1913, box 1, Fisher Papers; press memo, 9 January 1915, Lane Papers; Cato Sells, "Report of the Commissioner of Indian Affairs," *Interior Reports,* 1917; and Amos W. Hawk to Joseph J. Cotter, 22 February 1920, FS 22-44, RG 48, Interior Records.

46. Press memo, 15 July 1913, FS 1-127, RG 48, Interior Records.

47. Ibid.; Lane, "The Future of the Indian," *LaFollette's Magazine* VII (March 1915): 12.

48. Lane, address before the Commonwealth Club, 5 September 1913, Lane Papers.

49. Press memo, 19 March 1913, FS 1-127, RG 48, Interior Records.

50. Lane, *Interior Reports,* 1914, p. 114.

51. Cato Sells, "Report of the Commissioner of Indian Affairs," *Interior Reports,* 1917, pp. 3, 15; ibid., 1919, p. 70.

52. John Barton Payne, *Interior Reports,* 1920, pp. 9-10.

53. *New York Times,* 11 July 1920, p. 2; Randolph C. Downes, "A Crusade for Indian Reform, 1922-1934," *Mississippi Valley Historical Review* XXXII (December 1945): 331-54; Angie Debo, *A History of the Indians of the United States* (Norman: University of Oklahoma Press, 1970), chaps. 16 and 17; Lawrence C. Kelly, "The Navajos and Federal Policy, 1913-1935" (Ph.D. diss., University of New Mexico, 1961), pp. 64, 237, 240-43.

54. Shankland, *Steve Mather,* p. 7.

55. Donald C. Swain, "The Passage of the National Park Service Act of 1916," *Wisconsin Magazine of History* L (Autumn 1966): 4-7.

56. For my discussion of Mather and Albright, I have relied on Shankland, *Steven Mather,* Donald C. Swain, *Wilderness Defender* (Chicago: The University of Chicago Press, 1970), and Horace M. Albright, "The Reminiscences of Horace M. Albright" (Columbia University, Oral History Research Office, 1962).

57. Albright, "The Reminiscences of Horace M. Albright," pp. 72, 92-98; for a glimpse of Lane's willingness to permit Mather and Albright to make decisions on appointees, see Mather to Albright, 10 March 1919, FS 201-03, RG 79, Interior Records.

58. Elmo R. Richardson, "The Struggle for the Valley," *California Historical Society Quarterly* XXXVIII (September 1959): 249-57; Roderick Nash, *Wilderness and the American Mind* (New Haven: Yale University Press, 1967), pp. 161-81; press memo, 12 March and n.d. June, both 1913, FS 1-127, RG 48, Interior Records.

59. Lane to Mather, 13 May 1918; Mather to Lane, 1 December 1916, both FS 12-0, RG 48, Interior Records; for a brief discussion of the Yellowstone instance, see chap. 9; Shankland, *Steve Mather,* p. 195; Albright interview 1 April 1963; for a survey of the parks under Lane, see John Ise,

Our National Park Policy (Baltimore: The Johns Hopkins University Press, 1961), especailly p. 287.

60. Arno B. Cammerer to John Barton Payne, 18 March 1920; also see, Mather to Lane, 26 April 1918, both FS 0-207.0, RG 79, Interior Records.

CHAPTER 7

1. Jerome G. Kerwin, *Federal Water-Power Legislation* (New York: Columbia University, 1926), pp. 8-9, 128-30, and 153-54; typed undated manuscript in the Albert Shaw Papers, written by an Interior Department lawyer (see Lane to Charles D. Lanier, undated letter, Shaw Papers); U. S. Senate, 63rd Cong., 3rd sess., *Hearings before the Committee on Public Lands* (Washington, D.C.: Government Printing Office, 1915), Lane comments, pp. 813-15.

2. Lane statement, 16 June 1913, box 623, Pinchot Papers; Honoré Willsie, "Mr. Lane and the Public Domain," *Harper's Weekly* LVIII (23 August 1913): 7.

3. Willsie, "Mr. Lane," (30 August 1913): 6-7; Lane repeated the philosophy behind his waterpower principles on p. 7 of the 13 September 1913 issue.

4. Lane, *Interior Reports,* 1913, pp. 34-35; also see Lane to Albert Shaw, 20 December 1913, Shaw Papers.

5. Arthur S. Link, *Wilson: The New Freedom* (Princeton: Princeton University Press, 1956), pp. 129-30; Kerwin, *Federal Water-Power Legislation,* pp. 172-78, 180-87, 190, and 192; Lane to John R. Freeman, 23 February 1914; Lane to Elmer L. Corthell, 18 March 1914; Lane to George E. Chamberlain, 2 June 1914; clippings, Judson C. Welliver, "Wilson to Check Warring Factions," *Washington Times,* 30 June 1914; and Joseph P. Annin, "Wilson Behind Water Control," *Washington Herald,* 4 July 1914 and 17 July 1914; all in FS 2-194, RG 48, Interior Records; Lane to Wilson, 1 July 1914, series 2, Wilson Papers.

6. *Chicago Evening Post,* 7 July 1914; S. V. Stewart to Lane, 14 August; Oswald West to Lane, 13 August; George W. Hunt to Lane, 14 August, Lee Cruce to Lane, 14 August; George H. Hodges to Lane, 14 August; and W. C. McDonald to Lane, 26 August; all 1914 and all FS 2-194, RG 48, *Interior Records.*

7. U. S. Senate, 63rd Cong., 3rd sess., *Hearings before the Committee on Public Lands,* Lane comments, pp. 812-20; Lane, *Interior Reports,* 1914, pp. 16-17.

8. Ray Stannard Baker and William E. Dodd, *The Public Papers of Woodrow Wilson: The New Democracy,* vol. I (New York: Harper and Brothers, 1926), p. 218.

9. Link, *Wilson: The New Freedom,* p. 130; Kerwin, *Federal Water-Power Legislation,* pp. 186-95; Walter L. Fisher to Philip P. Wells, 13 December 1914, box 2, Fisher Papers.

10. Press release, undated but issued early in January 1915, Lindly Garrison Papers; Lane to Albert Shaw, 12 January 1915, Shaw Papers; Norman Hapgood, "Water Power and the Gang," *Harper's Weekly* LX (23 January 1915): 74.

11. Press memo, 10 February 1915, 28 April 1915, Lane Papers; clipping, *Washington Post,* 29 April 1915; Lane to Thomas Walsh, 22 July 1915, FS 2-194, RG 48, Interior Records; Lane to Albert Shaw, 10 May 1915, Shaw Papers.

12. *Boston Advertiser,* 9 September 1915; *Portland Oregonian,* 22 September 1915; "Resolutions Adopted by the Western States Water-Power Conference," 23 September 1915; Lane to Wilson, 2 December 1913; all in FS 2-194, RG 48, Interior Records; for an extensive clipping collection on the conference, see FS 2-194, RG 48, Interior Records.

13. Lane, *Interior Reports,* 1915, p. 19; *New York Times,* 23 December 1915, p. 8; Kerwin, *Federal Water-Power Legislation,* p. 231; Link, *Wilson: The New Freedom,* pp. 130-31; for conservationist sentiment in early 1916, see "Pinchot Exposes the Shields Bill," *The Public* XIX (11 February 1916): 130-31; editorial, *World's Work* XXXI (March 1916): 479-81; "Water Power," *Harper's Weekly* LXII (15 April 1916): 391; "Conservation in Peril," *New Republic* VII (13 May 1916): 32-33; for Lane's advice to Wilson and Lane's relationship with Ferris, see Lane to Wilson, 2 March 1916, series 2; Lane to Wilson, 20 April 1916, series 4; and Lane to Wilson, 27 June 1916, series 4; all Wilson Papers.

14. Lane to Wilson, 10 March 1916, series 2; Wilson to Lane, 13 March 1916, series 4; Lane to Wilson, 9 December 1916, series 2; and Lane to Wilson, 8 January 1917, series 2; all in Wilson Papers; press release, National Conservation Association, 23 December 1916, box 523, Pinchot Papers; Lane to Amos Pinchot, 29 December 1916, FS 2-194, RG 48, Interior Records.

15. Wilson to Lane, 10 November, series 3; and Lane to Wilson, 12 November series 2, 18 December, series 2, and 31 December, series 4; all 1917, all Wilson Papers; Lane to Newton D. Baker, 24 November 1917, FS 2-194, RG 48, Interior Records; Ray Stannard Baker, *Woodrow Wilson,* vol. VII (Garden City, N.Y.: Doubleday, Doran, and Company, 1931), p. 408.

16. Baker, Lane, and Houston to Wilson, n.d. January 1918, box 520; Pinchot to Lane, 21 January 1918, box 490; both Pinchot Papers.

17. Baker, Lane, and Houston to T. W. Sims, 27 February; Lane to Ferris, 28 March; William Kent to Wilson, 9 September; and Lane to Wilson, 3 October; all 1918, and all series 4, Wilson Papers; Lane to Albert Shaw, 7 March 1918, Shaw Papers.

18. Kerwin, *Federal Water-Power Legislation,* pp. 250-53; Belle and Fola LaFollette, *Robert M. LaFollette* (New York: The Macmillan Company, 1953), pp. 940-48; *New York Times,* 27 February 1919, p. 3.

19. Kerwin, *Federal Water-Power Legislation,* pp. 256-61.

20. Steve Mather, "Report of the Director of the National Park Service," *Reports of the Department of the Interior,* 1920, pp. 21, 30-32, 34; Horace M. Albright, "The Reminiscences of Horace M. Albright" (Columbia University, Oral History Research Office, 1962), pp. 82-84; for pressures on Wilson, see case file 1888, series 4, Wilson Papers.

21. Lane speech, "The American Spirit Incarnate," 21 June 1916, Lane Papers.

22. For example, see Lane to Wilson, 8 January 1917, series 2; Lane to Wilson, 31 December 1917, series 4; William Kent to Wilson, 9 September 1918, series 4; and Lane to Wilson, 3 October 1918, series 4; all Wilson Papers.

23. Gifford Pinchot, *Breaking New Ground* (New York: Harcourt, Brace and Company, 1947), p. 339; Pinchot drew the same conclusion on 28 February 1920, see Pinchot to N.J. Sinnott, box 686, Pinchot Papers; Lane to Frank W. Mondell, 13 February 1920, in Anne Wintermute Lane and Louise Herrick Wall, eds., *The Letters of Franklin K. Lane* (Boston: Houghton Mifflin Company, 1922), p. 338; Lane to Scott Ferris, 29 April 1914, reprinted in U. S. House of Representatives, 63rd Cong., 2nd sess., *Hearings before the Committee on Public Lands* (Washington, D.C.: Government Printing Office, 1914), pp. 5-7.

24. Lane, *Interior Reports,* 1913, pp. 13-17, 22; for a detailed Lane view on mineral leasing, see Lane, "Development of Western Oil, Phosphate, Coal, and Potash Lands," n.d. manuscript, box 1948, Pinchot Papers.

25. Lane to Andrious A. Jones, 11 April 1914, FS 2-187, RG 48, Interior Records.

26. Lane to Albert Shaw, 12 January 1915, Shaw Papers; Lane to Oswald West, 14 May 1915, FS 2-187, RG 48, Interior Records; J. Leonard Bates, "The Midwest Decision, 1915: A Landmark in Conservation History," *Pacific Northwest Quarterly* LI (January 1960): 26, 33.

27. For a summary of the act, see John Ise, *The United States Oil*

Policy (New Haven: Yale University Press, 1926), pp. 351-52.

28. Pinchot to N.J. Sinnott, 28 February 1920, box 686, Pinchot Papers; E. David Cronon, ed., *The Cabinet Diaries of Josephus Daniels* (Lincoln: The University of Nebraska Press, 1963), 24 February 1920; Lane to Frank W. Mondell, 13 February 1920, Lane and Wall, *Letters,* p. 338.

29. Daniels to Lane, 28 December 1915; Lane to Daniels, 30 December 1915; Lane to Daniels, 17 January 1916; and Daniels to Lane, 19 and 26 January 1916; all box 40, Daniels Papers; Thomas Gregory, "The Honolulu Case," typed manuscript, 27 February 1919, series 4, Wilson Papers.

30. Gregory to Lane, 12 April 1916, reprinted in U.S. Senate, 64th Cong., 1st sess., *Hearings before the Committee on Public Lands* (Washington, D.C.: Government Printing Office, 1916), p. 464; also see comments by Daniels, pp. 183-85 of the same report; Daniels to Wilson, 13 May 1916, box 13, Daniels Papers; Phelan to Wilson, 25 May; and Wilson to Phelan, 8 June; both series 4, Wilson Papers.

31. U. S. Senate, 65th Cong., 1st sess., *Hearings before the Committee on Public Lands* (Washington, D.C.: Government Printing Office, 1917), Daniels's comments, pp. 174-75; Daniels to Thomas Gregory, 26 February 1917; and Lane to Gregory, 24 February 1917; both series 4, Wilson Papers. For a glimpse of Lane-Daniels goodwill during this period, see Daniels to Lane, 24 January 1916; Lane to Daniels, 25 May 1916; and Daniels to Lane, 20 March 1918; all box 40; Lane to Daniels, 1 January 1921, box 48, Daniels Papers; Josephus Daniels, *The Wilson Era: Years of Peace* (Chapel Hill: The University of North Carolina Press, 1944), p. 116.

32. Wilson to Lane, 26 May 1916, series 3; and Lane to Wilson, 1 June 1916, series 2; both Wilson Papers.

33. Lane, *Interior Reports,* 1915, pp. 17-18.

34. Daniels to Wilson, 13 May 1916, box 13, Daniels Papers.

35. *New York Times,* 1 July 1916, p. 17; Lane to Pinchot, 1 July 1916, box 485, Pinchot Papers.

36. Lane press memo, 3 July 1916, box 512, Pinchot Papers; a month earlier, Lane had told Wilson that "the amendments that have been added to the bill in the Senate were added without my knowledge or approval." Lane to Wilson, 1 June 1916, series 2, Wilson Papers.

37. Pinchot to Lane, 15 July 1916; and Lane to Pinchot, 20 July 1916; both box 485, Pinchot Papers.

38. *New York Times,* 14 August 1916, p. 4; a copy of the letter is in

box 613, Pinchot Papers; Lane to William R. Wheeler, 21 August 1916, Lane and Wall, *Letters*, p. 222.

39. Joseph N. Teal to Lane, 30 August 1916, FS 22-60, RG 48, Interior Records.

40. Pinchot to numerous editors, 20 September 1916, box 533; and "Administration Conservation Record Is Defended by Norman Hapgood," *The Southern Lumberman,* 7 October 1916, clipping in box 686; both in Pinchot Papers; William Kent to Wilson, 13 November 1916, series 4, Wilson Papers; Fisher to Pinchot, 1 March 1917, box 8, Fisher Papers.

41. In 1920, Pinchot called Lenroot one of "the two biggest men in the United States west of Ohio." See address, 25 October 1920, box 1948, Pinchot Papers; Lane to Wilson, 1 June 1916, series 2, Wilson Papers.

42. Gregory to Lane, 5 August 1916, series 2; Lane to Gregory, 9 August 1916, series 4; Gregory to Lane, 17 August 1916, series 4; Wilson to Lane, 27 January 1917, series 3; Lane to Wilson, 29 January 1917, series 4; Wilson to Lane, 30 January 1917, series 3; and Gregory, "The Honolulu Case"; for the Honolulu case on the eve of Lane's departure from the Cabinet, see Lane to Wilson, 9 February 1920, and Wilson to Lane, 11 February 1920; both series 2; all Wilson Papers.

43. Wilson to Gregory, 19 February 1917, series 3; Gregory to Lane, 21 February 1917, series 4; Lane to Gregory, 24 February 1917, series 4; Gregory to Claude A. Swanson, 26 February 1917, series 4; and Daniels to Gregory, 26 February 1917, series 4; all Wilson Papers; Daniels, *The Wilson Era: Years of War and After* (Chapel Hill: The University of North Carolina Press, 1946), pp. 247-48.

44. Wilson to Lane, 31 December 1917, series 3; and Lane to Wilson, 2 January 1918, series 4; both Wilson Papers.

45. Daniels to Wilson, 3 January 1918; Lane to Wilson, 4 January 1918; and Scott Ferris to Wilson, 23 April 1918; all series 4, Wilson Papers; Cronon, *Cabinet Diaries,* 1, 4, 9, 10, 12, and 19 January 1918. For a detailed study of the oil question, 1909-21, see J. Leonard Bates, *The Origins of Teapot Dome* (Urbana: University of Illinois Press, 1963). Bates draws numerous conclusions about Lane's personality and actions that differ markedly from mine. He maintains, for example, that Lane entered the Interior Department a progressive and left a conservative, that Gifford Pinchot's 1916 criticisms were valid, and that Lane was a threat to the naval oil reserves.

46. Lane to F. H. Newell, George Otis Smith, and other bureau chiefs, 12 June 1913, FS 2-153, RG 48, Interior Records.

47. John De Novo, "Petroleum and the United States Navy before

World War I," *Mississippi Valley Historical Review* XLI (March 1955): 641-56.

48. Lane, "Land is Land: An Ancient Fallacy Exposed," *The Independent* LXXVIII (6 April 1914): 21; Press memo, 1 May 1915, Lane Papers; Daniels, *The Wilson Era: Years of Peace,* p. 379; Lane to Wilson, 1 June 1916; and Lane to Daniels, 1 August 1917; both series 2, Wilson Papers.

49. George Otis Smith, typed manuscript, 21 June 1917, FS 1-242, RG 48, Interior Records; Cronon, *Cabinet Diaries,* 18 June 1917.

50. Lane to Gregory, 24 February 1917, series 4, Wilson Papers.

51. For some of Lane's promotion of greater use of electric power, see *New York Times,* 23 November 1916, p. 16, 3 February 1919, p. 6, and 16 February 1919, p. 12; Lane, "A River of Electric Power," *The Literary Digest* LXI (24 May 1919): 22-23.

52. Lane to Van H. Manning, 24 September 1919, Lane and Wall, *Letters,* pp. 315-16; Lane, *Interior Reports,* 1919, p. 21.

53. For the need of conservation, see Lane, "Some Results of This War," *Harper's Weekly* LX (3 April 1915): 318; Lane, "Economic Preparedness," *Scientific American* CXIV (4 March 1916): 237; Lane, "The Nation's Needs of Petroleum and of a Petroleum Policy," typed manuscript, 29 December 1919, Lane Papers; Lane speech to the Conference on Natural Gas Conservation, 15 January 1920, Lane Papers; Lane, "The Oil Age and Its Needs," *The Independent* CI (17 January 1920): 89-90, 121-23; Lane, *Interior Reports,* 1919, 19-21.

54. Gerald D. Nash, *United States Oil Policy, 1890-1964* (Pittsburgh: University of Pittsburgh Press, 1968), pp. 20-21.

55. John De Novo, "The Movement for an Aggressive American Oil Policy Abroad, 1918-1920," *American Historical Review* LXI (July 1956): 864; also see, Lane, *Interior Reports,* 1919, pp. 22-24; Lane, "The Nation's Need of Petroleum and of a Petroleum Policy"; Lane, "The Oil Age and Its Needs"; *New York Times,* 11 May 1920, p. 25, and 11 October 1920, p. 23.

56. Lane, "Land is Land," p. 21; Lane, "Some Results of This War," p. 318; Lane to Albert Shaw, 6 February 1919, Shaw Papers; Lane to Van H. Manning, 24 September 1919, Lane and Wall, *Letters,* p. 316.

57. *New York Times,* 24 December 1913, p. 10; Lane, *Interior Reports,* 1914, p. 12; Lane to Wilson, 5 February 1920, Lane and Wall, *Letters,* p. 337; Lane, "The Oil Age and Its Needs," p. 89; Pinchot to Will H. Hays, 8 November 1919, box 686, Pinchot Papers.

58. For Lane's summary of his secretaryship, see Lane to Wilson,

28 February 1920, FS 22-44, RG 48, Interior Records; for an evaluation of Lane's secretaryship by the leading scholar of Woodrow Wilson, see Link, *Wilson: The New Freedom,* pp. 134-35. In contrast to Bates (see fn. 45), Link views Lane as a progressive who made important "contributions to the cause of wise conservation."

CHAPTER 8

1. Arthur Link, the dean of Wilson scholars, had concluded that "in early September 1913, . . . the President virtually stopped discussing any important question at Cabinet meetings because, as he told his friends, he simply could not trust Lane to keep the secrets of state." *Wilson: The New Freedom* (Princeton: Princeton University Press, 1956), p. 75.

Ray Stannard Baker, whose multivolume work about Wilson won a Pulitzer Prize, wrote that Wilson believed "that Secretary Lane . . . was responsible for the 'leaks.' The result was that Wilson began to be reticent in his discussion of highly confidential matters in Cabinet meetings." *Woodrow Wilson,* 8 vols. (Garden City, N.Y.: Doubleday, Page, and Doubleday, Doran, 1927-39), IV: 297-98.

Arthur Walworth, in his Pulitzer Prize-winning biography of Wilson, wrote that "Wilson's increasing reluctance to take his Cabinet into his confidence resulted in part from leaks of information that Wilson and other officials attributed to Secretary Lane's inclination to chat with newsmen and foreign diplomats after Cabinet meetings." *Woodrow Wilson,* 2 vols. (New York: Longmans, Green, and Company, 1958), I: 323n.

For Wilson giving his Cabinet members freedom to run their departments, see House Diary, 21 February 1913, 14 December 1916; David F. Houston, *Eight Years with Wilson's Cabinet* 2 vols. (Garden City, N.Y.: Doubleday, Page, and Company, 1926), I: 89; Link, *Wilson: The New Freedom,* pp. 76-77.

2. House Diary, 4 November 1913.

3. For examples, see ibid., 15 April 1914, 26 April 1914, 29 September 1914, 6 April 1915, 4 January 1917, 7 August 1917, 24 September 1918, and 2 March 1920.

4. Ray Stannard Baker interview with Lindley Garrison, 30 November 1928, Ray Stannard Baker Papers.

5. Notes on cabinet meetings found in Lane's files, dated 23 October 1918, p. 293, and 12 March 1918, p. 267, in Anne Wintermute Lane and

Louise Herrick Wall, eds., *The Letters of Franklin K. Lane* (Boston: Houghton Mifflin Company, 1922).

6. Houston, *Eight Years with Wilson's Cabinet,* II: 186.

7. Lane to George W. Lane, 1 April 1917, Lane and Wall, *Letters,* p. 243; Notes on cabinet meetings found in Lane's files, dated 1 November 1918, Lane and Wall, *Letters,* p. 296.

8. E. David Cronon, ed., *The Cabinet Diaries of Josephus Daniels* (Lincoln: The University of Nebraska Press, 1963), 30 November 1917 and 11 December 1917; also see 1 June 1917, 29 March 1918, 2 April 1918, and 30 April 1918.

9. Notes on cabinet meetings found in Lane's files, dated 1 March 1918, Lane and Wall, *Letters,* p. 266.

10. Ray Stannard Baker interview with Thomas W. Gregory, 14 and 15 March 1927, Baker Papers.

11. Houston, *Eight Years with Wilson's Cabinet,* II: 87.

12. William G. McAdoo, *Crowded Years* (Boston: Houghton Mifflin Company, 1931), pp. 193-94.

13. House Diary, 22 December 1913.

14. Ibid., single entry dated 18, 19, 20 December 1913, and 29 December 1914.

15. Wilson to Redfield, 11 February 1923, William C. Redfield Papers.

16. Ray Stannard Baker and A. Howard Meneely interview with Newton Baker, 6 April 1928, Baker Papers.

17. House Diary, 18 August 1917.

18. The only cabinet members who made this assertion were Gregory and William B. Wilson, but they did so years later. See Ray Stannard Baker, "Memorandum of Conversations with Former Attorney General Gregory," 14 and 15 March 1927; interview with William B. Wilson, 12 and 13 January 1928, Baker Papers.

19. Lane to Bryan, 6 November 1912, p. 111; Lane to John H. Wigmore, 8 January 1913, p. 122; Lane to Walter H. Page, 12 March 1913, pp. 133-34; and Lane to Ernest S. Simpson, 26 November 1912, pp. 114-15, all Lane and Wall, *Letters.*

20. Lane to Adolph C. Miller, 4 December 1912, pp. 117-18; Lane to Joseph N. Teal, 20 January 1913, p. 124; and Lane to House, 22 January 1913, pp. 125-26, all ibid.

21. Lane to Mitchell Innes, 26 February 1913, pp. 127-28, ibid.

22. Lane to Benjamin Ide Wheeler, 23 December 1912, p. 119; also see Lane to John H. Wigmore, 20 January 1913, pp. 122-23; both ibid.

23. Lane to Joseph N. Teal, 20 January 1913, p. 124; also see Lane to John C. Burns, 3 March 1915, p. 167; both ibid.

24. Lane to Albert Shaw, 12 March 1913, Sahw Papers; Lane to Walter H. Page, 12 March 1913, Lane and Wall, *Letters*, p. 133.

25. Lane to House, 21 July 1913, House Papers; Lane to Fairfax Harrison, 10 June 1913, Lane and Wall, *Letters*, p. 138.

26. House Diary, 1 April 1913; Lane to Wilson, 21 April 1913, series 3, Wilson Papers.

27. Honoré Willsie, "Mr. Lane and the Public Domain," *Harper's Weekly* LVIII (13 September 1913): 6.

28. Lane to Samuel G. Blythe, 6 January 1912, p. 87; Lane to Sidney E. Mezes, 15 February 1912, p. 88; and Lane and Wall commentary, p. 199; all in Lane and Wall, *Letters*.

29. House Diary, 19 December 1912, 24 August 1913, 28 November 1913, and 30 September 1914; *New York Times*, 13 July 1914, p. 2; Lane to Wilson, 14 July 1914, series 2; Wilson to Lane, 15 July 1914, series 3; both Wilson Papers; Josephus Daniels, *The Wilson Era: Years of Peace* (Chapel Hill: University of North Carolina Press, 1944), pp. 540-41.

30. Tattler, "Franklin Knight Lane," *The Nation* CII (20 January 1916): 70; "Resolution of the Bar Association of San Francisco Endorsing Secretary Lane for Appointment to the Supreme Court," January 1916; Daniels to Lane, 24 January 1916, both box 40, Daniels Papers; *New York Times*, 7 January 1916, p. 11; Wilson to Phelan, 11 January 1916, series 3, Wilson Papers; Lane to Carl Snyder, 22 January 1916, p. 200; and Lane to his wife, 5 February 1916, p. 202; Lane and Wall, both *Letters*.

31. Lane to Sidney E. Mezes, 4 July 1916; and House to Wilson, 13 July 1916; both House Papers; Phelan to Wilson, 8 July 1916, series 4; and Wilson to Phelan, 12 July 1916, series 4; both Wilson Papers.

32. Lane to Frank Reese, 2 July 1913, Lane and Wall, *Letters*, pp. 138-39.

33. Lane to Edward E. Leake, 26 May 1914, ibid., pp. 152-53; Phelan to Joseph Tumulty, 6 November 1914, series 4, Wilson Papers; Robert E. Hennings, "James D. Phelan and the Wilson Progressives in California" (Ph.D. diss., University of California, Berkeley, 1961), pp. 215-16; also see Lane to Wilson, 21 October 1914, series 4, Wilson Papers; Lane to House, 20 November 1914; House to Lane, 23 November 1914, both House Papers.

34. Lane to his wife, 4 July 1916, Lane and Wall, *Letters*, p. 216; Hennings, "James D. Phelan," p. 298.

35. George Mowry, *The California Progressives* (Berkeley: The University of California Press, 1951), pp. 254, 248-49; Johnson won

the primary by 20,000 votes and the election by a surprising 296,815 votes.

36. Lane to his wife, 4 July 1916, Lane and Wall, *Letters,* pp. 216-17; *Washington Times,* 21 August 1916, clipping, FS 1-144, RG 48, Interior Records; Franklin K. Lane, Jr., to Keith W. Olson, 21 February 1963, Olson files.

37. Lane to Wilson, 8 July 1916, Lane and Wall, *Letters,* pp. 211-12; Henry Morgenthau, *All in a Life-Time* (Garden City, N.Y.: Doubleday, Page, and Company, 1922), p. 242.

38. Lane to Frederic J. Lane, 6 June 1916, p. 210; and Lane to Wilson, 28 August 1916, pp. 224-25; both Lane and Wall, *Letters;* Lane to House, 28 October 1916, House Papers; Lane, "What Would They Have Done?" *New York Times,* 15 October 1916, sec. VII, p. 2, and 25 October 1916, p. 5; Lane speech at Syracuse, New York, 24 October 1916, Lane Papers.

39. Lane to R. M. Fitzgerald, 12 November 1916, pp. 228-29; and Lane to Frank I. Cobb, 11 November 1916, pp. 227-28; both Lane and Wall, *Letters.*

40. Lane to Benjamin Ide Wheeler, 14 November 1916, p. 230; and Lane to William R. Wheeler, 6 June 1914, p. 153; both ibid.; Cronon, *Cabinet Diaries,* 13 May 1913.

41. House Diary, 11 May 1913; Lane to House, 21 July 1913, House Papers; Daniels, *The Wilson Era: Years of Peace,* p. 184; Adolph Miller to Benjamin Ide Wheeler, 16 May 1914, box 2, Miller Papers; Lane to Wilson, 13 March 1916, series 2; for examples of advice, see Lane to Wilson, c. July 1913, 26 May 1915, 5 June 1915, and 9 September 1915; all Wilson Papers.

42. Henry N. Hall, "The President's Mexican Policy," interview with Lane, 16 July 1916, Lane Papers.

43. *New York Times,* 24 August 1916, p. 8; also see *Richmond Times Dispatch,* 24 August 1916; *St. Louis Republic,* 25 August 1916; and *Syracuse Journal,* 24 August 1916; all clippings in FS 1-144, RG 48, Interior Records.

44. *Papers Relating to the Foreign Relations of the United States, 1917* (Washington, D.C.: Government Printing Office, 1926), pp. 916-38; Arthur S. Link, *Wilson: Campaigns for Progressivism and Peace* (Princeton: Princeton University Press, 1965), pp. 51-55, 328-36; H. Bruere, "The Reminiscences of H. Bruere" (Columbia University, Oral History Research Office, 1949), pp. 138-39; Hugh Scott, *Some Memories of a Soldier* (New York: The Century Company, 1928),

pp. 529-30; Lane, "Remarks at a Luncheon to the Joint American-Mexican Commission," 4 September 1916, found in Lane, *The American Spirit* (New York: Frederick A. Stokes Company, 1918), pp. 24-26; Lane to his wife, 24 July 1916, p. 217; Lane to Frederic J. Lane, 29 September 1916, p. 227; Lane to Alexander Vogelsang, 29 September 1916, p. 226; and Lane to Benjamin Ide Wheeler, 14 November 1916, p. 230; all Lane and Wall, *Letters;* for representative correspondence, see Wilson to Lane, 31 August 1916, series 3; Lane to Wilson, 6 October 1916, series 2; Lane to Wilson, 20 December 1916, series 2; and Lane, George Gray, and John Mott to Wilson, 3 January 1917, series 5A; all in box 1, Newton D. Baker Papers.

45. New York Times, 18 August 1914, p. 13, and 26 June 1915, p. 1; Lane, "Some Results of This War," *Harper's Weekly* LX (3 April 1915): 318.

46. Lane to John C. Burns, 22 January 1915, Lane and Wall, *Letters,* p. 164; Lane to House, 5 May 1915, House Papers; for additional criticisms of Britain see Lane to Burns, 3 March 1915, p. 166; 13 March 1915, p. 169; 29 May 1915, pp. 173-74; and 30 July 1915, p. 179, all in Lane and Wall, *Letters.*

47. Lane to his wife, 22 July 1916, p. 214, ibid.; *New York Times,* 25 October 1916, p. 5.

48. Quoted in Edward Marshall, "War's Heavy Aftermath of Cost," *New York Times,* 4 July 1915, sec. IV, p. 11; Lane speech, Brown University, 21 June 1916, Lane Papers; also see Lane to John C. Burns, 30 July 1915, Lane and Wall, *Letters,* p. 179; Lane, *Interior Reports,* 1915, p. 3.

49. Lane to House, 5 May 1915, House Papers; Lane to Frederic J. Lane, 21 July 1915, Lane and Wall, *Letters,* pp. 177-78; McAdoo, *Crowded Years,* pp. 339-41.

50. Lane to George W. Wickersham, 18 July 1915, p. 176; Lane to John F. Davis, 2 August 1915, pp. 180-81; Lane to Frank I. Cobb, 8 May 1916, p. 207, all Lane and Wall, *Letters.*

51. Lane, "Concerning Foreign Affairs," *Harper's Weekly* CXII (4 March 1916): 224; also see Lane to Frederick J. Lane, 21 July 1915, p. 177; Lane to Eugene A. Avery, 2 August 1915, p. 180; and Lane to John H. Wigmore, 8 December 1915, p. 188; all Lane and Wall, *Letters.*

52. Lane speech, Syracuse, New York, 24 October 1916, Lane Papers; Baker, *Woodrow Wilson,* VI: 237-38; Daniels, *The Wilson Era: Years of Peace,* p. 581.

53. Daniels, *The Wilson Era: Years of Peace,* pp. 581, 594; Robert

Lansing, "Memorandum of the Cabinet Meeting, March 20, 1917,"
Lansing Diary, vol. II, Robert Lansing Papers; Lane to Geroge W. Lane,
25 February 1917, Lane and Wall, *Letters,* pp. 239-40.

54. Lane to George W. Lane, 16 February 1917, p. 236; 25 February
1917, pp. 240-41; and 1 April 1917, pp. 242-43, all Lane and Wall, *Letters;*
also see Lane to George W. Lane, 9 February 1917, pp. 233-34; 10 February 1917, p. 235; 20 February 1917, p. 238; and 6 March 1917, pp. 241-
42; all Lane and Wall, *Letters; New York Times,* 21 March 1917, p. 10;
Cronon, *Cabinet Diaries,* 30 March 1917; and House Diary, 1 February
1917.

CHAPTER 9

1. For Lane sentiments on why the United States was fighting a war,
see Lane, "Foresight and Cooperation," speech at a meeting of State
Councils of Defense, 2 May 1917, *The American Spirit* (New York:
Frederick A. Stokes Company, 1918), p. 60; *New York Times,* 3 May,
p. 1; 26 May, p. 4; 5 June, p. 2; 6 July, p. 5; and 24 August, p. 3, all
1917; 6 July 1918, p. 8; "Why We Are Fighting Germany," speech before
the Home Club, 4 June 1917, Lane Papers; "All for Liberty," *St. Nicholas*
XLIV (August 1917): 876-77; speech delivered in Oklahoma, 28 September 1917, FS 1-188, RG 48, Interior Records; "The New Americanism,"
5 July 1918, *Addresses and Proceedings of the 56th Annual Meeting of
the National Education Association of the United States, 1918,* p. 105.

2. Lane, "Three Flags in the Same Colors," speech at the Belasco
Theater, 1 May 1917, *The American Spirit,* p. 66.

3. Lane to George W. Lane, 3 May 1917, in Anne Wintermute Lane
and Louise Herrick Wall, eds., *The Letters of Franklin K. Lane* (Boston:
Houghton Mifflin Company, 1922), p. 250; for similar sentiments, see
Lane, "Three Flags in the Same Colors," pp. 65-66; *New York Times,*
3 May 1917, p. 1; 6 July 1917, p. 5.

4. *New York Times,* 6 July 1918, p. 8; Lane to George W. Lane,
3 May 1917, p. 250; and Lane to Edgar C. Bradley, 18 December 1918,
p. 305, both Lane and Wall, *Letters.*

5. Lane to J. Cosgrave, 21 December 1917, p. 263; also see Lane to
John Lyon, 15 March 1918, p. 278; both in Lane and Wall, *Letters;* Lane
speech, 28 September 1917, FS 1-188, RG 48, Interior Records.

6. Lane to George W. Lane, 15 April, pp. 246-47; and Lane to Frank I. Cobb, 12 April, p. 245; both 1917 and both Lane and Wall, *Letters.*

7. Notes on Cabinet meetings found in Lane's files, dated 1 March 1918, pp. 266-67; also see Lane to Robert Lansing, n.d. August 1917, pp. 255-56; and Lane to John Lyon, 15 March 1918, p. 279; all ibid.

8. Lane to George W. Lane, 15 April 1917, p. 247, ibid.; E. David Cronon, ed., *The Cabinet Diaries of Josephus Daniels* (Lincoln: The University of Nebraska Press, 1963), 17 July 1917.

9. The seven named were Daniel Willard, president of the Baltimore and Ohio Railroad; Hollis Godfrey, president of Drexel Institute; Howard Coffin, chairman of the Committee on Industrial Preparedness of the Naval Consulting Board; Dr. Franklin Martin, director-general of the American College of Surgeons; Bernard Baruch, financier; Julius Rosenwald, vice-president of Sears, Roebuck, and Company; and Samuel Gompers, president of the American Federation of Labor.

10. For the Council of National Defense and the Advisory Council in general and Lane in particular, see Franklin H. Martin, *The Joy of Living,* Vol. II (Garden City, N.Y.: Doubleday, Doran, and Company, 1933), pp. 43-45, 49-51, 62-63, 68-69, 89-90, 116, 121-22; and 145; Bernard Baruch, *The Public Years* (New York: Holt, Rinehart, and Winston, 1960), pp. 24-26, 35-39, 41-44, 47-48, and 282; Josephus Daniels, *The Wilson Era: Years of War and After* (Chapel Hill: The University of North Carolina Press, 1946), pp. 195-96, 212-13, 586, and 589-90; Samuel Gompers, *Seventy Years of Life and Labor,* vol. II (New York: E. P. Dutton and Company, 1925), pp. 352, 360-61, and 366-67; Frederic Paxon, "The American War Government," *American Historical Review* XXVI (October 1920): 54-76; Grosvenor B. Clarkson, *Industrial America in the World War* (Boston: Houghton Mifflin Company, 1923), pp. 10-64, 81, 285-86, and 385-86; Lane and Wall, commentary, pp. 248-50, Lane and Wall, *Letters;* Lane to Newton D. Baker, 11 July 1918, box 40, Daniels Papers; House Diary, 26 and 27 April 1917; Cronon, *Cabinet Diaries,* 19 April 1917, 30 April 1917, 27 December 1917, 3 January 1918, 22 July 1918, and 24 September 1918; Baker to Clarkson, 2 October 1925, Grosvenor Clarkson Papers; Lane to George W. Lane, 16 February, pp. 236-37; and 15 April, pp. 246-47, both 1917; Lane to Daniel Willard, 7 November 1918, pp. 300-301; and notes on cabinet meetings found in Lane's files, dated 11 November 1918, p. 300; all in Lane and Wall, *Letters.*

11. Baruch, *The Public Years,* p. 42.

12. Margaret L. Coit, *Mr. Baruch* (Boston: Houghton Mifflin Company, 1957), p. 157; Martin, *The Joy of Living,* vol. II, pp. 89-90; commentary,

Lane and Wall, *Letters,* pp. 248-49; Baruch, *The Public Years,* pp. 41-42; Clarkson, *Industrial America,* pp. 28-29.

13. For examples, see Martin, *The Joy of Living,* vol. II, p. 145; Daniels, *The Wilson Era: Years of War and After,* pp. 212-13; Cronon, *Cabinet Diaries,* 24 September 1918; commentary, Lane and Wall, *Letters,* p. 250.

14. Actually Gompers did not arrive in New York until the evening of March 17 as he had been resting for the weekend in Atlantic City, out of reach of the press and telephone, and was late learning of his appointment.

15. *New York Times,* 20 March 1917, p. 4.

16. Ibid., and 21 March 1917, p. 10.

17. For the strike settlement and Lane's role, see *New York Times,* 17 March, pp. 1, 4; 18 March, p. 1; 20 March, p. 4; and 21 March, p. 10, all 1917; Gompers, *Seventy Years of Life and Labor,* vol. II, pp. 146-47; Martin, *The Joy of Living,* vol. II, pp. 107-8; commentary, Lane and Wall, *Letters,* pp. 244-45; Frederick Palmer, *Newton D. Baker: America at War,* vol. II (New York: Dodd, Mead, and Company, 1931), pp. 97-98; William G. McAdoo, *Crowded Years* (Boston: Houghton, Mifflin Company, 1931), p. 451; Cronon, *Cabinet Diaries,* 16 March 1917; Newton D. Baker to Lane, William Wilson, Daniel Willard, and Samuel Gompers, 16 March 1917; Elisha Lee to Lane, William Wilson, Willard, and Gompers, 19 March 1917; "Statement Awarded by the Committee of the Council of National Defense," 19 March 1917; and W. G. Lee to Lane, 27 March 1917; all FS 1-53, RG 48, Interior Records; Elisha Lee et al. to Wilson, 7 March 1917; W. G. Lee to Wilson, 16 March 1917; J. Tumulty to Wilson, 16 March 1917; Lane to William B. Wilson, 17 March 1917; and Willard to Wilson, 17 March 1917; all series 4, Wilson Papers.

18. *New York Times,* 3 May 1917, p. 1; *New York Evening Post,* 2 May 1917, p. 1; commentary, Lane and Wall, *Letters,* pp. 249-50; Lane to Frank I. Cobb, 5 May 1917, p. 233; and Lane to Will Irwin, 21 July 1917, p. 255, all Lane and Wall, *Letters;* Stanley Washburn, "The Reminiscences of Stanley Washburn" (Columbia University, Oral History Research Office, 1950), pp. 156-57.

19. Lane to Wilson, 29 March; Wilson to William J. Harris, 31 March; Harris to Wilson, 7 April; and Wilson to Harris, 9 April; all 1917 and all series 4, Wilson Papers.

20. "The Committee on Coal Production," *Coal Age* 11 (12 May 1917): 817-19; Francis S. Peabody to Lane, 25 April; Lane to W. S. Gifford, 26 April; Peabody to Gifford, 12 May; and John White to the Council of National Defense, 21 May, 23 May; all 1917 and all FS 1-53, RG 48, Interior Records.

21. Lane speech before meeting of coal producers, 26 June 1917, Lane

Papers; *New York Times,* 27 June 1917, p. 1.

22. Press memo, Office of the Secretary of the Interior, 28 June 1917; and John F. Fort to Wilson, 30 June 1917; both FS 1-53, RG 48, Interior Records.

23. Lane remarks at the conclusion of the conference, 28 June 1917, Lane Papers; Lane to Peabody, 28 June; Peabody to Gifford, 30 June; and Fort to Wilson, 30 June; all 1917 and all FS 1-53, RG 48, Interior Records.

24. Newton D. Baker to Charles Seymour, 26 September 1921, box 20, Baker Papers; Cronon, *Cabinet Diaries,* 29, 30 June 1917; *New York Times,* 2 July, p. 6; 3 July, p. 1; and 14 July, p. 6; all 1917; Dix W. Smith to Lane, 26 June; Thrasher Hall to Lane, 27 June; W. J. Spaulding to Lane, 1 July; and Richard Edmonds to Lane, 2 July; all 1917; and all FS 1-53, RG 48, Interior Records; Daniel R. Beaver, *Newton D. Baker and the American War Effort, 1917-1919* (Lincoln: University of Nebraska Press, 1966), pp. 64-66.

25. Newton D. Baker to Charles Seymour, 26 September 1921, box 20, Baker Papers; Daniels, *The Wilson Era: Years of War and After,* p. 244; Lane to J. S. Cullinan, 5 July 1917; and Lane to Frederic A. Delano, 6 July 1917; both FS 1-53, RG 48, Interior Records.

26. Arthur S. Link, *The American Epoch* (New York: Alfred A. Knopf, 1955), p. 209; also see editorial in *Denver News,* 18 January 1918, clipping in FS 1-53, RG 48, Interior Records.

27. Wilson to Fort, 2 July 1917, FS 1-53, RG 48, Interior Records; House Diary, 15 August and 19 December, both 1917; Baker to Seymour, 26 September 1921, Baker Papers; Lane to Robert Lansing, 14 May 1921, Lane and Wall, *Letters,* p. 463.

28. *New York Times,* 9 December, p. 2; and 14 December, p. 1; both 1917; Mary Synon, *McAdoo* (Indianapolis: The Bobbs-Merrill Company, 1924), p. 312; I. Leo Sharfman, *The American Railroad Problem* (New York: The Century Company, 1921), pp. 90-99.

29. House Diary, 19 December 1917; *New York Times,* 17 December 1917, p. 3.

30. *New York Times,* 19 January, p. 1; 29 January, p. 7, both 1918; Sharfman, *The American Railroad Problem,* p. 120; General Order No. 5 of the Railroad Administration, 18 January 1918; minutes of the Railroad Wage Commission, 21 January 1918, FS 1-197, RG 48, Interior Records.

31. William G. McAdoo, *Crowded Years,* (Boston: Houghton Mifflin Company, 1931), pp. 488-91; Sharfman, *The American Railroad Problem,* pp. 121-22, 153-54, and 174-77.

32. House Diary, 19 May 1918; *New York Times,* 5 December 1918,

p. 1; McAdoo, *Crowded Years*, p. 504; K. Austin Kerr, *American Railroad Politics, 1914-1920* (Pittsburgh: The University of Pittsburgh Press, 1968), pp. 93-96.

33. Lane speech, 31 May 1918, Lane Papers; also see Lane speech, 19 April 1918, Lane Papers; McAdoo, *Crowded Years*, pp. 384-88, 391, and 406-10; *New York Times*, 24 October 1917, p. 3; and 8 April 1918, p. 6; Lane, The Message of the West," *The American Spirit*, pp. 85-94; McAdoo to Lane, 28 September 1917; Wilson to Lane, 29 September 1917; and Lane to Glenn Shaeffer, 6 October 1917; all in FS 1-188, RG 48, Interior Records.

34. Henry Morgenthau, *All in a Life-Time* (Garden City, N.Y.: Doubleday, Page, and Company, 1922), pp. 250-52.

35. Lane to George W. Lane, 3 May 1917, Lane and Wall, *Letters*, p. 252.

36. Lane to Theodore Roosevelt, c. July 1918, series 1, Roosevelt Papers.

37. Wilson to Lane, 25 February 1918, series 3, Wilson Papers; John Ise, *Our National Park Policy* (Baltimore: The Johns Hopkins Press, 1961), pp. 301-2; Robert Shankland, *Steve Mather of the National Parks* (New York: Alfred A. Knopf, 1954), pp. 202-6; Horace M. Albright, "The Reminiscences of Horace M. Albright" (Columbia University, Oral History Research Office, 1962), pp. 413-17.

38. Clarkson, *Industrial America in the World War*, pp. 385-86.

39. Lane to Wilson, 31 May 1918, Lane Papers.

40. Cronon, *Cabinet Diaries*, 31 May 1917; William B. Wilson, "Report of the Secretary of Labor," *Reports of the Department of Labor, 1915* (Washington, D.C.: Government Printing Office, 1916), pp. 44-45.

41. Frederick C. Howe, *The Land and the Soldier* (New York: Charles Scribner's Sons, 1919), pp. 100-101, 128; Elwood Mead, "Government Aid and Direction in Land Settlement," *American Economic Review* VII (Supplement, March 1917): 72-98; Paul K. Conkin, "The Vision of Elwood Mean," *Agricultural History* 34 (April 1960): 88-97.

42. Harry Slattery, one-time secretary of the National Conservation Association, and in May 1918 a special assistant to Lane, drafted Lane's original soldier settlement plan. See Slattery to John J. McSwain, 12 November 1919, Slattery Papers.

43. Kent to Wilson, 27 May; Wilson to Kent, 31 May; and Kent to Wilson, 3 June; all 1918 and all Slattery Papers.

44. See Kent to Wilson, 26 June, Slattery Papers; for a biting attack upon the timing, origin, and motive behind Lane's letter to Wilson, see "Lane and Mondell—Real Estate," *The Public* XXII (2 August 1919): 819-21.

45. For Lane's motives, see Lane to E. S. Pillsbury, 30 July 1918, Lane and Wall, *Letters,* pp. 291-92; Lane, "When They Come Home," *The Nation's Business* VI (September 1918): 22-23; Lane, "Putting Two and Two Together," *The Independent* XCVI (26 October 1918): 121, 139; Lane, "A Chance for Every American," *Everybody's Magazine* XXXIX (December 1918): 51-52; Lane, "Work and Homes for Returning Soldiers," *Review of Reviews* LIX (March 1919): 269-70; Lane, "Farms for the Returning Soldiers," *Current Opinion* LXVI (March 1919): 194; Lane, "Out of the Army Back to the Land: With the Help of the United States Government," *Touchstone* V (June 1919): 223; Lane to Wilson, 28 February 1920, FS 22-23, RG 48, Interior Records.

46. Lane quoting Wilson in letter to Edward H. Loveland, 3 March 1919, FS 1-201, RG 48, Interior Records.

47. Lane to Wilson, 31 May 1918, Lane Papers; also see Lane to R. L. Watts, 10 April 1919, FS 8-80, RG 48, Interior Records.

48. U. S. House of Representatives, 66th Cong., 1st sess., *Hearings before the Committee on Irrigation of Arid Lands* (Washington, D.C.: Government Printing Office, 1919), Lane statement, "Report of the Secretary of the Interior on H.R. 487," 10 January 1919, p. 37; for the social side of Lane's proposals, see Lane, "Farms for Returned Soldiers," *Scientific American* CXIX (9 November 1918): 373, 382; Lane, *Interior Reports,* 1918, p. 9; Lane, "Out of the Army Back to the Land," p. 220; *New York Times,* 11 January 1919, p. 4; and 26 April 1919, p. 14.

49. For support of Lane's plan, see *New York Times,* 25 January, p. 10; 27 February, p. 3; 26 April, p. 14; 29 May, p. 28; 19 December, p. 14; and 28 December, sec. IX, p. 5, all 1919; U. S. House of Representatives, 66th Cong. 1st sess., *Hearings before the Committee on the Public Lands* (Washington, D.C.: Government Printing Office, 1919), Lane statement, 28 May 1919, pp. 30-52; Howe, *The Land and the Soldier;* Elwood Mean, *Helping Men Own Farms, A Practical Discussion of Goverment Aid in Land Settlement* (New York: The Macmillan Company, 1920); Ray Stannard Baker and William E. Dodd, *The Public Papers of Woodrow Wilson: War and Peace,* 2 vols. (New York: Harper and Brothers, 1927), I: 314-15; U. S. Senate, 65th Cong., 2nd sess., *Report No. 580,* pp. 1-2, 5-7; A. P. David to John Barton Payne, 6 April 1920, FS 8-80, RG 48, Interior Records.

50. *New York Times,* 8 June 1919, p. 21; "Lane and Mondell-Real Estate," pp. 819-22; Lane to Mead, 18 October 1919, FS 8-80, RG 48, Interior Records; Lane, "A Mind's-Eye Map of America," *The National Geographic Magazine* XXXVII (June 1920): 507; Lane to John Finley, 4 May 1921, Lane and Wall, *Letters,* pp. 453-54; for agricultural opposition

to Lane's plan, I relied on Bill G. Reid, "Proposals for Soldier Settlement During World War I," *Mid-America* XLVI (July 1964): 172-86; "Agrarian Opposition to Franklin K. Lane's Proposal for Soldier Settlement, 1918-1921," *Agricultural History* XLI (April 1967): 167-79; and "Franklin K. Lane's Idea for Veterans' Colonization, 1918-1921," *Pacific Historical Review* XXXIII (November 1964): 447-61.

51. Lane file, Interstate Commerce Commission Library.

52. *New York Times,* 15 September 1918, sec. IV, p. 4.

53. Wilson to Lane, 13 July 1914, series 3, Wilson Papers; House to Lane, 10 August 1914, House Papers; "The Progress of the World," *Review of Reviews* L (August 1914): 146; *New York Times,* 14 June 1915, p. 9; for a copy of Lane's speech, see *Review of Reviews* L (August 1914): 147; for Lane Flag Day observances see FS 1-164, part I, RG 48, Interior Records.

54. For typical Lane views on the American spirit before the war, see his speech at Brown University, 21 June 1916, Lane Papers; and his address before the National Conference on Americanization, 4 February 1917, found in *New York Times,* 5 February 1917, p. 4.

55. For example, see Lane to Frederick Dixon, 7 October 1915, Lane and Wall, *Letters,* pp. 185-86.

56. Lane to Wilson, 14 March 1918, found in *Interior Reports,* 1918, pp. 29-31; also see Lane to George W. Lane, 16 February 1918, Lane and Wall, *Letters,* pp. 270-71; *New York Times,* 16 March 1918, p. 22.

57. Lane, "What Is It to Be an American," *The National Geographic Magazine* XXXIII (April 1918): 354.

58. Lane, "What Is an American?" *The Declineator* XCIII (August 1918): 2; for other Lane views on education and Americanism during the summer of 1918, see Lane, "The New Americanism," pp. 106-8; *New York Times,* 25 August 1918, sec. IX, p. 10; 14 September 1918, 11; Lane to Frank I. Cobb, dated "1919," Lane and Wall, *Letters,* pp. 326-27.

59. Lane, *Interior Reports,* 1918, p. 14.

60. Ibid., pp. 13-24; Lane, "The Living Flame of Americanism," *The New York Times Current History* XIV (July 1921): 608-10; Lane, "How to Make Americans," *The Forum* LXI (April 1919): 400-406.

61. Lane, "A Chance for Every American," p. 51; *New York Times,* 12 January p. 18; 27 January, p. 8, both 1919, Lane, "How to Make Americans," speech at the Americanization Banquet, Washington, D.C., 14 May 1919, Lane Papers; Lane, "What I Mean by Americanization," *Ladies Home Journal* XXXVI (May 1919): 33, 146; Lane, "What Americanization Means," *The Forum* LXII (September 1919): 370-71; Lane, "Americanization," *World Outlook* V (November 1919): 14-15; Lane to

Henry P. Davison, 23 November 1919, pp. 321-22; and Lane to Hamlin Garland, 31 December 1919, p. 333; both Lane and Wall, *Letters; New York Times,* 11 January 1920, sec. VIII, p. 6; Lane, speech to the Twentieth Century Club, 3 February 1920, Lane Papers; Lane, "A Mind's-Eye Map of America," pp. 479, 504-7, 510.

62. Interview with Lane by unnamed person, undated manuscript, Lane Papers.

CHAPTER 10

1. *New York Times,* 31 October 1918, p. 6; Lane to Wilson, 17 October 1918, series 2, Wilson Papers; Lane also wrote letters of endorsement to several senators.

2. Lane to Samuel G. Blythe, 13 November, pp. 302-3; Lane to James H. Hawley, 9 November, pp. 301-2; also see notes on Cabinet meetings found in Lane's files, dated 1, 5, 6 November, pp. 296-99; all 1918 and all in Anne Wintermute Lane and Louise Herrick Wall, eds., *The Letters of Franklin K. Lane* (Boston: Houghton Mifflin Company, 1922); Josephus Daniels, *The Wilson Era: Years of War and After* (Chapel Hill: The University of North Carolina Press, 1946), p. 307.

3. Oswald Villard, *Fighting Years* (New York: Harcourt, Brace, and Company, 1939), pp. 355-56; Joy Humes, *Oswald Garrison Villard: Liberal of the 1920's* (Syracuse University Press, 1960), pp. 36-39; Donald Johnson, "Wilson, Burleson, and Censorship in the First World War," *The Journal of Southern History* XXVIII (February 1962): 46-58.

4. For Lane's fears, see Lane to George W. Lane, 11 September 1919, pp. 312-13; Lane to E. C. Bradley, 2 October 1919, p. 317; Lane to Eleanor Roosevelt, n.d. November 1920, p. 372; and Lane to Benjamin Ide Wheeler, 18 November 1920, p. 370; all Lane and Wall, *Letters.*

5. Lane to Walter H. Page, p. 277; and Lane to John McNaught, p. 284; both 16 March 1918 and both ibid.

6. Lane to E. S. Pillsbury, 30 July 1918, p. 291; Lane to Frank I. Cobb, dated "1919," p. 326; both Lane and Wall, *Letters;* Lane, "Farms for the Returning Soldiers," *Current Opinion* LXVI (March 1919): 194; and Lane to James Cox, 25 July 1920, p. 384, Lane and Wall, *Letters.*

7. For Lane's postwar views on socialism, Bolshevism, and the need for change in America, not already cited, see Lane, speech at the Victory Dinner of the Representatives of Women's Clubs, Woodley Courts, Washington, D.C., 13 February 1919; and untitled typed statement, 27 April 1919; both in Lane Papers; Lane to Mrs. Ralph Ellis, dated March 1919,

pp. 383-87; Lane to E. S. Martin, 23 August 1919, pp. 311-12; Lane to E. C. Bradley, 2 October 1919, p. 317; Lane to Isadore B. Dockweiler, 25 September 1920, pp. 355-56; and Lane to D. M. Reynolds, dated February 1921, p. 427; all Lane and Wall, *Letters;* Lane, "A Mind's-Eye Map of America," *The National Geographic Magazine* XXXVII (June 1921): 510.

8. Lane, "How to Make Americans," *The Forum* LXI (April 1919): 405; Lane, "Americanization," *World Outlook* V (November 1919): 15; *New York Times,* 25 June 1920, p. 11.

9. Lane to Frank I. Cobb, dated 1919, pp. 326-27, Lane and Wall, *Letters;* Oswald Villard, "Franklin K. Lane," *The Nation* CXII (1 June 1921): 788.

10. Lane to George W. Lane, 30 January 1919, Lane and Wall, *Letters,* p. 307; Josephus Daniels to M. G. Woodward, 5 December 1927, box 620, Daniels Papers; Daniels, *The Wilson Era: Years of War and After,* p. 352; Lane speech before the Merchants' Association at the Hotel Astor, New York City, 16 January 1919, reported in the *New York Times,* 17 January 1919, p. 2.

11. Lane to George W. Lane, 1 May, p. 309; and 11 September, p. 314; both 1919 and both Lane and Wall, *Letters;* Lane to Bainbridge Colby, 19 April 1919, series 4, Wilson Papers; *New York Times,* 4 April, p. 2, and 31 July, p. 3, both 1919.

12. Lane speech, "League of Nations," Lane Papers; Lane to E. C. Bradley, 2 October 1919, Lane and Wall, *Letters,* p. 317.

13. Henry Morgenthau, *All in a Life-Time* (Garden City, N.Y.: Doubleday, Page, and Company, 1922), p. 300; *New York Times,* 13 February 1920, p. 8; Lansing Diary, 16 December 1919; John M. Blum, *Joe Tumulty and the Wilson Era* (Boston: Houghton Mifflin Company, 1951), pp. 230-36; Lane to James Cox, 25 July 1920, Lane and Wall, *Letters,* pp. 344-45.

14. Lane to Thomas A. Bynum, 26 June 1916, Lane Papers; Lane to Wilson, 23 January; Wilson to Lane, 31 January, both series 5B; and Lane to Wilson, 12 August, series 2; all 1919 and all Wilson Papers.

15. *New York Times,* 29 August 1919, p. 4; 7 October 1919, p. 1.

16. Wilson to Homer L. Ferguson, September 1919, series 3, Wilson Papers; *Proceedings of the First Industrial Conference,* 1919 (Washington, D.C.: Government Printing Office, 1920), 5-7.

17. *Proceedings of the First Industrial Conference, 1919,* pp. 9, 16-18; *New York Times,* 7 October 1919, p. 1.

18. *Proceedings of the First Industrial Conference, 1919,* pp. 19-21.

19. *New York Times,* 7 October 1919, p. 1.

20. Ibid., 22 October and 23 October, both 1919, both p. 1.

21. Lane to M. A. Mathew, 3 November 1919, Lane and Wall, *Letters*, p. 320; in addition to the *Proceedings*, for coverage of the conference, see Lane to Joe Tumulty, 19 October; Lane to Wilson, 19 October; Wilson to Lane, 23 October; Lane to Wilson, 23 October; Lane to Tumulty, undated but probably written 23 October; Ida Tarbell to Lane, 28 October; and Martin Glynn to Tumulty, 23 December, all 1919; all series 4, Wilson Papers; *New York Times*, 26 October 1919, p. 1.

22. Lane to James Cox, 25 July 1920, p. 347; Lane to Benjamin Ide Wheeler, 18 November 1920, p. 370; and Lane to D. M. Reynolds, dated February 1921, p. 427; all Lane and Wall, *Letters*.

23. Lane to John H. Wigmore, 8 December 1915, p. 188; and Lane to Francis R. Wall, 27 November 1915, p. 187; both ibid.; *New York Times*, 7 January 1919, p. 5.

24. Lane to E. C. Bradley, dated January 1919, Lane and Wall, *Letters*, p. 306; *New York Times*, 7 January 1919, p. 5.

25. *New York Times*, 14 January and 22 January, both 1919 and both p. 6; Lane to William Boyce Thompson, 20 May 1919, Lane and Wall, *Letters*, p. 310; *The Roosevelt Memorial Association* (New York: The Roosevelt Memorial Association, 1921), pp. 7, 9, 33.

26. Roosevelt to Lane, 30 November 1914, series 2; Roosevelt to Lane, 23 July 1918, series 3A; and Roosevelt to William Allen White, 22 November 1918, series 3A; all Roosevelt Papers.

27. *New York Times*, 19 December 1919, p. 14; *New York World*, 19 December 1919, p. 12; *New York Tribune*, 19 December p. 12; also see *Brooklyn Eagle*, 18 December; *New York Post*, 19 December; *Springfield Republican*, 19 December; *Syracuse Journal*, 18 December; *Sioux City Journal*, 19 December; *Denver News*, 29 December; *Richmond Times-Dispatch*, 19 December; *Richmond Journal*, 19 December; *Baltimore News*, 18 December; *Chattanooga News*, 18 December; *Sacramento Union*, 19 December; all 1919 and all clippings in FS 22-44, RG 48, Interior Records; "Mr. Lane and the Cabinet Crisis," *The Nation* CX (3 January 1920): 844.

28. *Portland Telegram*, 9 February; *Organized Labor*, 14 February; *Christian Science Monitor*, 10 February; *New York Post*, 10 February; *Baltimore Sun*, 1 March; *Washington Post*, 9 February; all 1920 and all FS 22-44, RG 48, Interior Records; editorial, *The World's Work* XXXIX (February 1920): 268.

29. For Lane's repeated mention of the need for a larger income as the reason for his resignation, see Lane to George W. Lane, 28 November 1919, pp. 322-23; Lane to John C. Burns, 29 December 1919, p. 325; Lane to Cary Grayson, 5 January 1920, pp. 335-36; and Lane to Frank W. Mondell, 13 February 1920, p. 338; all Lane and Wall, *Letters*.

30. Lane to George W. Lane, 28 November 1919, p. 323; for example, see Lane to Hugo K. Asher, 3 January 1920, p. 335; both ibid.

31. For representative views on Lane's financial plight, see Lane to Hugo K. Asher, 22 October 1912, p. 108; Lane to William R. Wheeler, 6 June 1914, p. 153; Lane to Mrs. Magnus Anderson, 24 December 1915, p. 191; and Lane to Dan J. O'Neill, 24 December 1919, p. 332; all in ibid.

32. *New York Times,* 28 September 1919, p. 18; Lansing Diary, 6 October 1919, 23 February 1920; Lane to Cary Grayson, 5 January 1920, Lane and Wall, *Letters,* p. 335; copies of Lane's resignation and Wilson's acceptance appeared in the *New York Times,* 8 February 1920, section I, p. 5.

33. Lane to George W. Lane, 28 November 1919, Lane and Wall, *Letters,* p. 322; Lawrence F. Abbott, "A Passionate American," *The Outlook* CXXCIII (1 June 1920): 205-6; *New York Times,* 1 January, p. 27; 16 January, p. 15; and 18 February, p. 6, all 1920; David Lawrence to Lane, 31 December 1919, Lane Papers.

34. Lane to Wilson, 28 February 1920, FS 22-44, RG 48, Interior Records; also see *New York Times,* 1 March, p. 1; 2 March, p. 10; and 14 March, sec. VII, p. 2, all 1920.

35. *New York Times,* 11 July 1920, sec. 2, p. 2; Lane to Adolph C. Miller, pp. 414-15; Lane to D. M. Reynolds, dated February 1920, p. 428, both in Lane and Wall, *Letters;* Lane, "The Cabinet," typed manuscript dated January 1921, Lane Papers.

36. *New York Times,* 15 February 1920, sec. II, p. 1; 24 November 1920, p. 5; and 2 March 1921, p. 28; Lane to John W. Hallowell, 12 November 1920, Lane and Wall, *Letters,* p. 361.

37. Lane to Benjamin Ide Wheeler, 14 November 1916, p. 230; also see Lane to E. C. Bradley, dated January 1919, p. 306; both Lane and Wall, *Letters.*

38. Lane quoted in commentary, p. 356, ibid.; Lane to Phelan, 1 November 1920, Phelan Papers; also see Lane to Benjamin Ide Wheeler, 28 October 1920, Lane and Wall, *Letters,* p. 359.

39. Lane to Robert Lansing, 10 November 1920, p. 362; and Lane to Benjamin Ide Wheeler, 18 November 1920, p. 371; both Lane and Wall, *Letters;* also see Lane to Phelan, 18 November 1920, Phelan Papers.

40 Herbert Hoover, *The Memoirs of Herbert Hoover; Years of Adventure, 1874-1920* (New York: The Macmillan Company, 1951), pp. 200, 265; Hoover, *The Ordeal of Woodrow Wilson* (New York: McGraw Hill Book Company, 1958), pp. 7-8; Lane to Hoover, 19 December 1916; Hoover to Curtis Lindley, 20 December 1916; and Hoover to Lane, 4 January 1917; all Hoover Papers.

41. Lane to E. C. Bradley, 2 October 1919, p. 317; Lane to George

W. Lane, dated December 1919, p. 331; and Lane to Hugo K. Asher, 3 January 1920, p. 334; all Lane and Wall, *Letters.*

42. For Hoover and the Democrats in 1920, see Wesley Bagby, *The Road to Normalcy* (Baltimore: The Johns Hopkins University Press, 1962), p. 43; House Diary, 5 November 1919; for Lane's view of Hoover, see Lane to Benjamin Ide Wheeler, 18 November 1920, pp. 370-71; Lane to Wheeler, 1 January 1921, p. 402; Lane to John W. Hallowell, 21 February 1921, pp. 421-22; and Lane to Curt G. Pfeiffer, 22 February 1921, p. 422; all Lane and Wall, *Letters.*

43. For Lane's declining health and death, see the many comments in his letters from July 1920 to May 1921, found in pp. 342-465; Lane and Wall, *Letters;* C. A. Severance to Frank B. Kellogg, 7 May 1921; and William J. Mayo to Herbert C. Hoover, 23 May 1921; both Hoover Papers; for Lane's views of his son's bride and wedding, see Lane to Curt G. Pfeiffer, 22 February, p. 423; and Lane to James D. Phelan, 2 May, pp. 449-50; both 1920 and Lane and Wall, *Letters.*

44. Lane to James Cox, 25 July 1920, pp. 346-48; Lane to James S. Harlan, 5 March 1921, p. 430; Lane to Alexander Vogelsang, p. 462; and manuscript fragment written on 17 May 1921 and found in Lane's room, p. 465; Lane died at 6:10 a.m., 18 May 1921; all Lane and Wall, *Letters.*

45. Hoover to Lane, 8 March 1921; and Hoover to William J. Mayo, 11 May 1921; both Hoover Papers.

46. *New York Times,* 19 May 1921, p. 14; editorial, *The World's Work* XLII (July 1921): 214; *Washington Post,* 19 May 1921, clipping in FS 22-44, RG 48, Interior Records; Villard, "Franklin K. Lane," p. 788; also see editorials, "The Far West Has Lost Its Best Friend," *Sunset Magazine* XLVII (August 1921): 13; and "The Passing of Two Great Americans," *The Independent* CV (4 June 1921): 590.

47. *New York Times,* 6 November 1921, p. 19; 24 August 1924, p. 4; 9 January 1930, p. 24; "Franklin K. Lane Grove Dedicated," *The Timberman* (September 1925), FS 22-44, RG 48, Interior Records; Thomas M. Woodward to Harold Ickes, 8 May 1943, RG 48, Interior Records.

48. *New York Times,* 9 July, p. 9; 23 September, p. 5; and 15 October, p. 12, all 1921; Herbert Hoover to Daniel Willard, 9 June 1921; and Adolph C. Miller to Edgar Rickard, 29 June 1921; both Hoover Papers; Adolph C. Miller to Paul M. Warburg, 28 November 1921, box 2, Adolph C. Miller Papers; Horace M. Albright to Keith W. Olson, 4 June 1964, Olson's files; the securities of the trust fund now form the financial basis for the Franklin K. Lane Memorial Foundation at the University of California.

49. Mark Sullivan, "Public Men and Big Business," *The World's Work* XLVII (April 1924): 610; *New York Times,* 20 March 1928, p.2.

Location of Manuscript Collections Cited

The Papers of Newton D. Baker, Library of Congress
The Papers of Ray Stannard Baker, Library of Congress
The Papers of William E. Borah, Library of Congress
The Papers of Josephus Daniels, Library of Congress
The Papers of Walter L. Fisher, Library of Congress
The Papers of Felix Frankfurter, Library of Congress
The Papers of Lindly Garrison, New Jersey State Historical Society
The Papers of Henry George, New York City Public Library
The Papers of Herbert Hoover, Hoover Presidential Library
The Papers of Edward M. House, Sterling Library, Yale University
The Papers of Franklin K. Lane, Bancroft Library, University of
  California, Berkeley
The Papers of Robert Lansing, Library of Congress
The Papers of Adolph C. Miller, Federal Reserve Board Library
The Records of the National Park Service, National Archives
The Papers of F. H. Newell, Library of Congress
The Records of the office of the Secretary of the Interior, National
  Archives
The Papers of James D. Phelan, Bancroft Library, University of
  California, Berkeley
The Papers of Gifford Pinchot, Library of Congress
The Papers of Theodore Roosevelt, Library of Congress
The Papers of Albert Shaw, New York City Public Library
The Papers of Harry Slattery, Duke University Library
The Papers of William Howard Taft, Library of Congress
The Papers of Benjamin Ide Wheeler, Bancroft Library, University of
  California, Berkeley
The Papers of John H. Wigmore, School of Law Library, Northwestern
  University
The Papers of Woodrow Wilson, Library of Congress

A Note on Sources

After publishing some three hundred of Lane's most important letters
a year after his death, his widow destroyed the thousands of letters and
manuscripts Lane had saved during his lifetime. In 1948, Anne Lane
presented to the University of California, Berkeley, a carton of items
that had turned up during the intervening years. The Lane Papers, consisting mostly of press releases and speeches, number about two hundred
and fifty items. These papers are also available on microfilm, totaling
two reels, at Butler Library, Columbia University.

Fortunately for the historian, a variety of written records that Lane
produced survived, in addition to the volume of letters his wife published
and the miniscule collection at Berkeley. For almost three and one-half
years, from the spring of 1891 to the summer of 1894, Lane wrote daily
editorials for his newspaper. the *Tacoma Daily News.* From December
1894 to June 1895, he occasionally wrote columns for *Arthur McEwen's
Letter.* In 1902, the City and the County of San Francisco published
The Official Opinions and Communications of Franklin K. Lane, covering
his first four years as city and county attorney.

The annual reports of the Interstate Commerce Commission, 1906-
1913, and the *Interstate Commerce Reports* for the same years contained
Lane's writings. In addition, the Interstate Commerce Commission Library
held two folders of Lane items, some of which are not available elsewhere.
Unfortunately, of the eight commissioners who served with Lane, for all
or part of his tenure, only one preserved manuscripts. This collection,
the papers of Balthasar H. Meyer, housed at the State Historical Society
of Wisconsin, Madison, Wisconsin, included no mention of Lane.

Lane's seven annual reports as secretary of the interior were rich sources
of information and revealed his philosophy, his suggested conservation

programs, and his view on some public questions. The voluminous records of the Office of the Secretary of Interior, Record Group 48, located at the National Archives, included incoming and outgoing correspondence, some newspapers clippings, proceedings of conferences, and various reports.

During the last twenty-three years of his life, Lane published close to forty articles. They ranged over many subjects including Alaska, Americanism, foreign policy, and railroad regulation, and appeared in journals such as *Harper's Weekly, The National Geographic Magazine, Outlook,* and *Scientific American.* In 1918, the Frederick A. Stokes Company of New York published a small volume of Lane's speeches, *The American Spirit.*

Numerous manuscript collections contained Lane material. Indispensable for the Cabinet years were the papers of Woodrow Wilson and Edward House. The papers of Newton Baker, Ray Stannard Baker, Josephus Daniels, Robert Lansing, Theodore Roosevelt, and William Howard Taft, were vital, although less so than the Wilson collection. In addition, the papers of Gifford Pinchot, F. H. Newell, and Walter L. Fisher proved essential for conservation matters. The John H. Wigmore Papers, the Benjamin Ide Wheeler Papers, and the Herbert Hoover Papers afforded assistance for special periods in Lane's life.

Among the influential persons whose activities touched upon Lane's career and life and who left published memoirs were Bernard Baruch, Josephus Daniels, Oscar King David, Samuel Gompers, Herbert Hoover, David F. Houston, Frederic C. Howe, Franklin H. Martin, William G. McAdoo, Henry Morgenthau, Fremont Older, Gifford Pinchot, Theodore Roosevelt, and Oswald G. Villard. Horace M. Albright's "The Reminiscences of Horace M. Albright" (Columbia University Oral History Research Office, 1962) advanced understanding of Lane's personality and of the Interior Department under Lane's direction.

Three unpublished doctoral dissertations and one masters thesis furnished help in the areas indicated by their titles. The dissertations were Peggy Heim, "Financing the Federal Reclamation Program, 1902 to 1919: the Development of Repayment Policy" (Columbia University, 1953); Robert F. Hennings, "James D. Phelan and the Wilson Progressives in California" (University of California, Berkeley, 1961); and Edward Fawsitt Staniford, "Governor in the Middle: The Administration of George C. Pardee, Governor of California, 1903-1906" (University of California, Berkeley, 1955). In researching his masters thesis, "The Career of Franklin K. Lane in California Politics" (University of California, Berkeley, 1936), Henry W. Wiens interviewed Lane's sister and brother.

The *San Francisco Bulletin* and the *San Francisco Chronicle* were valuable sources for Lane's political career in San Francisco. For Lane's years in Washington, the *New York Times* provided the most complete coverage. The Department of Interior records and several other manuscript collections contained newspaper clippings from numerous cities.

For the secondary works I used and for a complete guide to sources, please consult the notes to the text.

Index

About the Author

Keith W. Olson is associate professor of history at the University of Maryland in College Park. He is the author of *The G.I. Bill: The Veterans and the Colleges* as well as articles in such journals as *American Quarterly,* the *Historian,* and the *Wisconsin Magazine of History.*